QUEER CHILDHOOD

SEXUAL CULTURES

General Editors: Ann Pellegrini, Tavia Nyong'o, and Joshua Chambers-Letson
Founding Editors: José Esteban Muñoz and Ann Pellegrini

Titles in the series include:

For a complete list of books in the series, see www.nyupress.org

Queer Childhoods

Institutional Futures of Indigeneity,
Race, and Disability

Mary Zaborskis

NEW YORK UNIVERSITY PRESS
New York

NEW YORK UNIVERSITY PRESS
New York
www.nyupress.org

Library of Congress Cataloging-in-Publication Data
Names: Zaborskis, Mary, author.
Title: Queer childhoods : institutional futures of indigeneity, race, and disability /
Mary Zaborskis.
Description: New York : New York University Press, [2023] | Series: Sexual cultures |
Includes bibliographical references and index.
Identifiers: LCCN 2023005925 | ISBN 9781479813872 (hardback ; alk. paper) |
ISBN 9781479813896 (paperback ; alk. paper) | ISBN 9781479813919 (ebook other) |
ISBN 9781479813926 (ebook)
Subjects: LCSH: Gay youth. | Sexual minority youth. | Sexual minority youth—Institutional
care. | Children of minorities—Institutional care. | Sexual minorities—Identity. | Queer theory.
Classification: LCC HQ76.27.Y68 Z33 2023 | DDC 306.76/60835—dc23/eng/20230209
LC record available at https://lccn.loc.gov/2023005925

This book is printed on acid-free paper, and its binding materials are chosen for strength
and durability. We strive to use environmentally responsible suppliers and materials to the
greatest extent possible in publishing our books.

Manufactured in the United States of America

10 9 8 7 6 5 4 3 2 1

Also available as an ebook

To Liz—queer gratitude always

CONTENTS

Introduction

Institutionalizing Children, Queering Childhoods

Is it surprising that prisons resemble factories, schools, barracks, hospitals, which all resemble prisons?
—Michel Foucault, *Discipline and Punish*

A total institution is like a finishing school, but one that has
many refinements and is little refined.
—Erving Goffman, *Asylums*

The Children of Queer Theory

Children animate the field of queer studies. Long before Lee Edelman
asked queer folks to "fuck . . . the Child," children—literal and figural,
dead and alive, queer and non-queer—have been fundamental to queer
thought.[1] Through "the child," the field has generated its theories,
understood its histories, and worried over its futures.

   Genealogies of queer theory show that the predecessors of the field
fixated on the child. Children are one of the key figures through which
Michel Foucault constructed a history of sexuality.[2] Gayle Rubin looked
at laws around children's interactions with sexuality to demonstrate how
cultural norms determining "good sex" and "bad sex" emerged.[3] Women
of color feminist scholars like bell hooks, Cherríe Moraga, Audre Lorde,
Gloria Anzaldúa, and Patricia Hill Collins turned to the child as an
agent of sexuality, experience, and knowledge in the 1970s and 1980s.[4]
The "queered girl icon" was a sign for sexual revolution in some strains
of 1980s and 1990s feminist activism.[5] In 1993, Eve Sedgwick provoca-
tively opened one of the founding texts of queer theory, *Tendencies*, with
the claim that the deaths of queer youth were the "motive" for "everyone

1

who does gay and lesbian studies."[6] And in contemporary queer theory, beyond the Edelman polemic, children have been central to the field's investigations into how U.S. citizenship is imagined and secured, how subjects are interpellated into and by capitalism, and how gender, sexuality, race, and kinship are constructed.[7]

Contrary to popular belief, children—well, at least *some* children—are the hill (or perhaps the Brokeback Mountain) upon which queer theory has been willing to die over and over and over—to prove its points, its relevance, and its legitimacy. And yet, despite these recurring mountain deaths, queer theory is still here. And the children seem to be, too.

But are they? Or, more precisely, which children are here; and where, exactly, are they? In "Childlike: Queer Theory and Its Children," Michael Cobb succinctly observes queer theory's consistent turn to the child: "something about children—less as actual beings and more as what they are made to signify—livens up queer theory."[8] When invoked, children often do not represent actual children but rather are "made to signify" something else; their presence references something *besides* children, indicating that something other than children is actually at stake.

Paradoxically, children are often absent where they are present in queer theory. Cobb explains how children are deployed and "forced to do some incredible things . . . [and] are pressured to do the work of placeholders for so much political, cultural, [and] affective activity."[9] In fact, "a child can stand in for almost anything; with a child . . . anything is possible."[10] The child's ability to function as a pluripotent shapeshifter across domains transforms the child into a figure with seemingly limitless potential, perhaps in ways similar to, borrowing Ramzi Fawaz's phrasing, "the shape-shifting qualities of erotic desire and embodiment in all its forms."[11] The only referents "the child" might not be able to bring fully into being are actual children.

Even when the actual child has been at the heart of analysis—as we see with Foucault and Rubin, for example—it appears as one in a range of minoritizing figures to make universalizing claims about sexuality. These universalizing claims can be useful but might collapse differences that importantly distinguish children and childhood experiences—of time, labor, pain, sexuality, desire, and affect, among others. Even Kathryn Bond Stockton's queer child describes *all* children's sexuality— Stockton provides a "lens by which to see *every* child as queer," a useful project for illuminating the reality of childhood sexuality and strangeness in the face of its denial, but one that of necessity abandons some children in the name of all children.[12]

Metaphorized children are also absent literal children. Paul Amar observes that "critiques have so powerfully interrogated how gender/race/colonial/indigenous subjects, as adults, are infantilized. But oddly, these critiques have tended to avoid confronting the agency of the quintessential subject of infantilization itself, the child."[13] Concepts of childhood and the ways child subjectivity can be abstracted to understand power dynamics have been useful to the field.[14] However, literal children are often left out of, displaced from, or overshadowed by larger political stakes in queer analyses. For all the field's supposed investments in the child—which are, of course, in contradistinction from heteronormative society's overly sentimental, phobic-driven attachments to children—we still know very little about actual children in queer theory.

Queering Childhoods

This project participates in a recent turn in the field of queer studies to study and center children with a lowercase c—that is, to investigate material realities of children who populate history (LGBTQIA and otherwise) and the contemporary moment. In its efforts to examine historical and literary children and their queer futures, *Queer Childhoods: Institutional Futures of Indigeneity, Race, and Disability* exposes the queering effects of educational institutions that delimited criminalized, disabled, Black, and Native children's sexual, social, and economic lives starting in the mid-nineteenth century and through to the contemporary moment. In so doing, *Queer Childhoods* parts ways with queer theory's mobilization of the child that too often elides children with Children—that is, the child invoked is often a symbolic Child and has largely operated as an abstract, figural projection to advance queer scholarship. In his seminal text, *No Future: Queer Theory and the Death Drive*, Edelman argues that we must reject the future intended for and legitimized by invocations of these Children because "queer resistance" is an impossibility in a society driven by "reproductive futurism."[15] Implicit in his argument is that children, reproduction, and the future are opposed to queerness and that investment in any of these as values (or valuable) is conservative and politically uninformed. To invest in the child is to recapitulate inequities, especially against sexual minorities and those who do not participate in state-sanctioned family making.

Edelman's polemic evades grappling with the existence of queer children, and José Esteban Muñoz famously critiqued Edelman's call to dismiss the Child by reminding us that not all children are imagined to have a future—"the future is only the stuff of some kids," more often than not white, economically stable, straight, able-bodied children.[16] And since the deployment of the figural Child affects the material lives of actual children, we cannot wholesale dismiss the Child—not all children get to gather under the banner of the Child, not all calls for the future are actually in the service of protecting children, and not all children are guaranteed a future. In his engagement with Emma Pérez's *Decolonial Imaginary*, Antonio Viego also takes a critical approach to Edelman's rejection of futurity, arguing that we cannot "dismiss 'futurity' outright when the blighted past struck from the historical record always already seems to place a Chicano future in jeopardy."[17] Chicano futurity—and Native futurity, Black futurity, disabled futurity, immigrant futurity, poor futurity, queer futurity, trans futurity—is not a given historically or in the present. As Nat Hurley has argued, children do not hold an exceptional status in these populations: "life chances are unevenly distributed among brown, black, poor, or queer or trans youth."[18] Being a child is not enough to guarantee or protect one's future if that child is racialized, criminalized, colonized, disabled, migrant, and/or queer. As Jacob Breslow states, "Childhood [for some] means living within forced dependency, being dismissed, pushed out of the public sphere, and understood as incapable, immature, and in need of discipline."[19]

Like Breslow's project in *Ambivalent Childhoods*, *Queer Childhoods* is interested in not recuperating, affirming, or asserting one's right to childhood but rather revealing how minoritarian childhoods have been integral to the future of a nation not intended for them. Breslow argues the idea that childhood is a

> straightforwardly productive object . . . is structured by a twin fantasy . . . that childhood, in its contemporary political life, is itself separable from the very things that we have come to understand as race, gender, sexuality,

and nation; and that the persistence and force of racism, transmisogyny, heteronormativity, and the violences of the border are not themselves co-produced with childhood as well.[20]

In other words, the presumption that children and childhood are universal categories of innocence, protection, and sentimentality obscures the vital and co-constitutive role that many children have played in shaping the contours of citizenship, belonging, race, and sexuality in North America.

And since, as *Queer Childhoods* argues, "the future" is often invoked precisely to disguise the harms, inequities, and maneuvers that will orient children toward limited opportunities, we must pause and interrogate its deployment and attachment to a range of children across the historical record and present. In other words, "the future" is not a static or self-evident concept or temporal form; it does not always already signify openness, progress, and possibility. *Queer Childhoods* reveals that many minoritized children rhetorically linked with the future became tethered to state-sanctioned modes of being meant to curtail what their futures could look like. When "the future" is invoked in relation to children, we must pay attention to both the adults *and children* being disciplined by that invocation. Edelman is right—queers are "collectively terrorized" by the Child, and many children (in and beyond this project) are part of that queer collective.[21]

Critiques against Edelman have been lodged on the abstract, theoretical level—but who are some of these children left behind (and terrorized), and what futures, if any, do they get? How do other vectors of identity disrupt or inform the linkage between children and futurity? When is the future emancipatory, and when is it a product of coercion? How is futurity itself a temporality that is produced, granted, and offered to vulnerable persons and communities? Who can celebrate the future and under what conditions? What tenets in the field of queer theory are contested when we take seriously the experiences of children in different historical, regional, and social positions? Sarah Chinn has observed that "queer approaches to childhood are less invested in history and far more interested in psyche," while childhood studies' investment in history has led to "an odd lack of ideological critique."[22] Addressing the above questions, *Queer Childhoods* also bridges these gaps in queer and childhood studies by bringing queer theory to bear on historically situated children. By broadening where we locate queer children and queer childhoods in American history and culture and turning to the extant archives of their lives, this book extends the work of queer studies by (1) challenging the presumed static relationship between children and futurity by providing textured, multidimensional cases of children who were promised expansive political, social, and economic opportunities but trained for limited futures in institutions; (2) disrupting the presumption that "queer" is uniformly and universally positive and liberating; (3) engaging with incomplete, mediated records of childhoods, even if that engagement yields politically ambiguous and even painful outcomes that do not affirm the field's position as that which always opens and enables political and theoretical possibilities; (4) and rejecting previous claims of opposition between queerness and institutions as well as between queerness and norms by showing how institutions inducted children into contextually produced normativity *precisely to* queer them.[23]

In five chapters and an epilogue that examine the histories, dynamics, and legacies of institutions that targeted marginalized children, *Queer Childhoods* examines the lived and literary experiences of children who attended reform schools, schools for the blind, African American industrial schools, and Native American boarding schools in the United States and Canada. I examine institutions established in the nineteenth and early twentieth centuries, with a focus on materials in the twentieth century and contemporary moment. I argue that institutions queered children by training them in gender and sexual norms that they were not intended to inhabit after they completed their education; this training enabled their labor, sexualities, and reproductive capacities to be controlled in part outside the institution because of the ideological, affective, and material educations that children internalized at schools.

I identify these educations as queering processes in particular because they functioned to leave children outside of what J. Jack Halberstam calls "heterotime"—that is, a linear timeline bound with marriage and reproduction, driven by the rhythms of capitalism.[24] Laura Wexler argues that these norms in which Native American, Black, and immigrant children were trained upheld the "universal superiority of the middle-class white

Christian 'home' that erased . . . those groups' own traditional mode of living."[25] These norms, however, were instilled so these children could be not "future householders" but rather "domestic servants in the homes of others" and other subservient positions.[26] Norms were not abstract or transportable across racialized, criminalized, and disabled bodies. Julian Carter has historicized the rise of norms in the United States, arguing that at the turn of the twentieth century the "modern, normal person was defined in large part through a powerfully racialized understanding of sexuality . . . [the normative] represented an ideal of specifically heterosexual whiteness, not simply a statistical composite."[27] Norms were "ideals," ones that could be projected onto diverse populations as that to which to aspire but that could be realized only by bodies that were heterosexual and white. The racialized, able-bodied heterosexuality that inflected these norms ironically queered children. They were educated to believe inhabiting white bourgeois gender and sexual norms was one of the only viable paths toward citizenship, sociality, and futurity, and this education ensnared them in an askew, impossible relation to norms. Assimilation, reform, and progress would fail, but the attachment to impossible norms continued to shape their bodies, sexual capacities, labor, and orientation to the state. Norms, then, sustained these children in a queer temporality—norms enabled the continual production and inhabitation of queer childhood, and norms preserved a queer relation to the state that kept these children exploited, violated, and suppressed. It positioned them toward limited economic, social, and political futures in order to both produce and maintain dominant white, able-bodied, heterosexual culture. Queerness was a manufactured exclusion intended to leave children in the margins.[28]

Queer Childhoods transforms the field's conversation around the child by bringing our focus from children to child*hood*. In the same vein as the queer turn to temporality that shifted from identifying, analyzing, and theorizing queer figures to instead the institutional and naturalized structures that have prescribed and regulated the timelines and rhythms of gendered and sexual bodies and subjects,[29] I propose that we can expand our theoretical, material, and historical engagements with children and sexuality by bringing queer theory's focus on temporality to bear on childhood. The temporal turn in queer studies has not fully accounted for certain kinds of subjects and historical periods. The doubly vulnerable subject of the institutionalized historical child requires a particular model of queer thought offered through temporality. Instead of reparatively looking for the presence of LGBTQIA (proto- or otherwise) children in history, literature, and/or sexologically marked archives, I examine historically produced queer child*hoods*. I analyze queer childhoods as temporal forms executed and managed by the state in order to arrest the development of children from particularized groups into proper heterosexual and reproductive adult citizens that would nonetheless support the "national heterosexuality" by providing a docile supply of domestic and industrial labor.[30] In a 1995 issue of *GLQ*, Elspeth Probyn observed the "queer turn to childhood," already apparent and worthy of comment in the nascent field of queer theory.[31] She critiqued this turn as too invested in linear, unbroken lines of continuity that are always already impossible and instead suggested the field apprehend "childhood . . . as event."[32] This mode allows us to see childhood as non-teleological, neither bound to a fixed origin position nor strictly belonging to the individual who endured a singular childhood. Rather than recuperating queer children, *Queer Childhoods* insists on a mode of reading the *times* of childhood as queer in ways that challenge how the field has attached queerness to children and apprehended the political and social potential of queer temporalities.

Unmooring childhood from children allows the field to find queer childhoods in ways that are not dependent on genealogical models for identification—mining queer childhoods in histories and contexts that are not part of a gay liberation lineage and that may have no contemporary counterparts that could readily gather under any of the banners of LGBTQIA identity, community, or activism. The queerness these children encounter and endure is not one that necessarily, in the words of Chinn, "provide[s] valuable solace" or can "breathe new and queer-positive life into them."[33] In so doing, *Queer Childhoods* looks at a different kind of queer childhood and a different kind of child in queer studies: the ones whose management and segregation away from perceived or real nonnormative sexualities as well as successful heteronormative reproductive futurity nonetheless was foundational to constructing the temporalities of queer life and theory. My separation here of children from childhood is not a critical move that re-metaphorizes childhood but rather is an emphasis on how the *time* of childhood can endure, recur, rupture, fragment, or continue to follow and haunt children and their affiliates even as their bodies and subjectivities age. I provide neither the recuperative "now-found" queer child predecessor in queer history nor the future gay adult but rather the queer child who could be assimilated into neither gay subjectivity nor guaranteed heterosexual success. Instead, I argue, producing particular experiences of queer childhood was a state-run disciplinary tactic to manage populations deemed threatening to the social and political order. Queer childhoods disciplined vulnerable children as they entered state-determined trajectories for life outside the institution—trajectories that would help secure the bounds of racialized, sexualized, able-bodied citizenship and the future of a nation that would not recognize or treat them as fully human or fully a part of the citizenry.

Thus, this is a project about queer children, but more importantly, it is an argument about queer childhoods: how temporal experiences have been institutionally manufactured by the state during the time of childhood in an effort to mitigate economic, social, and political possibilities for subjugated populations. The temporal parameters of queer childhood were not determined by children's time in schools; queer childhood would continue to shape (but not overdetermine) how children inhabited their bodies and sexualities upon leaving the schools. This queerness is discernible only through a temporal approach because it *looks* sexually normative—identity approaches to queerness and queer children do not capture the ways these children's bodies, sexualities, and reproductive capacities were vehemently targeted and managed in schools to align with unattainable white, settler-colonial, bourgeois norms. The field must include investigations of these children because their experiences reveal how the institutionalization of these children was a biopolitical project of population management *that pivoted on children's sexualities.* The children's attempts to replicate norms looked like respectability, assimilation, and/or progress, and these appearances occlude the ideological and repressive tactics that attempted to reorient children's relationships to their bodies and sexualities in order to limit the ways they entered the future. The queer childhoods produced in these schools have enabled the forward-moving, progressive timeline of the nation—these childhoods have secured American futures in which children (and the adults they become) have not been full-fledged citizens or participants. Scholarship on queer temporality, and this project's participation in that scholarship by shifting our focus from children to childhood, is crucial for seeing how children's institutional and sexual experiences are constitutive pillars for ongoing white supremacy, settler colonization, and violences against racialized, colonized, and disabled persons.

I construct an archive of queer childhoods produced and managed in and by institutions to restrict future social, economic, and political opportunities for minoritarian youth. Through finding queer childhoods in normative, sanitized institutional spaces and materials—dry annals, rote hygiene regimens, tedious daily schedules—I show how these childhoods were central to the state's formation and preservation of mainstream white, racially assimilated, and productive heterosexual culture. This move reveals the violent intimacies that can exist among queerness, institutions, and processes of normalization. In my archive, institutions are not opposed to queerness; they *produce* queerness. Queerness *looks* socially and sexually normal in schools and like a proper gendered and sexual identity: before and after photos that capture Native children in a properly domestic setting wearing settler clothing, criminalized Black girls attending a picnic with the local boys' reform school, blind children attending a school dance, or Black children avowing Christian-inflected morals of family and industry. Queerness emerges in these educations in racialized, gendered, and classed norms that institutionalized children could not fully inhabit because of their race, criminal status, or disability. What appears as a gendered and sexual identity evidences the production of a temporality.

Of course, queer theory and its predecessors have always been invested in interrogating the ways that the state has managed populations marked as sexually deviant, as well as the ways the state and its institutions have produced and policed categories of sexual difference. My intervention focuses on how the queerness that the state produced is not the identity category of outsider (sexual or otherwise) but the temporal categories of abeyance, non-futurity, non-reproduction, liminality, regression, and fixity. These temporalities manifested in individuals, communities, and sociopolitical figures who were, on the one hand, failed heterosexual, reproductive subjects but not recognizably queer in the identity sense, but who nonetheless appear across records, literature, and historical moments as signs of the state's division of populations into normative, (re)productive citizens who can access open futures and others who help maintain the superiority and futurity of that population without being guaranteed access to it themselves.

This approach to queerness draws on Jasbir Puar's theorizing in *Terrorist Assemblages*, in which she defines queerness as a biopolitical process by which the state targets and manages deviant populations. The institutions I examine reveal, in Puar's words, "queerness as a process of racialization [that] informs the very distinctions between life and death, wealth and poverty, health and illness, fertility and morbidity, security and insecurity, living and dying."[34] In this way, queerness is what Kara Keeling describes as "an epistemological category—one that involves life and death questions of apprehension and value production."[35] Schools managed children's embodied and affective experiences in order to shape their relationship to economic security, sexual expression, reproduction, health, and political rights outside of the school. This management and the contours of the education are what I discern as "queer." "Queer" doesn't name the material outcome of the schools—whether children are reproductive or not reproductive, for example—but it names the temporal experience produced within these schools that altered children's relationship to their bodies, sexuality, and ability to inhabit the future as sexual beings and laborers.

"Queer" as temporal and in a vexed relation to norms, however, has a close proximity to "queer" as identity in the archives I examine. *Queer Childhoods* is deeply intertwined with gay and lesbian history. Queer childhoods were being produced in boarding schools at the same time homosexuality was being invented, punished, and "treated" in clinics, prisons, and hospitals. Sexual deviance was being marked and responded to *in both child and adult institutions*, with the goals and outcomes for each segregated population differing. Children viewed as sexually deviant by virtue of their race, criminality, and/or disability were institutionalized, taken out of society in order to impede their sexual and reproductive development—children could return to society when affective ties and intimacies had been quashed, when bodily and sexual relationships had been reprogrammed, and/or when they acquired skills that would permit them to join a menial labor force. Institution-alization was an attempt to *prevent* sexually deviant adulthoods, which were imagined as a threat to the economic productivity of the newly industrializing America. Adults viewed as sexually deviant were put in the corresponding adult institutions, no longer schools but exclusion-ary sites that suspended their futures and development. Heather Love explains that queer adults "have been seen across the twentieth century as a backward race. Perverse, immature, sterile, and melancholic: even when they provoke fears about the future, they somehow also recall the past."[36] Queer adults' supposed threats to the future justified their institutionalization, with less energy and resources expended toward integrating them back into the social and economic orders. Confine-ment and segregation from the population produced these adults as "modernity's backward children"; they were identified as backward and childlike in order to *make* them backward and childlike.[37] Both children and adults perceived as sexually deviant were targeted by the state, and their relationships to state-sanctioned capitalist-driven heterotime were managed through institutionalization. Children could exit institutions once queer childhood had been successfully produced, a temporality that would limit their sexual and reproductive capacities—not necessar-ily fully extinguish but reconfigure them so that children's relationships with their bodies, sexual desires, and sexual expressions were triangu-lated with the institution, which had a chilling effect on children in their attempts to build connections, community, and intimacies outside the schools. Adults' ability to exit institutions was not as clearly mapped, and many were instead required to inhabit a state-produced queer child-hood in the institution as "modernity's backward children."

Queerness does emerge in the identity sense (sometimes centrally, sometimes peripherally) across all of my case studies—for example, children being separated at schools for engaging in real or suspected same-sex intimacies, girls who are tomboys, boys who are sissies, youth who identify as gay, and children growing into gay adults. While I ex-plore how these different instances of queerness inform the disciplining of children and the time(s) they can occupy, this is not a project about recuperating or finding LGBTQIA children in the archives. Many of the children in these schools may indeed have been, would be, or would have been LGBTQIA (by historical and/or present standards).[38] I am not abandoning identity but looking to queer temporal forms that informed how children's sexualities, desires, and affects could develop, and how this designed development was key in determining children's opportunities in the future.

Institutionalized children's queerness was instantiated through rigorous educations in gender and sexual norms, a formulation that puts pressure on the ways the field has conceptualized the political possibilities of queerness in relation to norms. In their introduction to the "Queer Theory Without Antinormativity" issue of *differences*, Robyn Wiegman and Elizabeth Wilson observe how the field of queer theory has been invested in its oppositional relationship to normativity: "The critical force of queer inquiry lies in its capacity to undermine norms, challenge normativity, and interrupt the processes of normalization—including the norms and normativities that have been produced by queer inquiry itself."[39] The "critical attachment" that practitioners have to antinormativity has led to an ossified binary relationship between queerness and norms—queer is doing its work only if it's disrupting some contextualized norm because queerness and norms are ontologically distinct and antonymic.[40] *Queer Childhoods* shows the entangled relationship between queerness and norms and how queerness can be harnessed, mobilized, and produced by seemingly normative institutions and sexually normalizing processes in order to manage racialized, criminalized, and disabled populations. Queerness might not always be that which liberates, invents, imagines, and makes possible—queerness can also debilitate, confine, and harm. Just as norms are not static but defined according to their contexts (e.g., cultural, historical, regional, institutional), queerness is not static but can be in varied dynamics with norms, and these entanglements are especially visible at the material and granular level of the archival and textual.

Institutionalizing children—in schools for the blind, in reform schools, in Native American boarding schools, in African American industrial schools—yielded queer childhoods. The shape of queer childhood took different forms. For some children, it meant cathecting to trauma. For others, it meant creating a split between body and mind after having mastered "those technologies of discipline central to the formation of sexual subjectivity: namely, the cultivation of the self and the responsibility to self-govern."[41] In an effort to "self-govern," the body remained attached to childhood and the mind was permitted to advance to the role of adult parent, assuming responsibility and strict oversight of their supposedly perpetual, incorrigible, untrustworthy bodily desires and impulses. Another form of queer childhood was an evacuation of interiority, a placeholder that negated libidinal energies and left one with a compromised sexuality that had an orientation toward serving the state. This sexuality was carefully, painfully acquired through an education in gender and (hetero)sexual norms.

Queer childhood was an asymptotic curve toward an adulthood that would likely never be reached, an inhabiting of gender and sexual norms always already inaccessible because they emerged from a white, bourgeois, able-bodied settler context, one that did not intend to fully accommodate those whose race, criminal status, and disabilities marked them as deviant. Liminality, restraint, disavowal, deferral, and displacement were central features of queer childhoods for racialized, criminalized, and disabled children. Children were temporally and spatially dislocated. Once bound to institutionally produced queer childhoods, their mobility, both literal and figurative, was restricted even as they entered lifeworlds after and outside the institution. Queer childhood meant the institution was never truly left behind—children might physically leave schools, but they didn't fully move beyond the institution and instead were bound to and by the experiences, traumas, and educations that shaped and defined institutional life. Queer childhood derailed them from the reproductive-driven, teleological, progressive temporal mode of the state. While not all queer childhoods were non-reproductive and nonsexual, the force of education oriented them severely away from these life outcomes and social possibilities. Keeling opens up *Queer Times, Black Futures* by asking, "If we were never meant to survive *as such*, what do we do with [what Saidiya Hartman calls] 'the time that remains,' while we suffer, while we rejoice, while we exist within conditions not entirely of our own making, yet still open, currently defined by, but not simply confined by, flesh that dies and lives in its time?"[42] *Queer Childhoods* brings these temporal and material questions to bear on institutionalized children by considering how survivors of institutions navigated futures whose conditions were shaped and produced by their confinement. These children left schools and their futures were "informed by life lived *after* the historical accumulation of queer deaths."[43] Queer childhood was a violently constructed temporal form that, on its surface, appeared as respectability, assimilation, reform, and progress—gifts of education. And while these educations looked like triumphs in white heterosexual norms—Native American children wearing "civilized" clothing, blind children playing with doll houses, Black juvenile delinquent girls participating in courtship rituals—lurking beneath these celebratory images were psychic and sexual losses, calculated attempts to sever children's connections to sexual and reproductive capacities through lessons, textbooks, curricula, and kinship with the state.

By locating these queer childhoods in state archives and institutions, I expose a queer social history entangled with genocide, eugenics, and racialized violence. To apprehend these temporalities and histories as queer requires a recapitulation of queer's mobility and possibility across cultural and historical contexts. In *Disturbing Attachments*, Kadji Amin observes the impulse of scholars of queer theory toward a "utopian, coalitional mode," a mode that has led to "idealization" of its objects—and of queer theory itself.[44] This latter idealization is one that Joshua Chambers-Letson, Tavia Nyong'o, and Ann Pellegrini remind readers of and caution against in the foreword to the tenth anniversary edition of Muñoz's *Cruising Utopia*. Muñoz was also concerned with the "overly hopeful or romanticizing readings of *Cruising Utopia* . . . [and] expressed disappointment that his defense of utopia was enthusiastically read by some as uncritical optimism."[45] Synthesizing Muñoz's theorizing, they continue, "Queerness, blackness, brownness, minoritarian becoming, and the utopian imaginary . . . cohere around a certain 'failure to be normal.' . . . Hope may not be commensurate to reality; our hopeful actions may not produce—may not ever produce once and for all—the hoped-for end"—but operating on hope, even impossible hope, can enable "a queer ethics for living through the gaps between what we need and what we get, what we allow ourselves to want and what we can survive and transform in the now."[46] Muñoz's articulation of hope—as an unattainable orientation and as a survival strategy—is not a celebration of the future or an overappraisal of the potential that can emerge from trying to navigate the challenges of "living through the gaps." Hope can assist in survival and transformation, but this does not mean queerness or the utopia that queer can orient one toward are affirmative or the horizon of optimism and idealization.

Part of what makes "queer" endlessly irresistible is the way it can orient practitioners against the grain in ways that feel, and indeed often can be, politically and intellectually valuable. Amin worries that this feature of queerness, however, has become a norm in the field, one that has limited queerness to attach only to those objects that can be redeemed, recuperated, and/or made valuable. Amin argues, "In Western modernity, sexual and racialized deviance has been pathologized, violently policed, and subjected to normalizing disciplines in prisons, hospitals, and schools. As a result, the cultures, knowledges, and life-worlds of denigrated groups have been stigmatized and rendered monstrously unintelligible. A powerful tendency within scholarship has been to respond to this damaging legacy of shame and stigma by loudly idealizing the alternatives that emerge from deviance."[47] Like Amin, I am concerned that "loudly idealizing the alternatives that emerge from deviance" calcifies "queer" so that it can be identified only after it has been confirmed that it *has* potential. In these scenarios, queerness can be named as such only if it attaches to bodies, practices, and modes that can be read as socially disruptive and politically resistant, celebrated and liberated positions in relation to the dominant order. Puar describes how the "ideal queer" has been imagined as one who operates as if they have a "freedom from norms."[48] This idealization of queerness's liberatory potential supports the notion of "queerness as automatically and inherently transgressive."[49] Puar further argues that this view of queer as transgressive "enacts specific forms of disciplining and control, erecting celebratory queer liberal subjects folding into life (queerness as subject) against the sexually pathological and deviant populations targeted for death (queerness as population)."[50] In other words, recognizing queerness only in its liberatory forms does not just occlude but enables queering processes that harm and subjugate populations not envisioned as ideal citizens in the nation precisely because of the gendered and/or sexual narratives attached to them.

What would happen if queerness did not always free, but sometimes harmed? If it was not always freely chosen or inhabited, but sometimes a constructed and coerced social position that contributed to the maintenance of white supremacy?[51] What if queerness is not as opposed to the state and its institutions in all times and places, and in fact can be produced within and co-constitutive of those spaces? This is not to say that queerness is *only* state-sanctioned and bound with violent institutions, but rather to say that we must recognize queerness in *all* of its deviant and alternative forms, even the ones that upset the hopes and aspirations practitioners have for the potential of both the field *and* queer. In *Feeling Backward*, Love identifies the risk of focusing only on that which affirms queerness: In "dwell[ing] at length on the 'dark side' of modern queer presentations . . . it is not clear how such dark representations from the past will lead toward a brighter future for queers. Still, it may be necessary to check the impulse to turn these representations to good use in order to see them at all."[52] Regina Kunzel makes a similar point when she observes that the field at times struggles with "the question of who counts as a proper subject in queer history"— speaking specifically to her work on sex in prisons, she explains that "the prison's association with criminality and especially with sexual coercion and violence push against the parameters of a history often motivated by the impulse to recover and celebrate gay identity and community."[53] Limiting queerness to those objects that are decisively on the correct side of politics, resistance, and activism risks reinstating the very power structures and dynamics queer theory seeks to dismantle—creating divisions between "good" queers and queerness and "bad" queers and queerness, stigmatizing or refusing recognition of persons, places, or experiences in ways that look like gatekeeping, and romanticizing queer work in ways that amplify critiques of the split between theory and lived experience. In other words, identifying queerness in sites, populations, and practices that leave us with versions of queerness that are politically ambivalent and not guarantors of a "brighter future"—queer social forms that are abusive, queer affect that is irredeemably damaged, alternative relations to time bound with hopelessness, sterility, and death—is a method that opens up the racial, class, and cultural locations of queer in ways that reveal the field's uneasy relation with critical race studies, Black studies, disability studies, Indigenous studies, and carceral studies.[54]

Refusing to locate queerness in these sites reinscribes the field's racialized norms and gives credence to these other fields' critiques of queer theory's limitations—sticking to that which affirms and validates the field's politics "in the name of respectability or assimilation."[55] Amin names this unease, rhetorically asking, "If the subjects of queer culture are no longer out-and-proud gay and lesbian activists fighting to destigmatize and diversify sexual practices and intimate forms, but rather nineteenth-century Chinese immigrants forced to live in residentially segregated, crowded, and insalubrious conditions, refugees and undocumented migrants struggling under conditions of debility and 'slow death,' and drug addicts, then to what extent can scholars ethically celebrate the alternatives they innovate?"[56] In other words, identifying queer subjects in historical and institutional sites not associated with gay liberation puts pressure on the ways that the field "celebrates the alternatives," as if alternatives and deviations were absolutes, universals that signify only as politically and socially good. Locating queerness elsewhere risks generating alternatives and deviations that are beyond redemption or repair. What happens to the field's theorizing and its political aspirations to call these queer?

In examining the ways that queerness can be linked to harm and in putting pressure on the positive valences often attached to queerness in the field's theorizing, I am seeking not to make queer more capacious or to emphasize its pessimisms or disruptive qualities (although these potential features of queerness emerge at different moments throughout *Queer Childhoods*). There is pleasure in pursuing queer's potentialities; like the child, queer can be a pluripotent shapeshifter, a placeholder for the ideals, desires, and aspirations of a field that has an increasingly ambivalent relationship to the academy. This is not about condemning the pleasure of queerness or denying queer's potential and the way it can reveal regulatory tactics and provide tools and approaches for dismantling the structures that restrict, harm, and dehumanize persons. This investigation, rather, is inviting us to reflect on how queerness is not ontologically pure, universal in its applicability, or outside of state formations. I am seeking to productively examine the intersection of queer childhood and queer temporality studies in order to expand the sites, times, and figures with whom the field can engage, while holding steadfast to queer's capacities to be *both/and*—indeed, the *both/and* of queerness is present in *Queer Childhoods*, as pleasure, desire, and excess are often copresent and even emerge out of regulatory tactics in ways that refuse recuperation, celebration, or repair.

This examination and the attempt to work outside a recuperative mode of queer thought also inform the methodology of this project. The chapters examine instances of queer childhood in historical and literary records, a method that enables, in Laura Soderberg's words, the "combining [of] institutional discourse's focus on multiplicity with literature's attention to singular subjectivity."[57] In other words, these materials give us different access to and perspectives on the scale of institutional discipline and violence. In Soderberg's investigation of children in nineteenth-century institutional archives and literary texts, she "attend[s] to their overlapping languages while respecting that they [records and literature] often prioritize different questions."[58] The case studies in this project each find different inroads to trying to understand the production of queer childhoods in schools, knowing that none is complete and that each has its own limitations. I don't interpret the historical and the literary as equivalent in the kinds of realities they reflect, construct, and imagine; rather, I see each as able to contribute to understandings of what institutions thought they were doing and how students experienced and responded to these educations, and I consider the possibilities and limitations of each case's materials across my chapters.

In pairing archival records and literary material, I may be getting at the contours of some children's experiences through the lens of the institution (in the case of archival materials), the grown adult, or the adult who has lived with the legacy of these institutions (in the case of literature). However, I am not able to recuperate or fully access children's voices, expressions, and perspectives. I have critiqued the field's invocation of figural children and argued for more *actual* children in the field's theorizing. This study examines the disciplining of actual children and some of the effects of this discipline on the adults they grew into, but these are fragmented and highly mediated inclusions of children; some dimensions of children are absent in this project, and these absences are built into histories of race, sexuality, and disability. I admire scholars who have taken a "critically fabulative" approach to the absence of voices and experiences in the archive, following Saidiya Hartman's call to "advanc[e] a series of speculative arguments and exploit . . . the capacities of the subjunctive (a grammatical mood that expresses doubts, wishes, and possibilities) . . . to tell an impossible story and to amplify the impossibility of its telling."[59] Critical fabulation is one rich and productive method for approaching experiences of race, sexuality, and disability in archives. While I am not taking a critically fabulative approach in my theorizing and interpretation, many of the literary texts I examine arguably are—through drawing on their own and/or historical experiences, these authors are creatively responding to experiences and legacies of harm. Their responses are not necessarily in the service of healing, redeeming, or repairing. They explore the disciplining of these schools at the micro level—at the level of the body, affect, habits, desires, and erotics—and finds ways to tell "impossible stor[ies]" of queer childhoods and their effects. Through examining historical materials alongside these literary texts to understand productions of queer childhoods, I acknowledge the limitations of my archive in what we can fully know about children. I respect these limits by resisting the queer urge to speculate, project, or impose my own ideals and hopes onto these children.

Educations in Erotics

Promises of futurity were a trap that enabled the institutions I examine to orient children toward limited futures where their bodies, sexualities, and labor were partly under institutional control—schools continued to exert an ideological, affective, and material force on children upon leaving the schools. These schools were preoccupied with managing children's bodies and sexualities—children's bodies and sexualities were the entry point for orienting these children and their communities toward stagnancy, liminality, and death. In the mid- to late nineteenth century, candidates for these institutions were educated to believe that elements of their culture, person, or background were blocking them from attaining citizenship, humanity, and capital in the future. They were told that through education, they could be liberated into futures preserved for ideal U.S. citizens. Native American children were taught their Indigenous conceptualizations of gender, sexuality, and kinship were backward and sinful. Black children were taught their bodies and sexualities were dirty, excessive, and shameful. Juvenile delinquents, and especially girls, were often sentenced to reformatories for sexually related crimes. Children with disabilities were taught their bodies were the product of moral weakness, signs of sexual impropriety from their ancestors or themselves manifested in their bodies.

Children, then, were marked as queer—out of heteronormative, productive, processional time before entering the school by virtue of their race, criminality, and disability. This marking was a biopolitical marking, as theorized by Puar—it was through perceived sexual deviance that children were suspended from full inclusion in the nation. Puar writes that "national recognition and inclusion . . . is contingent upon the segregation and disqualification of racial and sexual others from the national imaginary."[60] The "segregation" of these children understood as "sexual others" from the nation in educational institutions helped constitute the bounds of who could be recognized and included as citizens. In these segregated schools, though, children were told in implicit and explicit ways that their sexual otherness *could* be resolved to some extent. Children were made aware of their marked queerness so they would recognize themselves as backward, feel shame when that happened, and realize they needed reform and rehabilitation through education.

Moreover, as *Queer Childhoods* shows, the schools queered children through disciplining their bodies, affects, and habits. Children were taught that if they learned and practiced white bourgeois norms of sexual propriety, hygiene, and courtship, they could leave the institution and enter the social and political orders as heterosexual citizens. But these children would never be straight citizens in the state's eyes—they were trained in norms the institution did not intend for them to enact outside of the schools. Their educations were "in productive tension with the legal and cultural structures that insisted some children . . . would never be able to move through the lessons of the schoolroom to the contracts of adulthood."[61] Schools enacted a dynamic David Kazanjian examines in *The Colonizing Trick*—schools participated in "the systematic production and maintenance of hierarchically codified, racial and national forms [that] actually enabled equality to be understood as formally and abstractly universal" by promising children access to those universal rights through education but in actuality maintaining their status as lesser because of their racialized, disabled, and/or criminalized sexualities.[62] If children were to have a future outside the school, it would be primarily as laborers, a category imagined—or at least desired by the state—as incompatible with sexuality and reproduction.[63] Elizabeth Freeman argues that "failures or refusals to inhabit middle- and upper-middle-class habitus appear as, precisely, synchrony or time out of joint."[64] Freeman reminds us to think of "the body erotic . . . not only in terms of its possibilities for making sexual cultures but in terms of its capacities for labor."[65] Children's state-designed failures to inhabit these bourgeois norms enabled the "expenditure of bodily energy" toward labor.[66]

In taking children from their communities of origin and placing them in institutions for a long period of their youth, schools effectively orphaned children, supplanting their families of origin with the institution. The convergence of state and family at the site of these children's schools "contest[s] romanticized notions of privacy and family as outside capitalist relations of exploitation and domination"—the schools' claims that they could function as home for children enabled this management and exploitation of their present and future labor.[67] Schools produced what Kyla Schuller terms "the biopolitics of orphanhood, in which civilized children precipitate the vitality of life itself, while the primitive are relegated to positions of service that will enable their imitation of sexed and sexual norms of civilization."[68] Institutionalized children's "imitation" of bourgeois settler gender and sexual norms strengthened and upheld "national heterosexuality," but they were still considered "primitive"—these norms were to be embodied primarily in subjugated economic positions. Heterosexuality, then, was the means through which the state oriented children toward limited futures. And boarding schools were the mechanism through which these children were managed and oriented toward these limited childhoods; boarding schools produced the experience of queer childhood.

Queer Childhoods examines the production of racialized queer childhood, criminalized queer childhood, and disabled queer childhood with the understanding that one version of childhood often inflected another—for example, criminalized queer children who were also racialized queer children experienced a different queer childhood than white juvenile delinquents. In Kathryn Bond Stockton's *The Queer Child, or Growing Sideways in the Twentieth Century,* she proposes four versions of the queer child, one of which is the "child queered by color."[69]

While children are often synonymous with innocence, the child queered by color—that is, the racialized queer child—is incapable of that innocence.[70] The innocent child is free of a past, which is understood as "antithetical to childhood."[71] Yet the child's very innocence is the product of adults' desire for a "preferred past."[72] Adults narrate some children as blank slates not because they are but because adults want them to be.

However, racialized queer children, as well as criminalized and disabled queer children, are queered by specific and historical pasts—and this matters not only because it is *matter* but also because the specificities of history became part of the erotic specificities of such queered children's bodies, affects, and habits. Native children were (and continue to be) queered by a settler-narrated past, disabled children by a eugenicist understanding of heredity, and Black children by pathological understandings of race as predetermining a child for violent capacities and menial labor. These children were incapable of innocence because of settler, white-supremacist, and eugenicist ideologies that viewed children and their communities as backward and dangerous—that is, queer. Being queered by these histories positioned children for educations that would further queer them through disciplining their bodies, affects, and habits.

This disciplining was an erotic education, and the process of educating children in erotics produced queer childhoods. I understand erotics in the Foucauldian sense—in volume 1 of *The History of Sexuality*, Foucault argues that while sexuality was not named in Victorian England, sensations, pleasures, and habits came to constitute what we now understand as sexuality. Sensations, pleasures, and habits, then, became eroticized—they could be understood only as part of one's sexuality. This eroticization was in the service of political and economic subjection. In *Discipline and Punish*, Foucault describes this way in which institutions take hold of bodies as a kind of "microphysics"—the body is infiltrated at the most local level through training, force, and ideology in order to gear it for "economic use."[73] This infiltration is discernible in bodies through "forms of habit," "behavior," "movements, gestures, [and] attitudes."[74]

Similarly, in these late nineteenth- and twentieth-century institutions, schools eroticized children's pleasures, sensations, habits, affects, and practices through routine and repetition. Students learned that these erotics were constitutive of a backward, dirty, and/or pathological sexuality. They also learned how to alter these erotics so as to align with a state-sanctioned sexuality—one recognizable as white, straight, settler, and able-bodied, seen as synonymous with moral aptitude. These erotics were supposed to distance, restrict, or mitigate children's relationship to sexual expression desire. In this way, their educations in erotics were educations in celibacies, in the way that Benjamin Kahan proposes: celibacy is about not "absence" but "an organization of pleasure."[75] Education organized children's pleasure in an effort to restrict its expression in the future.

Producing institutional erotics was key to biopolitical population management. Schuller argues that in the nineteenth century "nonstate actors such as churches, domestic homes, private reform societies, slave auctions, health movements, synagogues, and club societies inaugurated sentimental technologies of biopower that combined atomizing measures of disciplinary castigation and/or redemption and populational tactics of managing risk and economic productivity. In other words, the tasks of the biopolitical state evolved out of the private institutions of sentiment."[76] The schools I examine were among these "private institutions of sentiment" that consolidated and harnessed sentimental views of ostensibly universal but white, abled-bodied, heterosexual childhood and deployed them in order to discipline children to whom that sentiment would not be extended. Schuller understands these institutions as products of "biophilanthropy," arguing that "biophilanthropy works via the steady accumulation of impressions that will redirect a class or race from foreordained death and force it to persist, as a newly proletarianized group, for the economic and moral health of the settler colonial project" and was contingent upon "eradicating family connections."[77] Biophilanthropical institutions would take these children and "thrust . . . new hereditary material on them and allowing traces of parental lineage to wither."[78] Schuller fascinatingly reveals how not determinism but rather "pliability" was the predominant view of race and poverty in this era.[79] Schools, it seemed, preached determinism but took pliable approaches to children; affects, sensations, and ideologies were implanted in children to *retroactively confirm the deterministic view of their racialized, disabled, and criminalized sexualities.* Schuller asserts that "biophilanthropy is a particular deployment of making live, taking place at the level of sensory experience, that recruits children from surplus populations who threaten the health of the wage economy."[80] Schools took these children who threatened the future of the nation and through educations of their body at the level of sensations, affect, and feeling— erotics—found ways to manage their sexual and reproductive lives to, at best, contribute to the economic health of the nation and, at worst, not pose a reproductive threat as adults through abuse, harm, and sterility.

This education in erotics looked straight, but in fact heterosexual norms and values enabled students to leave the institution oriented away from marriage and reproduction. Wexler explains that "the curricula of these institutions functioned . . . through the imposition of noncorpo-real, affect-based models of discipline based on the family values that marked the emergence of white middle class identity."[81] These "non-corporeal, affect-based models of discipline" were the erotics in which children were educated—they looked like "white middle class" affects, values, and habits and were imposed on racialized, criminalized, and disabled bodies to alter their relationship to futurity. In this way, power in the Foucauldian sense "penetrated and controlled everyday pleasure" through inculcating and monitoring "individual modes of behavior."[82]

This education in erotics necessarily impacted what roles children could occupy in the future as adults. Laura Briggs has explored how "taking children has been a strategy for terrorizing people for centuries" in America, and this strategy "attempts to deny [people] the opportunity to participate in the progression of generations into the future—to inter-rupt the passing down of languages, ways of being, forms of knowledge, foods and culture."[83] Briggs here encapsulates the genocidal component of "taking children." Institutionalizing them is a generational and re-productive disruption, both culturally and biologically. Briggs argues that taking children from their families and communities is a mode of "disrupted reproduction [that] produces new regimes of racialized rightlessness. Child taking is . . . a counterinsurgency tactic [that] has been used to respond to demands for rights, refuge, and respect by com-munities of color and impoverished communities, an effort to induce hopelessness, despair, grief, and shame."[84] The "racialized rightlessness" that emerges via state-produced orphaning in the form of institutional-izing children is also a "sexualized rightlessness" in my case studies because of the central role that sexuality played both in justifying children's institutionalization and then in determining their progress within and futures beyond the schools. The institutionally produced temporalities that emerged from "taking children" resonate with what Nicole Fleetwood calls "penal time," which captures the ways that "imprisonment fundamentally reconstitutes *being* in time. . . . Prison reconfigures time not only for the imprisoned but also for the intimate relations and social network of the imprisoned."[85] Like Briggs, Fleetwood here captures the ways that confining someone alters their relationship with time and futurity as well as that of communities from which they came. The targeting of children and production of queer childhoods was about orienting entire populations' relationship to futurity—a biopolitical tactic to slow communities' survival and flourishing.

Following theorization in queer temporality studies that deviations from future-oriented, heteronormative timelines are queer, these children ended up in a queer time outside the school. The institution counterintuitively accomplished this queering. In *Time Binds*, Elizabeth Freeman explains that institutions induct their subjects into "chrononormativity," defined as a "mode of implantation, a technique by which institutional forces come to seem like somatic facts," and "subjectivity emerges in part through . . . mastery over certain forms of time."[86] Schools are one example of chrononormative spaces that produce subjects who are in "synch with state sponsored narratives of belonging and becoming," and Freeman argues that queer temporality emerges when a subject "liv[es] aslant" to these narratives.[87] The boarding schools I investigate show children can "live aslant," willingly or not, within "state sponsored narratives"—the schools *produced* children who "lived aslant" so that they would never operate fully in "synch with state sponsored narratives"; these narratives were for populations of which these children were not a part. The schools educated children in a sexual normativity they would never fully achieve, and this education enabled a "violent retemporalization of bodies."[88] Asynchronicity with the rhythms of state-sanctioned sexual scripts was the time of their queer childhoods. Keeling argues that "the production of 'queer' is violent, material, and excessive to the management of control and sociability. 'Queer' is palpable, felt as affect. It is also not only an imposition but simultaneously a becoming."[89] The case studies in *Queer Childhoods* examine queerness not as "excessive to the management of control and sociability" but as constitutive of that management. The queer temporalities that children inhabited were outcomes of queering processes felt "palpabl[y]" at the level of erotics.

This might not be a queer time that the field of queer studies is used to recognizing—it is not liberatory but genocidal, violent, and exploitative across the cases in this study. Amin notes that while the field admits that not all queer time is "necessarily resistant, politically progressive, or even nonheteronormative," queer work on temporality "most often choose[s] to focus on these moments, pregnant with possibility . . . [that] open . . . alternate possibilities for the flourishing of queer erotic subjects and communities."[90] To explore queer temporalities that are not "pregnant with possibilities" and in fact are institutionally designed to inhibit "flourishing" is a move that queer scholarship on temporality makes possible in theory but that in practice has been underutilized, perhaps because it does not affirm queer's potential and in fact reveals instead its capacities to wound, brutalize, and deteriorate.

By recognizing training in white bourgeois gender and sexual norms like marriage and reproduction and the prohibition on children from fully approximating those norms, I do not mean to valorize heterosexuality, marriage, and reproduction. Rather, *Queer Childhoods* thinks about the ways children were oriented away from these options. I understand this "orientation" in the sense that Sara Ahmed proposes—a mode that "restrict[s] the capacity for other kinds of action."[91] Orienting children away from reproductive futurity did not necessarily open up alternate modes of being—their education "restricted" the possibilities available to them. They left schools alienated from their communities and families of origin having internalized shamed understandings of their bodies and sexualities. Such queer futures, bound to and accessed through queer childhood, put pressure on the fields of queer studies to be precise about the extent and range of the claims it makes and to be more attentive to the ways that queer studies looks different when it engages with fields like Indigenous, Black, and disability histories and studies. Madhavi Menon asks, "The burning question in relation to queer theory is whether or not its capaciousness has gone 'too far.' Does queerness have a specificity that can be grounded in particular bodies and practice?"[92] *Queer Childhoods* answers this question in the affirmative, but my analyses do not generate an affirmative queerness when I bring queer theory to bear on the "particular bodies and practice[s]" of institutionalized children and queer childhoods.

Queer studies can engage with these fields, but it must be prepared to acknowledge damage, limitations, and loss. Alternative kinship is celebrated in queer studies; when the institution supplanted the family and parented children in shame and abuse, that was queer kinship, but a violent reordering of kinship intended to estrange children from their families and bodies—instances of "kinship as a idiom of state power, white supremacy, and Western modernity."[93] In the introduction to their recently edited volume exploring kinship, sexuality, and race, Tyler Bradway and Elizabeth Freeman urge scholars to "avoid a simple dichotomy between queerness and kinship in which the former is detached from its temporal and historical entwinement, and even complicity, with the exclusions, violences, and abandonments of kinship."[94] Rejection of reproductive futurity is held as politically resistant gesture—but how do we understand populations that were violently denied a choice for reproductive futurities? The uniform embrace and idealization of the nonnormative and non-reproductive is ahistorical when it doesn't acknowledge that these are also outcomes of eugenic, racist, and genocidal knowledges bound with management of sexual deviance. This project returns to the question of the universalizing and the minoritizing by asking if queer studies can produce universalizing knowledge, and even if the field admits it cannot, how universalizing gestures are made in ways that dismiss entire fields and communities, affirming the racialized, classed, and able-bodied constraints of queer theory. This is meant not to condemn queer theory but to draw attention to the limits and contexts of the claims we can make.

Progressive Promises of Futurity

I ground my investigation on institutions that emerged, flourished, and/or gained new public and financial traction in the mid- to late nineteenth century, and particularly the Progressive Era, because of the convergence of children, futurity rhetoric, and institutions at this historical moment.

Social reformers, politicians, and newly formed state agencies claimed to invest in the futures of minoritized children. They appeared committed to finding a place in the social, political, and economic orders for children who either were new to the American citizenry or would face obstacles in their attempts to enter it. Jules Gill-Peterson, Rebekah Sheldon, and Kathryn Bond Stockton write in their introduction to the special childhood issue of *GLQ* that these adults imagined that "by taking children in the Progressive Era off the streets, out of factories, and placing them into mass schooling or institutions for juvenile delinquency, childhood was constituted as an ostensibly empty innocence based in deferral and delay: of work, of sex, and of civil rights."[95] In other words, these adults thought deferring children's access to work, sex, and full citizenship was in the service of protecting children and ultimately orienting them toward a path that would lead to American adult sexual, political, and economic life. This deferral created the time and experience of childhood. Dubbed the "child savers," these adults proselytized about the welfare and reform of children excluded from the categories of innocence because of their race, criminality (which often coded class, race, and national origin), or ability.[96] There was an "increasing emphasis on child welfare and its relationship to social stability and national prosperity," and these agents proposed residential educational institutions to be a solution for social problems the state was newly encountering because of the passage of the Dawes Act, waves of European immigration, post-Reconstruction migration, and industrialization.[97]

The Progressive Era was an epoch of faith in institutions—educational, artistic, governmental, and professional. Institutions were a product and agent of modernity. By World War I, because of "the birth of the great American symphony orchestras, museums, philanthropic foundations, the reorganization of American publishing, the development of serious national magazines and a cultivated audience to read them, and, in astonishing variety, the organization of the profession . . . the United States had developed a vigorous and truly American structure of high culture."[98] Institutions preserved and maintained "high culture," their presence signaling progress, mobility, modernity, and achievement of American values. Schools were founded by people who "trust[ed] in the efficacy of institutions to shape American life for the better."[99] Educational reformers pressed for compulsory education laws to open alternative futures for children who would have otherwise been destined for factories, if not prisons.[100] Wexler argues that institutions for minoritized populations were the material "afterglow of sentimentalization"— while literary sentimentalism was over around the 1870s, the founders of these sites "lag[ged] behind the literary imagination" in their establishment of social institutions later in the nineteenth century.[101]

These institutions would, in theory, help to secure futures for children imagined to be left out of promises of the future because of their race, criminality, or ability. Schools employed "tender violence," a phrase coined by General Samuel Chapman Armstrong, founder of the Hampton Institute, and theorized by Wexler as "the spirit of the kind of education . . . believed . . . necessary for the nation to undertake in order to prepare American ex-slaves and newly pacified Native Americans for citizenship."[102] "Tender violence" describes how the rhetoric of care and concern masked harm, abuse, and subjugation in these institutions. Unlike early nineteenth-century institutions such as prisons, almshouses, and asylums, the residential school became an increasingly popular strategy for training and managing these children. Many of these schools were overseen and regulated by the same government agencies as state welfare activities became centralized in the latter half of the nineteenth century; others were run by private institutions and charities, subsidized and, for some, eventually taken over by the state or merged with another institution.[103]

But the training and management of children did not open up futures beyond menial labor. Historians of the sociology of deviance have argued that Progressive Era institutions differed from earlier institutions because they employed strategies for training a labor force needed with the rise of industrialization and market capitalism. Institutions were a way to classify the "unproductive poor" from the "able-bodied poor," a distinction that determined what type of labor they would be trained to do.[104] These institutions "transcend[ed] charity [by] claiming to drive a wedge between the child's miserable past and his or her future"—in other words, institutions sought to alienate children from their origins for the ostensible purpose of social, political, and economic advancement.[105] Tova Cooper observes that while "education officials rhetorically promoted full civic, or political membership, in reality citizenship education programs usually trained new citizens for life in the civil rather than the civic sphere—that is, in the world of work rather than the world of political participation."[106] Promises of citizenship enabled reproduction of the working class—the rhetoric of expansive open futures enabled by work ethic, industry, and self-sufficiency secured limited futures that would guarantee some people's subservience. When these promises revealed themselves to be false and children encountered the "disappointing realities of Americanization," they couldn't return to their families from whom they "became alienated. . . . Older forms of community no longer provided citizens relief."[107]

More often than not, these children's futures as laborers enabled the social, political, and economic advancement of an already privileged subset of Americans. Disrupting kinship through the institution ensured that these students' affective ties would not interfere with their capacity for labor. In this way, queer temporality was embedded in capitalism but also had anticapitalist features because it was not intended to be reproductive. Like John D'Emilio's foundational claim that gay and lesbian identity could emerge only in relation to and out of industrialization and capitalism, queer temporalities were shaped by and within capitalist frameworks that mandated the productivity of its excess subjects while desiring for those subjects to disappear, die out, or occupy a disposable position.[108] These queer temporalities, though, negated the possibility of identity—arresting the development of identity was key to the production of this labor class; identity became unsutured from the body, oriented to the state. No identity meant no future.

Institutions justified kinship disruption by claiming that children's own families and communities were ill equipped to provide them with the physical and moral training necessary to become laboring U.S. citizens.[109] Residential schools were a way for institutions and their agents to intervene in kinship and manage children—schools were home, and the institutions and their agents acted as parent, reinforcing "the family as a disciplinary matrix . . . [whose] particular forms of social control [are linked] to colonialism and globalization."[110] The rhetoric of care, welfare, and reform enabled these institutions to wrest children from their communities; families gave up their children in exchange for the promise of expansive economic futures and better chances at entering the social and political order.[111]

However, these schools for the supposed rehabilitation and preservation of childhood innocence were factories for producing, managing, and exploiting the labor of marginalized populations. Gill-Peterson, Sheldon, and Stockton argue that "child labor was never eradicated by Progressive reforms, but merely reorganized and made less visible."[112] By "less visible," they index the fact that child labor masqueraded under different names—like apprenticeships, the outing system, manual training, farming, and domestic service. Native American boarding schools, reform schools, schools for the blind, and industrial schools all initiated these programs as part of their educational curriculum. Students engaged in unpaid, often strenuous labor. There was not a deferral of work in these spaces but rather a deferral of entry into the categories of U.S. citizenship—a deferral intended to be made semipermanent once students left the institution.

This training did not necessarily position children for economic futures, even limited ones. For example, Wexler points out that at the Hampton Institute, the training that students received was "outmoded almost as soon as it was learned. It was training for a second-class career at best and more likely for domestic service or low-level, nonunion labor. At worst . . . it was training for nothing at all."[113] Native American children would be sent back to their reservations with no way to enact the skills they received, but their education was considered "a success precisely because of its program of indoctrination in the white, middle-class, Christian domestic lifestyle."[114] Students' labor was often in the service of maintaining the institution.[115] While the division of labor was gendered outside the institution, single-sex institutions often did not abide by these divisions. Thus, in boys schools, some boys would perform domestic work that they were ineligible for outside the institution, while some girls engaged in farming and mechanics, labor they would be unlikely to be hired to perform beyond school.

We Other Boarding Schools

These schools are not as rare in the cultural imaginary as one might think they are at first blush—they are boarding schools, and our culture has been preoccupied with the historical and fictional elements of boarding school literature and culture since the nineteenth century, when the school story became a recognizable genre and staple in the canon of children's and young adult literature. *Queer Childhoods* asks what happens when we decenter elite European and American boys (and later girls) as the site of knowledge production for the relationship among children, sexuality, and institutions. What happens to this knowledge and the presumptions on which it operates when the boarding school is in the late nineteenth-century United States or Canada and its attendees are Native American, Black, criminalized, and/or disabled? This project is, in part, inspired by Ann Laura Stoler's *Race and the Education of Desire: Foucault's* History of Sexuality *and the Colonial Order of Things*. Stoler asks, "Why, for Foucault, [did] colonial bodies never figure as a possible site of the articulation of nineteenth-century European sexuality?"[116] She investigates how Foucault's renderings of sexuality are disrupted when colonial bodies are not imagined as "racially erotic counterpoints" to European bourgeois sexuality but are examined as "objects of knowledge" in their own right.[117] Similarly, I center these other boarding schools that were being established in North America for marginalized populations at the same time as many of their elite counterparts to see how they recalibrate presumptions over childhood sexuality and innocence, as well as the place of the institution in shaping children's sexualities and futures. The children in these schools are examples of what Soderberg would call "antisocial" children whose "childhoods . . . often go unnoticed because they are so far from what we conventionally recognize as childhood, most notably because they are cruel social narratives that harm the children they label."[118] The nineteenth century is rife with attempts to manage "children inhabiting a nation [who] were not necessarily its future citizens and might even be a danger to its future stability."[119] These antisocial childhoods (and the antisocializing institutions that fostered them) fundamentally "enforced the boundaries of population" and were crucial to nation building and development and to upholding hierarchies.[120]

The boarding school has been an important site and the children who attend important figures for historians of childhood and sexuality. In *Centuries of Childhood*, Philippe Ariès looks to fifteenth-century boarding schools as sites where modern notions of childhood innocence and its eventual corollary, childhood asexuality, emerged. Ariès notes that educators in these institutions recorded their anxieties over sexual behavior among students, especially masturbation. They worried masturbation was a product of the "scholastic confinement of the boarding-school"—in other words, there was a fear that the institution itself produced the perceived deviant behavior.[121]

This relationship between sex and space for the child in boarding school resonates with Foucault's *History of Sexuality*. Foucault pays attention to children to show that "between the state and the individual, sex became an issue, and a public issue no less."[122] Foucault explains that within boarding schools "the architectural layout, the rules of organization, and their whole internal organization . . . [reveal that] the question of sex was a constant preoccupation."[123] Without ever naming that "preoccupation," everything about the schools—from the "shape of the tables" to "the rules for monitoring bedtime"—all "refer . . . to the sexuality of children."[124] Fear about childhood sexuality was literally built into the schools' walls and pivoted on the "assumption that this sexuality existed, that it was precocious, active, and ever present."[125] Because of this fear of sexuality being expressed or practiced among children, adults in these institutions were forced to "take charge, in a continuous way, of this precious and perilous, dangerous and endangered sexual potential" in children.[126]

Both Ariès and Foucault reveal desires that adults held regarding the children attending these institutions—overwhelmingly wealthy white boys. Adults wished that these children would not act on sexual desire or engage in sexual practices, and enormous effort was exerted to prevent the expression of childhood sexuality. They both acknowledge the force that the institution exerted on children's sexuality—the pedagogues in Ariès's history feared it would encourage premature sexual capacity, while those in Foucault's formulation hoped the physical institution could impede the enactment of extant sexuality. The schools they examined served as models for American boarding schools that also worked to "preserve the innocence of childhood" in order to transform it "into a pure and responsible maturity."[127] Attempts to erase, deny, or thwart sexual expression and desire did not necessarily fully succeed, but they did shape the universalizing narratives that emerged around childhood sexuality.

Educational reformers and professionals began debating the efficacy of boarding schools as more were established primarily for boys who were wealthy and white throughout the nineteenth and twentieth centuries in the United States. In the nineteenth century, romanticist reformers praised these schools' rural settings as able to preserve childhood innocence imagined to be at risk of corruption as cities began to develop on the East Coast—racist and xenophobic anxieties were coded as concerns over the power of place as a contaminating agent.[128]

As boarding schools become totalizing residential spaces—that is, sites where students both lived and learned 24/7—institutions and their agents could monitor children's development by mimicking the family unit. This project was always oriented toward failure—there were too many students and not enough adults to surveil their every move. Opponents thought these schools replicated the worst parts of British culture that America was trying to eschew. They condemned these institutions for disrupting kinship, producing "un-American" values of elitism, and creating the conditions for students to develop immoral habits like drinking, gambling, and same-sex intimacies.[129] Educational historian James McLachlan argues that boarding schools ultimately impeded teleological, normative psychosocial development: "The history of the private boarding school is the story of the beginnings of the extension of the period of institutionalized dependency for the youth of the United States."[130] Institutionalized dependency of the populations that attended these types of boarding schools, however, did not result in economic or political disenfranchisement—students graduated from these institutions and went on to become leaders in politics, business, and the arts.

While reformers continued to debate the best institutions for the upper echelon of American society, some saw these potential and more pernicious aspects of boarding school life as adaptable for other populations and thus began the establishment of institutions like those examined in this study. In the 1840s, politician Robert Dale Owen proposed state boarding schools as a solution for educating the immigrant and Black children newly populating his state of Indiana.[131] These children were imagined as good candidates for boarding schools because their families were seen as incapable of completing the moral work necessary to mold their children into proper American subjects. Compulsory schooling became the law of states throughout the late nineteenth and twentieth centuries as reformers realized that "social control over children [and] restoration of order [c]ould be accomplished through

local primary and secondary schools rather than in distant institutions."[132] While most American children attending school were enrolled in local public schools, specialized schools emerged to handle
those children who political leaders and reformers decided needed to
be more intensely managed in order to indoctrinate them properly into
U.S. citizenship.

These institutions billed themselves as educational, but they were
sites for discipline and labor training. Both school-like and prisonlike,
these boarding schools straddled the boundary between ideological
state apparatus (ISA) and repressive state apparatus (RSA). As Louis
Althusser argues, all state apparatuses are both ideological and repressive, but the proportion between ideology and repression determines
its classification. ISAs are private institutions that function by ideology first, then repression.[133] RSAs are public (that is, state-controlled)
and function by force and punishment first, then ideology. But the
line between public and private was often blurred for these schools;
many were state-run or state-sponsored, while others were founded
as private schools taken over by the state. Those that remained private
were often at the mercy of white benefactors with close ties to the state
(e.g., politicians or their wives and philanthropists). Institutions were
a mechanism of the state to control populations deemed threatening to
the political order; the state passed these institutions off as benevolent
in order to mask their repressive techniques. Schools were invested in
disciplining children's minds and bodies, and they attempted to exert
control over both through education and violence. By converging the
institutions of school and family, the state helped to reduce the chances
for interpellation to fail. Althusser explains that the time from "infant
[to] school age . . . [is] the years in which the child is most 'vulnerable,' squeezed between the family State apparatus and the educational State apparatus."[134] Institution and its agents operated *in loco
parentis*.[135] By endowing the institution with this authority, the state
eliminated this dangerous "vulnerability," increasing their chances for
"drum[ming] . . . into [marginalized students] . . . a certain amount of
'know-how'" through their education programs.[136]

Erving Goffman's taxonomy of total institutions also provides a useful
lens for understanding the ambivalent position of these schools. Total
institutions are places "where a large number of like-situated individu-

als [are] cut off from wider society for an appreciable period of time together [and] lead an enclosed, formally administered life."[137] There are five types: institutions that provide care for those who cannot care for themselves; institutions that care for those considered an unintended threat, such as those with contagious illnesses; institutions that house those deemed a threat where "the welfare of the persons . . . is not the immediate issue," such as prisons; institutions that allow persons to "pursue some technical task and justifying themselves only on these instrumental grounds" such as "army barracks, ships, [and] boarding schools"; and institutions for those who retreat, often for religious purposes, such as convents.[138] Total institutions function ostensibly to protect, but the directionality of that protection is dependent—they are either protecting their members or protecting the world outside the institutions from their members. The boarding school is the only example in Goffman's taxonomy in which protection seems neutral—the language suggests they are a site for training and tasks. However, confinement and education of children in boarding schools for white, wealthy children was tied up with language of protection, particularly of innocence. And boarding schools for marginalized populations claimed to be protecting children through providing them with an expanded future. However, the mode through which children were closed off from their communities and families of origin and the ways in which they were trained for limited, if any, futures suggest that the social and political orders were being protected from these populations.

Method and Overview

Despite the fact that children at the boarding and industrial schools described here were educated in institutional erotics, these so-called progressive institutions nonetheless could not anticipate or discipline every affect, habit, and sensation of the child. *Queer Childhoods* is also concerned with how children were able to respond to educations that sought total control of their bodies through having bodily experiences unauthorized by the state, and what these responses mean for their experience of queer childhood. Bodily sensations and pleasures can be what Foucault terms "stumbling block[s]" to power and what Elizabeth Povinelli might call aspects of the flesh that are consequences of discipline but also "independent, unruly vector[s] at play within . . . biopolitics."[139] Erotics are what M. Jacqui Alexander might term types of "body praxis," practices and sensations that "position . . . the body as a source of knowledge within terms differently modulated than the materiality of the body and its entanglement in the struggle against commodification."[140] Alexander focuses on spiritual rituals that engage the body as the "means through which we come to be at home in the body that supersede its positioning in materiality, in any of the violent discourses of appropriation, and in any of the formations within normative multiculturalism."[141] In other words, the spiritual is one register for accessing a relation to the body, finding a "home in the body," that is otherwise foreclosed. I use Alexander to think not of the spiritual but of the eroticized sensations, pleasures, affects, and habits, as a way to approach how the body might act as a source of knowledge that exceeds the education produced in institutions, enabling ways to inhabit the body against which the state educates. This excess is another form of queerness that at once folds into and further exceeds the queering produced by the state institutions—insofar as it allows bodies of marginalized and disciplined children to escape their foreclosed futures through atemporal erotics in, of, and against the present.

The direction of power in institutions was not one-way, nor did it render children as entirely passive objects only to be acted upon. I understand institutions in the way that historian of deviance Bruce Bellingham proposes—not as "simply a thing—a site, a program, an apparatus," but as relational.[142] In other words, institutions had a force upon children, and children reacted to institutions and the work carried out by their agents. The institution was not static but constantly being acted upon and reshaped by children. Settler, white-supremacist, eugenicist erotics were being reconstituted and altered as they were being inhabited. Furthermore, surveillance of sexuality through institutional mechanisms like the "pedagogical report" or "family control" could produce a double bind of "pleasure and power"—institutions derived "pleasure [from] . . . exercising a power that questions, monitors, watches, spies, searches out, palpates, brings to light; and on the other hand, the pleasure that kindles at having to evade this power, flee from it, fool it, or travesty it."[143] In other words, institutions did not completely eradicate pleasure through discipline but rather produced new types of pleasure bound up with the punitive features of institutional life. It is in these pleasures, bodily sensations, and habits that Foucault locates potential "points of resistance."[144] Children's bodies, in this formulation, could serve as a resource for responding to institutional erotics in which they were being educated. While open to this possibility, my analyses do not assume these disruptions as recuperative or something that could redeem the pain, loss, and trauma of the boarding school. Robin James cautions us against seeking out and celebrating "resilience," which she critiques as "neoliberalism's upgrade on modernist notions of coherence and deconstruction" that make "crisis and trauma . . . actually necessary, desirable phenomena."[145] To automatically apprehend these disruptions in children's experiences as politically resistant, psychically liberating, or signs of resilience would be to dishonor the contexts and histories from which they emerge and to enact epistemological harm. I investigate them without imposing this burden of transformation or potential, even if doing so leaves me in a "politically ambiguous" position because it undoes neat stories of social control while not giving way to easy stories of resistance.[146]

I look at how students' bodies and sexualities were weaponized against them and also look at how children responded to this education through harnessing these eroticized affects, sensations, and pleasures. I am also concerned with asking what weight these erotics can carry in their violent contexts. Does a moment of pleasure for a Native American student undo any state-sanctioned genocide? Does a blind student's illicit touch of a fellow classmate disrupt eugenicist narratives that render them nonsexual? Does a juvenile delinquent's continued engagement in sex work after leaving a reform school resist institutional management of her body or give the institution evidence for her pathology? Does a Black student's deviation from one moment of a schedule count when they ascribe to routine and regimen the rest of the time? My investigation poses these questions of scale, knowing there may not be easy or immediately available answers. I resist the affirmative mode of queer studies to celebrate these moments; I can insist only that we acknowledge them. To endow them with value would be to instrumentalize queer childhood; resisting this impulse, despite the pull to make theoretical and political meaning of them, is an uneasy, uncomfortable position. Queer theory has trained me to find the "potential" and "open up possibilities"—do I fail the field by refusing to do so, or does the field fail queer childhood by requiring it to *do* something?

This book is divided into five chapters. Chapter 1 argues that early twentieth-century reform schools for Black girls in the United States educated children in heteronormativity to restrict their possibilities for entering the social order. Delinquency for Black girls in this era was bound up with excessive sexuality and perverse kinship. I examine institutional materials from the Virginia Industrial School for Colored Girls, a reform school for Black girls established in 1915, to show how the institution had to prove its students were capable of sexual reform despite their race and thus was preoccupied with gender and sexual propriety based on white middle-class norms. Schools promised reform through heterosexualization, and the Virginia Industrial School claimed to prepare children for marriage, domesticity, and reproduction. However, this was a false promise that attempted to trap Black girls in a form of indentured servitude to white middle- and upper-class families. While the school spoke with pride of students who left to get married, in reality many students aged out of the institution and became apprentices for local white families. The school deemed children's own families unfit, so a full return to home and kinship was impossible. The school trained girls in gender and sexual norms to displace them from their own economic, sexual, or reproductive futures outside the institution. This displacement was the queer childhood that restricted their movements and choices beyond the institution.

Chapter 2 investigates the historical moment in juvenile reform when the discourse shifted from saving juvenile delinquents to treating them. Pathological narratives began to explicitly inform institutional management of children's sexualities. I look at Claude Brown's *Manchild in the Promised Land* (1965), a fictional account based on Brown's time in and out of reform schools in the 1930s and 1940s. In the mid- to late twentieth century, social scientists reproduced excerpts from the novel in professional textbooks to support state-sanctioned narratives of racialized criminalized childhood. While the novel demonstrates how schools attempted to pathologize children's sexualities, Brown's descriptions of sexuality as neutral and quotidian do not affirm this pathologization. The novel traces schools' attempts to make the world outside the institution uninhabitable for its protagonist but demonstrates his attempts to access non-institutional spaces to construct a sense of home that permits sexuality. I consider how the queer childhoods produced for Black juvenile delinquent boys in the novel transform their sentences into an indefinite time when their bodies, sexualities, and reproductive capacities remain under state and local (white) community control. Attempts to find alternative spaces outside the school were limited by being temporally bound to criminalized queer childhood.

Chapter 3 argues that schools for the blind educated children to renounce their sexualities. I suggest this education effectively sterilized children—educating them to repudiate their bodies and sexualities made students non-reproductive. Schools, then, operated in conjunction with allied practices of medical sterilization—their ideological work was supposed to have the same result as repressive state apparatuses. I examine how schools educated children to understand their blindness as the result of sexual impropriety for which their penance was present and future sexual disavowal. Thus, children knew they were being educated in norms they would never access. I look at annual reports from the Perkins School for the Blind and Ruth Hayden's *Erma at Perkins* (1944), a fictional account of her time at the school, from 1900 to 1913. The characters in the text are Hayden's actual classmates at Perkins, with the exception of the titular Erma. The fictional invention of Erma in what Hayden calls a "true account" allows the text to respond to a eugenicist education. It is through Erma that the text explores the disciplining of gender, sexuality, desires, and reproductive capacities, as well as Erma's sustained struggle against the mandates of disabled queer childhood.

Chapter 4 argues that hygiene programs in African American industrial schools educated children to experience their sexualities as dirty and shameful. Hygiene programs helped secure Black queer childhood in these settings. Through examining materials of the Manassas Industrial School (1893–1938), I argue children's sexuality was viewed as contaminated by virtue of their race, and this metaphorical contamination translated to strict hygienic practices and regimens in the school. The slippage among contaminated sexuality, race, and bodies educated children to believe they had to renounce sexuality in order to attain work outside the institution; bodily and sexual capacities had to be recalibrated and directed toward labor. Like with schools for children with disabilities, children understood that this compromise had to be made for them to gain access to a future outside of the institution. I examine Tarell Alvin McCraney's *Choir Boy* (2015), a play that imagines how those persons and institutions who bear the legacy of industrial education manage sexuality and futurity in a contemporary boarding school for African American boys. The play navigates how the institution cleanses its students of homosexuality, which culminates in a violent encounter in the school's showers. Its form shows how these histories are living and embodied in the contemporary moment.

Chapter 5 argues that Native American boarding schools educated children to abandon Native understandings of kinship, gender, and sexuality. This state-enforced abandonment resulted in sexual orphanings. Orphaning children from Native conceptualizations of gender and sexuality alienated children from their bodies, which resulted in nonreproductivity. Sexual orphanings, then, were key to the production of Native queer childhood. I look at the history and mission of the Carlisle Industrial School, the first off-reservation Native American boarding school established in the United States in 1879, and center my analysis on Cree author Tomson Highway's *Kiss of the Fur Queen* (1998), a magical realist novel based on his time at a Canadian residential school in the 1950s and 1960s. The text shows how children, upon leaving school, were unable to return to the home communities from which they were alienated or move forward into white communities from which they were barred full entry. The novel's form invokes alternate times and spaces informed by Indigenous epistemologies; Cree understandings of temporality enable the exploration of potential within liminality, but the book doesn't conclude with a redemptive understanding of the queer childhoods that determine the life outcomes of its characters. In a coda to the chapter, I explore the ongoing legacy of the boarding school through Sherman Alexie's *Flight* (2007). Most of the schools I examine in this project were closed by the mid-twentieth century. Many recognize this as part of the deinstitutionalization movement. However, students didn't leave these institutions and return to their families and communities—rather these schools were subsumed or transformed into other institutions, such as foster care, prisons, hospitals, group homes, and wilderness programs and schools part of the so-called troubled teen industry, part of a trend known as "transinstitutionalization."[147] These children continue to be targets of policies that seek to erase their communities' presence under the guise of welfare. The institutions in this project offer a genealogy to contemporary state intervention into kinship and institutionalization of children deemed threatening to the political order—the state continues to manage these threats through false promises to protect children and their futures. *Flight* examines the violence of racializing indigeneity, a process that obscures colonization and enables a complete orphaning of the foster care child from Native pasts and futures.

In the project's epilogue, I reflect on my own personal attachments to the field of queer theory. I provide two versions of the answer to the question of why I approached this as a queer project. I first consider the challenges and imperatives for doing interdisciplinary queer work. I then consider how the desire for this to be a queer project is a product of my training and generation and an idealization that might be incurring damage as it works to identify and disrupt it.

Queer childhoods abound in the present. As I write this introduction, queer childhood is being violently produced at the border—children attempting to enter the United States to escape violent and precarious futures are being produced as orphans, separated from their families, and institutionalized in detention centers because of the supposed threat they embody and pose to the nation. In these centers, their bodies are under strict state surveillance and are being experimented on, denied basic care and nourishment, and sexually and physically abused. Many who are allowed to leave the camps aren't being united with their families of origin but rather are being illegally adopted by families pledging to raise them in white Christian homes. Still others are not accounted for—as of September 2021, the federal government had lost track of about one-third of these children. These children don't get to gather under the banner of the Child, and for those who access a future, it will be contingent on violently enforced loss, trauma, and assimilation—on experiencing and enduring queer childhood. Expanding where and how we apprehend queer childhood is about interrogating which children are invested in by whom and for whom. Confining migrant children is a multibillion-dollar industry that emerged out of and alongside the privatization of prisons, generating capital and grants for the organizations building these centers. Historically and in the present, marginalized children's bodies have been acted upon in order to preserve racialized, classed, able-bodied, and national boundaries. Children secure the future for white heterosexual citizenry. These queer children should be at the center of queer studies because they are at the heart of the nation, carefully manufactured objects who guarantee and support the future at the expense of their own. Their queer childhoods have enabled the life rhythms of racialized capitalist sexual normativity.

1

False Promises of Heterosexualization

Criminalized Black Queer Girlhood

This chapter examines the production of criminalized and racialized queer childhood for Black juvenile delinquent girls in an early twentieth-century reform school. The Black juvenile delinquent girl was excluded from the category of normative childhood because of her racialized sexuality. In *Aberrations in Black: Toward a Queer of Color Critique*, Roderick Ferguson builds on Chandan Reddy's work to suggest that queers of color have no place in the home of the family nor in the home of the nation. In the context of Black juvenile delinquent girls, their delinquency was a mark of queerness that denoted and confirmed their perceived sexual perversity and deviance. State agencies intervened into Black families' homes by removing children and giving them a temporary home in reform schools to limit the possibilities of ever feeling fully at home in the nation. Ferguson remarks that this is how the state has "control[led] . . . erotic impulses" among persons of color: the state must enter "privatized spaces of home and body," and "the body must be . . . placed within the hands of Man . . . [and] controlled by Mankind."[1] Criminalized Black girls were queered by delinquency and "always presumed to be immoral."[2] They are examples of how the state entered the private sphere and disciplined "erotic impulses" at reform schools, which were understood as public entities functioning as private homes or "institution[s] of intimacy" invested in regulating sexuality among a population to whom they never intended to grant the benefits of full citizenship.[3]

I consider the educational work that reform schools for racialized populations saw themselves attempting, seeing reform schools in a larger matrix of late nineteenth- and early twentieth-century institutions that justified the long-term separation and confinement of marginalized populations under the guise of welfare, reform, and assimilation as well as promises of a better future. Criminalized children have been excluded from twentieth-century and contemporary cultural narratives that have viewed youth as sexually innocent, deserving of protection, and beneficiaries of the future. I'm interested in how promises of recuperation, protection, and futurity to criminalized children actually enabled the continued denial of each, producing a queer childhood defined by yearning and impossibility.

Children were oriented away from expansive sexual and reproductive futurities in reform schools through educations in gender and sexual normativity. More than just providing educations in academic and industrial training, these institutions were preoccupied with educating the children in how to apprehend, inhabit, and express their bodies, sexualities, and desires. Like post-Reconstruction residential industrial schools established for noncriminalized Black youth (which I explore further in chapter 4), juvenile reformatories for Black children were invested in "reforming the black subject from degenerate and immoral primitive to the normative citizen-subject of the United States."[4] Ferguson argues that industrial education was an "alliance between sexual normativity and citizenship."[5] Industrial training was not just education in and management of labor but also training in white bourgeois gender and sexual norms, where "sexual normativity claimed to be able to draft African Americans into citizenship and humanity."[6]

Reform schools for African American children were hyperinvested in training children in this sexual normativity because the pathological sexuality assigned to all Black bodies was compounded by children's supposed criminality. Black girls especially were viewed as "inherently deviant, unfixable and dangerous delinquents."[7] This view, according to Kali Gross and Cheryl Hicks, "allowed judges, juries, and officers to excuse their unjust treatment of African American women based on the belief that African American women did not require the same protection because they lacked virtue."[8] Jen Manion explains that in early American carceral spaces, "racialized gender norms of patriarchal white supremacy structured the penitentiary, making the promise of American justice . . . elusive for black and immigrant women."[9] In other words, training in white gender and sexual norms set racialized girls and women up for an unfulfillable promise, as they would never be white—and thus could not fully enter the category of U.S. citizenship—in the eyes of the state.

The promise of citizenship through racialized sexual normativity was an impossibility, but it continued to structure carceral spaces throughout the nineteenth and twentieth centuries.[10]

I center the case of the Virginia Industrial School for Colored Girls to examine how this carceral institution educated criminalized Black girls in white gender and sexual norms and the sexual and temporal effects of this education. In 1915, the institution was established as the Industrial Home School for Colored Girls and opened in Hanover County, Virginia, for the care, education, and reform of Black juvenile delinquent girls.[11] Founded by social reformer Janie Porter Barrett, the school was one of the first U.S. reform schools for African American girls. It was supported by white and Black patronage until 1920, when it was taken over by the state.

The school used the rhetoric of welfare and sexual reform to orient children toward limited futures in the homes of wealthy and often abusive white families. Delinquency for girls and especially nonwhite youth in this era was bound with excessive sexuality and perverse kinship and was "virtually synonymous with sexual impropriety."[12] Thus, the school was preoccupied with how to manage the problem of Black girls' bodies and sexualities. The school claimed that a major solution to juvenile delinquency was to prepare children for marriage, reproduction, and homemaking; an engagement for one of these children was the hallmark of successful reform. I focus on how the schools promised reform through heterosexualization. I argue that this was a false promise that attempted to trap children in a form of indentured servitude to white middle- and upper-class families, sentenced to what Sarah Haley has called the "domestic carceral sphere."[13] While the school spoke with pride of students who left to get married, in reality most students were initially paroled (vs. initially married) and became apprentices for local white families. At times they were sent back to school because the families they were required to live with were violent or abusive toward them. The school deemed children's own families unfit, so a return to a prior home and kinship was impossible. There was no guaranteed exit from the school but rather a revolving door that kept children under the surveillance of the institution and its agents.

I understand this false heterosexualization that resulted in inaccessible white heterosexuality as producing and constituting girls' criminalized and racialized queer childhoods. Brigitte Fielder's theorizing on how "race is . . . relative" usefully illuminates how a mode of interracial kinship enabled the trapping logics of the school.[14] Fielder explores how race "is produced not in individual bodies themselves, but, crucially, in the relationships between them—in kinship relations that are not simply direct genealogies of racial inheritance from one generation to the next, but which work in decidedly gendered and non-heteronormative ways."[15] The school's education in white norms enabled through kinship disruption and supplanting—removing girls from their homes, repudiating their families of origin, and making school home and family— was a racializing process that endowed girls with a felt sense of white heterosexual norms that mitigated their relationship with their bodies, sexualities, and desires. Racialized sexual knowledges were transferred to the girls in order to suspend them in a strained relationship with their sexual expression and capacities. Queer childhood tethered girls to the institution in material and ideological ways; the internalization of and adherence to white heterosexual norms did not assimilate girls into white mainstream culture—rather, it helped to determine to what extent they could bolster white heterosexual norms through domestic labor. Refusal of these norms increased girls' chances of more institutionalization. Their queer childhoods were recursive and repetitious temporal forms. The future these girls could access was state-designed to curtail girls' mobility, independence, and freedom in adulthood. It also formalized their dependency on the state, a dynamic that Crystal Webster recognizes as "institutionaliz[ing] Black childhood as transgressive."[16] The school's production of criminalized and racialized queer childhood through making the school a site of kinship and transfer of racialized modes of inhabiting the body mandated aspiring to sexual respectability and gender propriety, and violating this mandate made students susceptible to further criminalization, pathologization, and institutionalization. In Saidiya Hartman's investigation of girls and women who were incarcerated at Bedford Hills, she asserts "the aim [of the institution] was civil death: the mortification of the self, everything a young woman had been and might be ended at the gates."[17] This formulation, when applied to the Virginia Industrial School, captures the ways the institution cut off one path to futurity through rigorous displacements from the body, sexuality, family, and community.

I focus on the first twenty-six years of the Virginia Industrial School (1915–41), which illustrate how sexuality was a preoccupation of the school in its founding years. Children's senses of home were constructed alongside and indeed bound with a sexual propriety that left them without home and with limited access to economic or reproductive futurity outside the institution. The institution functioned as an affective and material anchor that restricted the times and places accessible outside it. This era also illustrates the school's growing concern with pathology, and specifically "feeblemindedness" and mental health in the 1930s, which Regina Kunzel has termed a shift from "saving" to "treating" girls that was happening in many institutions for sexually delinquent youth at the time.[18] When girls were sent back to the school, it was usually because they were convicted of a sexually related crime; the school explained these girls were "feebleminded," a "diagnosis and categorization of social worth" that rescripted sexual delinquency from being a product of race to being a byproduct of racialized disability.[19] Girls who could not be absorbed into the national order and whose labor could not be exploited had to be pathologized, and their new destiny was more institutionalization and, for some, sterilization. The production of Black disabled queer childhood was a tactic to manage the perceived ongoing threat of Black girls' sexualities.

I read archival materials in order to discern the narratives the school told about itself to the world beyond the institution. I rely heavily on annual reports to help me construct this narrative. Annual reports were written by Barrett, who was involved in the day-to-day management of the institution, and they were addressed to the funding body that would determine the allocation and distribution of resources. The reports aimed to tell a story of progress to justify the institution's existence and to guarantee a renewal of funds that would enable it to continue operating. Reports usually included a narrative, divided into sections, about life in the institution, figures and statistics on the health of the student body, lists of materials produced by the institution through student labor, lists of donations, and budgetary reports. Students' voices were largely absent from these materials, and when they do appear (e.g., in the form of testimony), they're heavily mediated. In her work on carceral institutions in Chicago, Tera Agyepong notes how "staff members' and administrators' words shed light on how institutional policies . . . shaped the girls' experience of the institution."[20] These narratives impacted the material conditions and affective experiences of the girls in the school and provide insights into how the norms governing students' bodies and sexualities were key components of their educational experience.

In their introduction to the special "Gendering the Carceral State" issue of the *Journal of African American History*, Gross and Hicks contend that in "resurrecting and examining black women's historical skirmishes with the legal system and analyzing crime and violence, we identify judicial patterns of raced and gendered biases at the same time that we affirm black female humanity by committing their lives to the historical record. These are important steps in the ongoing struggle to remedy the racist failings of the U.S. criminal justice system and to protect the lives of African American women and girls."[21] Looking at the ways in which promises of sexual normativity worked to displace girls from the social order provides us with tools for interrogating the treatment and confinement of Black juvenile delinquent girls. In this chapter's conclusion, I reflect on how the history of the Virginia Industrial School illuminates contemporary state-sanctioned practices that continue to target and harm Black girls while utilizing the rhetoric of care and protection enabled by education.

The Industrial Home School to the Virginia Industrial School

The Virginia State Federation of Colored Women's Clubs, spearheaded by the efforts of social reformer and educator Barrett, provided the necessary funds for the school to open (i.e., purchase of land, construction of buildings, hiring and support of staff), with additional financial assistance for maintenance and expansion offered by the Virginia General Assembly. The school was managed by the Virginia State Federation of Colored Women's Clubs until 1920, at which point it was taken over by the state, largely for financial reasons and the state's "threatened stoppage of appropriations."[22] The Women's Club remained heavily involved, however, and Barrett served as the school's superintendent for its first twenty-five years, helping to manage the school's transition from private to state-run institution.

Juvenile reformatories of the late nineteenth and twentieth centuries were largely populated by and intended for white children.[23] Those who were at the forefront of juvenile justice reform in the Progressive Era were often white, as were those working in the government positions whom "the child savers" petitioned for resources and approval to establish reformatories. In *The Black Child-Savers*, Geoff Ward explains that "white child-savers typically enjoyed access to white government officials, industrial leaders, and other power brokers essential to advancing their civic initiatives, [while] the black child-savers proceeded from a subordinate social position and were engaged in a conflict movement, a contentious struggle against existing racial power relations," and "states routinely prioritiz[ed] the creation of white reformatories, or manufactories of white citizens, while refusing to provide equivalent services, if any at all, for black youths."[24]

Until the mid-nineteenth century, most children who were deemed delinquent, because of either their own behavior or that of their parents, were sent to prison. The desire to establish separate institutions for children came from fears both sexual and temporal that intersected in the space of the prison: reformers feared that children were being corrupted by adults in prisons, and they believed that children who committed crimes were more capable of redemption than their adult counterparts.[25] Children, then, needed to be segregated from adults to preserve their innocence, which was perceived to be lost by virtue of their criminality; this innocence, however, was seen as capable of rescue, and child savers worked to establish reformatories for children throughout the United States. Displacing children from their families to put them in institutions managed by the state and other organizations was a "new form of state intervention into children's lives, which relied on institutional interventions to care for poor and disabled children and reform children who committed crimes, [and] was distinct from nineteenth-century houses of refuge and reformatories because it was fueled by a distinct Progressive ideological movement and was intricately intertwined with juvenile courts."[26] The reform school ostensibly differed from its institutional predecessors precisely because of its stated investment in children's futures.

As reformers like Barrett noticed, the determination of which children could be reformed and which deserved protection from corruption was racialized. While white children's delinquency was also often sexualized, their delinquency was considered a product of their environment versus an inherent feature of their race.[27] Black children ended up in "adult prisons, the convict-lease system, [or] prolonged periods in detention."[28] White children of the same age and convicted of the same crimes attended reform schools.[29] When reformatories for Black children and other racial minority groups were established, they were often funded and managed by women's clubs and other private organizations and, like the Virginia Industrial School, were eventually taken over by the state.[30]

These schools' origins as private institutions backed by philanthropic organizations and individuals, however, made for an alternate experience within the school. More so than state schools for white children, these schools in their founding moments had components that resembled elite private boarding schools. For example, at the Virginia Industrial School, students celebrated Founder's Day, had organized athletic competitions between cottages, and had a system of merits signified by dress color, ribbons, and pins. These features of the school coexisted with other qualities usually absent from elite institutions: girls engaged in hard labor and were screened and often treated for sexually transmitted diseases upon arrival (and throughout their stay), and their graduation signified being paroled to the community. These more traditional features of the school were retained when the state took over. However, the state's final determination of the distribution of resources impacted conditions at the school, which was overcrowded, understaffed, and unable to monitor girls upon parole because the state refused to provide the school with a parole officer, despite an annual plea for one in the school's reports.

When the school was taken over by the state, its name shifted from the Industrial Home School to the Virginia Industrial School for Colored Girls.[31] This subtle change encapsulates how state control made the school less a "home" and more a site for managing Black girls so that their bodies, sexualities, and labor could be controlled by the state and its agents in the future. While the school's leaders struggled for the school to retain its homelike features, the state's final say on the distribution of resources created conditions that made it difficult to do so. A 1941 inspection conducted by the Children's Bureau of the State Department of Public Welfare noted that the "cottages are so large or so over-crowded that the atmosphere is institutional rather than home-like . . . The task of producing something like home life at Peaks . . . is further handicapped by the fact that cottage personnel is inadequate in numbers and not highly skilled. The house mothers have too many duties to perform to give sufficient attention to their relationships with the girls."[32] The inspection applauded the staff and administration's desire and intention to create homelike conditions for the girls, but the financial management of the school made it difficult to create space that didn't look and feel institutional or carceral. Aspirations for intimacy between staff and students were thwarted by sheer numbers—too many students and too little staff—as well as a lack of trained staff. The inspection continues,

> Something approaching home life, or at least life in a small enough group so that close personal relationships and guidance are possible, is considered fundamental. Much of what is meant by training is not a highly formalized process, but takes place naturally in the day-by-day cottage life. . . . While a cottage with even as few as twenty girls in it cannot come to simulate home life exactly, it can produce much of the atmosphere of a home and utilize many of the methods that make it possible for a good home to train children in the natural give-and-take of family life.[33]

Here, the inspection acknowledges that the girls were being trained not just with regard to skill and labor but also in quotidian ways on how to properly inhabit relationships, homes, and families. This affirms both that training for futures in domestic service was tied up with training in heterosexual and domestic propriety as well as the impossibility for the school to actually fulfill this promise of heterosexualization and future work in homes because of the underresourced institution.

In the following analysis, I do not intend to disparage or diminish the work that Barrett and her colleagues did to reform and care for these girls. Despite the nature of reformatories, scholars, including Geoff Ward, have argued that Black women's roles in the creation and maintenance of these institutions enabled "potentially *progressive* dimensions of racialized social control."[34] As Barrett frequently notes, she and her staff were working with a population of girls who "represent the group which society has discarded as a failure" and would be treated as such if not for institutions like the Virginia Industrial School.[35] During her twenty-five-year tenure, Barrett regularly used language in the annual reports that suggests her desire to treat the girls as her own daughters and teach them to treat each other as family: they were her "foster children," the institution was a "growing family," and the school annually celebrated Mother's Day, when the girls often honored the staff.[36] Creating a family in the school usually depended on demonizing the girls' families of origin; Barrett writes in the *Eighth Annual Report*, "Many of our girls have heard all their lives (often from their own mothers) that they are nothing and never will amount to anything and they believe it firmly. We have not only to make them want to be somebody, but we have to teach them how to develop that 'somebody.'"[37] Barrett claimed that the school did maternal work that the girls' own mothers were incapable of fulfilling. In Barrett's estimation, the school had to undo the bad mothering that made girls feel unworthy and then build up their worth and personhood.

Vilifying girls' families and communities of origin was routine and crucial in funneling the girls into a limited future disconnected from any sense of original home and kinship. The institution supplanted the home and family, which left the girls isolated and out of place when they had to leave: they had neither their family, home, or community of origin nor the one of the institution and instead were obligated to work in the service of someone else's home and family.[38] These eventual outcomes weren't necessarily the intention of Barrett and her colleagues; by all accounts, the attempts to create community and family within the school were sincere, and these women worked to make each girl feel cared for and connected to one another in the space of the school. I attempt to understand the impact of these quotidian moments of intimacy and care within the larger state-determined structure of neglect and criminalization of Black delinquent girls.

Criminalized Sexuality and Protection

Institutional reports and memories of the school's origin pinpoint World War I as the reason for an influx of students in the school's first years. At the time, a military training camp was established near the school, and soon after Black girls were being sent to juvenile courts for misconduct at the camp. They'd be sent from the courts to the school, and many were infected with sexually transmitted diseases upon arrival. In the school's

Fourth Annual Report, Barrett writes, "Since the day the special appropriation was given to our school by the Fosdick Commission and our State to take care of the girls who would be harmful to the War Camp communities, we have felt that we had a very important part in winning the war. We have realized that our part is not only to relieve the communities of the objectionable girl, but that we must make her a safe citizen and return her in due time to society."[39] The Fosdick Commission was established in 1917 to "ke[ep American troops] physically healthy *and* morally pure, free of the traditional degradation of training camp culture" and was especially concerned with managing and preventing the spread of sexually transmitted diseases in the training camps.[40] The commission and the state donated the money necessary to build the school's second cottage, Hanover Cottage, a "structure [that] was erected hurriedly for the housing of girls who showed a tendency to become a menace around the training camps during the world war."[41] For building the cottage the Fosdick Commission donated $20,000, matched by the state. Prior to World War I, the state had provided $3,000 to the school in its first two years and $10,000 in its third, amounts that were continually shifting because the state would respond to neighboring communities' objections to the school's existence by withdrawing or reducing pledged sums.[42] Thus, the state invested in these girls when it was an investment in persons *besides* the girls: in this case the military and, by extension, the nation.[43]

Barrett's reporting reveals that these girls' sexualities were both criminalized and perceived as a threat to the nation, not just by the Fosdick Commission but by the school's staff. The girls were seen as having an innate capacity for sexual deviance, and they had to be prevented from acting on their perceived nature. Questions of consent, coercion, violation, abuse, and violence were not posed, despite the fact that most of the girls admitted to the school during this time were well under the age of consent in Virginia.[44] The girls needed to be cared for to protect those persons, specifically men, with whom they might come in contact. The institution increased safety—not for girls but for those around them. The men and the nation had to be protected from these girls, narrated as a threat. But controlling Black girls' sexualities and specifically their interactions with military men was constructed as a condition of guaranteeing national security and U.S. power: it was a "very important part of winning the war." Black girls were not outside of the national framework; instead, managing their role within the nation was crucial to its strength. The strength of the nation, then, came at the cost of criminalizing Black girls.

Rhetoric of assimilation, citizenship, and national service pervades the reports and helped to assuage the fears these girls posed to those in proximity to the school as well as those in charge of distributing funds to the school. In the *Second Annual Report*, Barrett wrote, "These girls can be made an asset for the state and nation . . . all a normal girl needs is a chance."[45] The justification to reform Black girls related back to national service—their value was in their potential service, not in their present existence. Girls were educated to believe that the labor they performed, often strenuous, was for the state. For example, during World War I, there was a "labor shortage" and crops in the area around the school weren't being harvested.[46] Barrett tried to convince the school's neighbors that her students could work their crops for free. Some objected to having the girls anywhere near their property, referring to them as "trash" and "scum of the earth."[47] Barrett eventually convinced some neighbors, in part by negotiating that the girls were "perfectly willing to do the work for nothing. . . . Our pay will be the satisfaction of knowing that we are helping to conserve food for the soldiers."[48] Barrett wrote that she framed this to the girls as "an opportunity we have to prove that we love our country by raising all the vegetables we can. I have told them that . . . we are working for our country."[49] Girls did not like working the farm because of the harsh conditions, and Barrett admitted it was not the best form of preparation for girls' future after the institution because "they must earn their living in some other way when they leave the school."[50] So the girls' hardship and even sacrifice of future economic opportunity had to be endured to prove their devotion to the nation. Girls were taught their own well-being could be subservient to that of the nation. Their labor could be exploited by persons who saw them as "scum of the earth," but they must be "satisf[ied]" because this labor is helping soldiers. So, despite the fact that the girls were seen as future "assets" to the nation, they actually provided valuable labor in their present. There was a deferral in their recognized value, and this deferral enabled their exploitation.

This temporal confusion over when girls were seen as valuable relates to a similar confusion over their ability to be or become citizens. At school, girls would strive to make each week's honor roll for good behavior, and these girls were "considered the first citizens of our community, and . . . permitted to wear a small American flag to the [daily] Assembly."[51] The school was invested in "teaching the fundamentals of good citizenship which our girls must know before they can fit acceptably into any community."[52] To be a citizen of the Virginia Industrial School was to be a citizen of the United States, and good behavior permitted one entry to citizenship (publicly via an American flag pin). Girls were being conferred citizenship in the space of the school, but they were actually not yet citizens in the eyes of the school because they did not yet know the "fundamentals." Barrett affirms girls were not yet citizens when she writes, "We can never lose sight of the fact that we are dealing with citizens of the future. The training they are given now will determine the kind of citizen they will be."[53] Whether or not they could be citizens depended on the labor they did at school.

Thus, citizenship was a condition for community membership, but the origin moment of citizenship appears confused. In the same report Barrett writes, "I am more and more convinced that next to character building must come training in home making, for this is the natural line of work the girls will follow; training along this line not only means opportunity and a useful life, but it also means better-care-for homes, where the training for citizenship begins. And whether they are caring for their own homes or those of someone else, if they do it well they are making a contribution to their country's welfare."[54] Here, Barrett explains the work of the school was to train girls in domestic service, seen as a "natural" course of events. The oscillation between whether girls were being trained to maintain their own home or others' captures the school's project of training girls in a white domestic heterosexuality they would not necessarily inhabit: their future was more likely to be in proximity to these norms and helping to maintain them through domestic service. This future in domestic service was important for the nation because homes are "where the training for citizenship begins." Barrett might be saying that citizenship for the girls would not begin until they were working; citizenship, elsewhere described as being inculcated in the school, actually would not occur until girls were part of the economic order and "contribut[ing] to their country's welfare," despite the fact that they had already been doing this work. Students were operating under a promise of citizenship, which wasn't guaranteed. Outside of school, they would realize that they had to "live down the stigma of having been committed to a penal institution."[55] They would be employed in homes that shared the belief they were "scum of the earth." They would not be guaranteed full entry to citizenship.[56]

Reform through Heterosexualization

In addition to appeasing fears about the girls through narrating their capacity for citizenship, the threat girls posed was further extinguished through a vehement assertion of proper heterosexuality. While the school was a single-sex institution, the annual reports include accounts of interactions with nearby boys schools, all narrated as having a didactic purpose. For example, in the *Fourth Annual Report*, Barrett wrote, "A new feature was added to our recreation list when the honor boys of the Boys' School invited the honor girls to a watermelon feast. . . . The feast was carefully supervised by the officers from both schools and it was wholesome and bracing for both. It gave an opportunity to find out what the girls needed to know about how to conduct themselves when in the company of the boys, and the same is true of the boys."[57] Here, surveilled heterosexual interaction was imagined to contribute to and strengthen morality of students' minds and bodies. This education in heterosexuality had to be included in the annual report to convince people that perceived inherent sexual delinquency was being reformed in the school; heterosexual interaction was proof that girls were educable and that delinquency was not natural but a result of circumstance. Barrett knew that a significant amount of "time and energy" was expended to plan the celebration, but "it was doubly worth [it]. . . . They looked forward to the trip for days and talked about it for weeks afterward and planned to be good all the year so they could go next time."[58] The understaffed and overworked institution saw this event as a worthy investment because it was crucial to heterosexualize these children. The motivating force of the event shows how heterosexuality helped to structure discipline and reform in the school.

Other examples of interactions with boys schools occur in the reports, all included to show that these girls were capable of sexual reform—sexual delinquency wasn't a lifelong, inherent condition but something that could be improved. In the *Sixth Annual Report*, Barrett wrote that a complement to the summer event was the New Year's Party: "[It] has proved in every way helpful to both boys and girls. The girls are given instructions about how to conduct themselves in the presence of young men and the boys are given similar instructions."[59] Barrett continues, "These gatherings give them an opportunity to put into practice what they have been taught and help to develop them naturally."[60] Heterosexuality had to be indoctrinated into children, and events like this "helped" and gave opportunities for staff to provide roadmaps for proper gender and sexual propriety. That which was manufactured must appear "natural." The preoccupation with heterosexual interaction reveals a concern for girls' sexual capacities, and specifically capacities for deviance, and a desire to straighten them. Propriety routed through heterosexuality was a safe guarantor of reform.

Rhetoric around marriage also reveals a desire to straighten girls. Marriage became synonymous with futurity outside the institution. A student could leave the school when she was paroled, aged out, transferred to another institution under state control (a hospital or the State Board of Public Welfare), transferred to an industrial school for non-criminal African American children, ran away, or got married.[61] Paroled students were still followed by the school, but the number of students and lack of a parole officer made it impossible to track many of these students' fates—paroled students' fates reveal themselves most visibly in the annual reports, when the number of returned parolees is included in the population statistics.

However, a student could be fully extricated from the school and its surveillance (even if not a full or thorough surveillance) if she married. Such marriages were few and far between according to the school's ledgers, but Barrett wrote in detail about several weddings over the course of the first twenty-five years of the annual reports. For example, in the *Fourth Annual Report*, Barrett wrote about the wedding of a student who was paroled close to the school, so many students were able to attend: "She married a soldier boy, a very nice fellow for whom eight months in training camps had done wonders. . . . The whole affair was just as dignified and pretty as could be. I don't believe that there was a girl present who did not feel that it was a very fine thing indeed to marry honorably, the lesson I meant to drive home."[62] Barrett used the wedding of this former student as a lesson in heterosexual futurity. The inclusion of the husband's status as a soldier in the training camps acknowledged a strange union between two groups—one criminalized for their sexual behavior, one exempt from any responsibility for sexual interactions that may have resulted in the other's criminality. If the student had interacted with this soldier prior to enrolling in school, she would have been a menace, endangering him and the nation; now she was no longer a threat, and their interactions could occur in a state-sanctioned union. Training camp had "done wonders" for the young man, which parallels how the school reformed the young woman. The marriage suggests that the student had been incorporated into the national order—she was held as a model to the state for what reform could look like for these criminalized children, and she was also a model for other students for why they should work hard at the school. Heterosexuality was a promise to motivate girls' labor in the present.

In addition to the rhetoric around marriage and heterosexual interaction, the annual reports' medical statistics reveal a fear of girls' capacity for and enacting of sexual deviance. In each annual report, the school includes the number of students tested for sexually transmitted infections, most commonly syphilis and gonorrhea, upon entering the school; the number tested for sexually transmitted diseases throughout the year; and the number and types of treatments given for sexually transmitted diseases. Despite the large number of treatments administered every year, and even girls having to leave the school in its early years because their infections were so severe, as well as the inclusion of these statistics in each annual report, Barrett's narrative includes repeated claims regarding the overall health of the student body.[63] This repeated insistence on health in spite of large numbers of sexually transmitted infections suggests a desire to sanitize the narrative around these girls because of the stigma attached to these infections.[64] Numbers suggest that sexually transmitted epidemics were routine, but Barrett's refusal to report this reality in narrative form (despite her narrative being submitted with these statistical reports that suggest otherwise) reveals a refusal to acknowledge that what was perceived to be sexual deviance might be occurring in the school. Barrett constructed a story of sexual propriety and health to present to those in charge of the school's resources in order to prove these girls were capable of sexual reform. Heterosexuality and sexual propriety were justification for the school's existence and proof of its usefulness to the state. This narrative, on one hand, was in the service of getting more resources for the school, which would ultimately help the girls. On the other hand, it contributed to the ideology that Black girls' sexualities and bodies were dangerous, wrong, and shameful. Girls' sexualities and bodies were permitted if they fit into a narrow sanitized heterosexual vision, which was offered to them as something to desire since it signified futurity and life beyond the institution. What was a narrative for the state was absorbed as a promise for the girls, which came at the cost of sexual shame and indoctrination into a heteronormative order into which they would not necessarily gain entry.

Lurking beneath this preoccupation with heterosexuality was a fear of same-sex intimacies. At first glance, homosexuality seems absent from the official records of the Virginia Industrial School. While the annual reports intermittently include a list of infractions and behaviors for which girls lose privileges, homosexuality never appears on the list.[65] However, the 1941 inspection reported that homosexual behavior did occur and discussed what happened when a girl engaged in homosexual acts: "When homosexuality is reported the superintendent counsels with the girl, and if the affair is considered serious enough, she may be placed in Virginia Cottage in an individual room. Whatever class standing she has is lost until she shows desire to control herself and get along without close supervision."[66] The same report later mentions, "Homosexual problems are dealt with sensibly, the major emphasis being on counselling. The girl offending in this way is assigned to a single room."[67] The inclusion of homosexual behavior and its systematized consequences in the inspection versus its absence from the annual reports contributes to a reading that Barrett wished to sanitize girls of sexual deviance and impropriety in the official record, despite what was actually happening in the institution. Other scholarship on contemporaneous single-sex reform schools suggests that sexual interaction between the girls was common and was seen either as harmless friendship or as a result of situational homosexuality—in other words, the institution produced these intimacies and ostensible perversities, and staff had to discern which behavior was threatening and which could be rendered harmless.[68] Barrett's school seemed to follow the same logic—girls were punished if "the affair [was] considered serious enough," suggesting degrees of physical intimacy among students. Students were "dealt with sensibly" through "counselling": homosexuality is a window into seeing the school's shift to becoming more concerned with psychological health, treatment, and pathology.

There might be occluded mentions of homosexuality in the annual reports in discussions of disciplinary responses to students' infractions. Barrett's disciplinary model repudiated physical punishment and instead used a system of rewards and privileges, which could be conferred or taken away depending on a student's behavior. The one seeming exception to this model was the Thinking Room, first mentioned in 1919.[69] This Thinking Room may be the "individual room" girls were sent to when they were suspected of engaging in homosexual behavior. Girls could be sent to the Thinking Room for up to a month, and here they were required to live in silence and survive on minimal sustenance— meals could be delivered only after a girl had completed work—in order to "get straight with the world."[70] In the *Sixth Annual Report*, Barrett describes the room in more detail:

> If at any time a girl's behavior is so disgraceful that she has to be locked up in the "Thinking Room" she has to wear a brown dress. The activities of the "brown-dress girl" must be confined to road improvement work, which consists of carrying from the gravel pile to the roads on the grounds a certain number of buckets full of gravel which varies according to the nature of her misdemeanor. If her spirit is good she may carry as many as three or four bucketsful at a time. . . . If her spirit is ugly she has to bring up the gravel a half-bucketful at a time.[71]

While described elsewhere as a site of meditation, the room here seems to represent punishment in hard labor, isolation, and publicly visible exclusion. While Barrett doesn't explicitly state which infractions constitute "behavior . . . so disgraceful," homosexuality may be one of the unnamed actions that isolated a girl to this single room. That a single room could be maintained for this purpose in an institution that was chronically overcrowded suggests the urgency of this particular form of punishment.

After Heterosexualization?

The promise of marriage and heterosexual futurity in exchange for abandonment of imagined sexual deviance and regaining of sexual health was not guaranteed. While the girls were educated in heterosexual interaction and motivated by the reform granted through marriage, their futures outside the institution were overwhelmingly in the homes of white families as domestic servants. Barrett writes of many girls' marriages in the annual reports, but the ledgers report that only three girls left the institution between 1915 and 1939 for marriage.

The discrepancy between the number of marriages reported in the annual reports versus the number recorded in the school's official ledgers might be because the former includes students who were paroled. However, given Barrett's lamentation of her inability to follow up with most girls when they were paroled and the lack of inclusion of other data or reports of paroled students (other than general statements of their success and a few individual cases) calls into question from where these numbers were coming. Even the paroled students' marriages were being reported. The fact that they were included in the statistics for marriage but not for other outcomes routinely included in the annual reports, like reports on sexually transmitted disease, suggests a desire to augment the data that show success in heterosexuality and occlude the data that could signify sexual delinquency. In the *Eighth Annual Report*, Barrett wrote, "Twenty-one of the girls have married. I am much pleased to report this for it shows that some of our ideals and standards for home life have taken root. We try to stress personal purity directly and indirectly at all times. Whether I find the couple living in one or two rooms or in a little cottage, I see their marks of the training we have given."[72] Who exactly these twenty-one girls were remains a mystery, but they were invoked to prove reform through heterosexualization: their marriage exemplified the success of the school's moral and sexual "training." Girls had very few options upon leaving the school. Barrett repeatedly wrote about how girls were not allowed to return home because their families had been deemed unsuitable or "not the right kind."[73] Concern over girls' returns to their families recurred across the reports.[74]

The school, then, worked to undo girls' senses of home. Girls were permitted limited contact with home, as incoming and outgoing mail had to be read and approved by a staff member. While visits were permitted monthly, Barrett believed them to be too "upsetting to the children" and encouraged parents to not visit and to trust that the "children [were] properly looked after and managed in the right way."[75] The school alienated children from their families of origin for the sake of reform and proper "manage[ment]." Barrett stated that the goal was such that "when [a student] goes out she is made to feel that the school is her home."[76] A student was disentangled from her roots and required to reorganize her frame of reference so that the institution was home. On one hand, making the institution home permitted the girls a sense of community and connection with those in the institution. On the other hand, this sense of home comes when a girl "goes out." Barrett constructed home *retroactively*—it was something girls were "made to feel" *after* they have left school. Home functioned as a trap that left girls with no home, other than a longing for the institution. Home was not a place but an affective mode oriented toward the state institution, which could provide a girl with only limited opportunities and subscribed to narratives of sexual delinquency and propriety. Girls' options were primarily domestic service in someone else's home, return to the institution, or placement in another institution if they were over eighteen. The longing for home, and the impossibility to feel at home in the time of childhood, was a key feature of their queer childhoods.

Domestic service was an economic opportunity for which the girls were trained. While Barrett noted that "each year finds a larger number of girls anxious to continue their academic work," most did not "hav[e] sufficient funds" to do so.[77] She discussed one student who received a scholarship to continue her education and reported that this student, upon graduation, would "com[e] back to us as a teacher of domestic science."[78] A future via education, then, was routed back to the institution and in the service of helping to funnel more girls into domestic labor. Domestic work was often a student's only initial option for life outside the institution. While at school she was invited to imagine and aspire toward other futures—for example, marriage, education, and citizenship. While domestic work didn't negate the possibility of attaining these, it was often a block, at least initially, toward accessing them. The role of the school was to restrict girls' sexualities in order to make their bodies valuable to the state. The school was a site to consolidate, control, and manage the distribution of Black labor. In her investigation of criminalized Black women in Georgia in the early twentieth century, Haley argues that through parole "black women were forced to labor as domestic workers for white families, giving new meaning to the concept of the prison of the home."[79] In the home, these women "were subject to constant surveillance and the threat of return to the prison camp for any transgression; private individuals served as police and warders."[80] Haley's argument maps onto the parole system of the Virginia Industrial School, which sentenced girls to "the prison of the home" that they were expected to maintain but not have themselves, and failure to do so meant a return to the institution. Girls were entrenched in "the domestic carceral sphere[, which] extended the period of black women's captivity beyond the minimum sentence imposed by judges and expanded the purview of the prison regime."[81] What was pitched as economic opportunity functioned to maintain discipline and surveillance over Black girls' bodies.

Thus, the desire to straighten girls materialized in outcomes where girls were oriented toward futures in domestic labor and, at times, other institutions; girls were more often paroled or returned to the institution than they were immediately married. This heterosexualization of girls considered queer by virtue of their sexual delinquency, then, was a false heterosexualization. The promise of heterosexuality tried to guarantee their service to the nation by training them to serve in white homes. This isn't to say that no children were married during or after their time working in domestic service, but this analysis reveals the ways children were trained in heteronormativity but oriented away from heteronormative futures through their education. Their heteronormative education was a mechanism for managing and limiting sexual capacities in their life outside the institution. Orienting children away from heterosexual futures through training in gender and sexual norms impacted their lives beyond the institution. They left school alienated from their communities and families of origin having internalized shamed understandings of their bodies and sexualities.

Constructing and Extinguishing Feebleminded Futures

If girls left school and were found to still be engaging in criminalized sexual activity, they would sometimes be sent back to the school. The annual reports' anxiety over the failure of reform in these girls ultimately reveals another future available to criminalized Black girls: one where the sexual threat they were narrated to pose to the nation was violently eliminated through the eugenic practice of sterilization. Increasingly, girls who returned to the school for reform failure were described as having diminished intellectual capacity, a description consolidated in the term "feebleminded." Kunzel notes that feeblemindedness emerged as a "diagnostic category" in the 1910s, was widely used when dealing with sexually deviant populations, and served as a "catchall term for those whose intelligence, as measured by newly designed tests, was 'subnormal.'"[82] For women, feeblemindedness "was defined almost exclusively in sexual terms," and Kunzel notes a confirmation bias at play around the diagnosis—professionals engaged in social work and reform expected to find feeblemindedness among sexually deviant populations and "found it with a vengeance."[83] The feebleminded label helped to mark when delinquency was treatable or incurable (i.e., pathological). It "placed them beyond the possibility of civilization."[84] Its deployment worked to criminalize girls whose sexualities were not fully suppressed, bodies not fully controlled, and labor not fully exploited upon being paroled from the institution. Sexual pathology became a result of constructed disability rather than race in order to distinguish who was capable of reform from those who were not.

The Virginia Industrial School's discussion and responses to students deemed feebleminded were part of a larger matrix of institutional responses to incarcerated persons, especially girls and women of color. Natalie Lira's *Laboratory of Deficiency* explores how reformers and those in professionalizing fields regarding social work "produced entire bodies of research that constructed Mexican-origin youth as inherently defective and prone to deviant behavior and economic dependence" in California in the 1920s to 1950s, which "translated into state policies of confinement and reproductive constraint."[85] These policies, in California and elsewhere, aimed to control the futurity of incarcerated girls and women constructed as disabled through restricting their mobility, fertility, and economic opportunities. In his discussion of the infamous *Buck v. Bell* case, Stephen Jay Gould notes how the decision that justified compulsory sterilization of Carrie Buck, who was labeled feebleminded, stemmed from the conviction that "feeblemindedness is inherited."[86]

Only heredity and pathology could justify this violent and violating policy—for "if decent food, upbringing, medical care, and education might make a worthy citizen of Carrie Buck's daughter, how could the State of Virginia justify the severing of Carrie's Fallopian tubes against her will?"[87] The stigmatization that attached to poor, racialized, and/or criminalized persons was being converted to ostensibly neutral, scientific knowledge.[88] Michael Willrich notes the "proliferation of criminological discourse linking criminality to hereditary 'mental defect,'" which fueled a "eugenic jurisprudence" intent on preventing the reproduction of Black people through targeting sexuality and reproductive capacities in institutional settings.[89] The state sanctioned this supposed objective knowledge, and it became a way to eschew responsibility and care toward vulnerable persons as well as to justify extremely repressive violations under the guise of care. In the case of Black juvenile delinquent girls, instead of considering the environmental factors that might contribute to girls' engagement in criminalized activity—lack of economic opportunity, vulnerability to coercion, desire to express autonomy—other frameworks were sought to explain the failure of the institution to contain and corral these girls' excessive sexualities and the reproductive threat they were imagined to pose.[90]

The Virginia Industrial School was concerned with feebleminded girls who enrolled in the school. In the *Second Annual Report*, Barrett lamented that feebleminded girls could not be made an asset to the state because of their limited capacity for labor as well as the fear of their contagion effect on the other students: "Of course we cannot expect the feebleminded children ever to be responsible, but they can be taught to work and can work well if carefully directed. It is a mistake, however, to try to train them with the other girls, because their influence is very demoralizing. We have quite a number in our group that ought to be segregated."[91] In the *Fifth Annual Report*, she explicitly stated that these girls have no hope for a future outside the institution: "It does not seem fair to parole girls who are mentally defective; there seems to be nothing else to do at present, however, but they cannot be expected to make their way."[92] In other words, feebleminded girls were being paroled despite the fact that Barrett didn't believe this was the best solution for them.

Why this might be is revealed in the *Sixth Annual Report*: "We need— and this is a crying need—mental tests for our girls. It is very difficult to ascertain whether our girls' failures are their own fault or that of those of us who have paroled them when they have not the mentality to make their own way."[93] Here, Barrett reveals a temporal confusion over when feeblemindedness made itself apparent: was it in school during coursework and training or once a girl had been paroled and then became a "failure"? Barrett's desire for mental tests was a desire to identify this feature at the time of entrance. Given that feebleminded girls were being identified before entry to the school by other agencies and still sent there, however, why does Barrett want to mark as many girls as possible at the time of entry—will they be treated differently? Trained differently? That feeblemindedness would then be a "fault" of the girls and not the school suggests the institution was anxious to pathologize *some* deviant girls in order to justify the role of the institution. Being able to distinguish between "normal" girls and "feebleminded" girls was a way to discern who was capable of sexual reform and who wasn't. These lines were blurry, however. The school was actively trying to find ways to explain "failures"—girls who could not successfully perform their labor on parole or abstain from aberrant sexual behavior on parole and had to come back to school or another institution.

Pathology was rendered a block to reform. In the *Eighth Annual Report*, Barrett expanded on this confusion regarding *when* feeblemindedness could be named: "Our difficult problem of discipline is made more difficult because of those girls whose mentality is low. It takes an expert to tell the difference between a child whose mentality *can* be developed and a feeble-minded one who cannot learn. Our institution will be seriously handicapped until it is relieved of the feeble-minded. I hope it will be made possible for all girls to be given a mental test as they enter."[94] Barrett's desire to label the girls came from a belief that their capacity to learn was minimal and so made the work of the school futile. She believed the institution was "seriously handicapped" while feebleminded girls were there—disability migrated from individuals to the space they occupied, and space itself was pathologized.[95] Barrett feared that girls who retroactively revealed themselves to be feebleminded were hurting the institution, and so she wanted to mark them from the outset in order to protect the institution. Survival of the institution came at the cost of demonizing a subset of the student and parolee population.

The threat that feebleminded girls were narrated as posing to the institution and its goals was amplified by the late 1930s. In the *Twenty-First Annual Report* Barrett wrote, "Numbers of these girls are feeble minded and if paroled are again a menace to society. Some proper place should be provided for this class and removed from institutions like ours. Their presence is also detrimental to the care and training of the other inmates."[96] Girls were retroactively made feebleminded when they failed parole by engaging in criminal (sexual) activity again and/or having to come back to school. The institution and its agents worked to demonstrate that criminalized girls were capable of reform, but here disability became criminalized and naturalized, and thus was seen as inherent and incapable of change.

Criminality moved from racialized bodies to racialized disabled bodies, and these bodies were produced as disabled when deemed to have failed at reform. The 1941 inspection provides some more insight into what happened to girls determined to be feebleminded while still at school: "Probably as high as 30 per cent of the population are girls awaiting transfer to the Colony. Occasionally a girl will be sterilized at the State Colony or the Central State Hospital and then returned to Peaks Turnout for training and later placement."[97] Girls rendered feebleminded were sent to another institution, where some were sterilized—they were then allowed to train again at the Virginia Industrial School. That girls were allowed to return and continue training suggests that their threat was extinguished when they were made incapable of reproduction. Their feeblemindedness didn't go away upon sterilization—the objections that they were disabling the institution and other girls occluded a greater fear about the capacity for racialized criminalized bodies to reproduce, which aligns with Gould's reading of *Buck v. Bell*.

Feeblemindedness was constructed in order to explain girls who continued to engage in sexually delinquent behavior even after their time in school. If girls continued to engage in this behavior, then the school was seen as a failure and the state would have no reason to continue to invest in it (or invest even less). The school found a way to exculpate itself of blame by placing the responsibility on the girls who failed, and specifically on their perceived mental capacities. Agents of the institution argued that the state should continue investing because some girls *did* leave the school and were absorbed into the national order through their domestic service. Girls who could not be absorbed into the national order and whose labor could not be fully exploited despite reform school had to be further pathologized, and their new destiny was continued institutionalization, for some, and sterilization.

This increased focus on feeblemindedness was part of larger trend toward focus on mental health in the institution and others like it in the 1930s and 1940s. "Mental health" was first used in the *Twentieth Annual Report*, and Barrett saw it as an important facet of girls' health to more robustly address in their program.[98] She realized that some girls were "temperamentally unfit" for the school because they were "victims of backgrounds or early experiences which are destructive of emotional equilibrium and need segregation and the analysis and guidance of psychiatrists. In the absence of such treatment and care, we are just about at our wits' end to know how best to bring about adjustment."[99] The school's admission procedures also changed at this time with the creation of the Children's Bureau of the State Department of Public Welfare. According to the 1941 inspection, the Children's Bureau acted as an intermediary agency that would administer tests to children and interview them in order to "diagnose" the girls and figure out the "trouble that got her into the school. The girl is given an opportunity to bring out her real feelings about her commitment and what she would like to do to make the most of it. She is informed as to what the school has to offer in the way of training for her future, and she is told how her behavior and work effort will figure in her release."[100] These diagnostic interviews ascertaining girls' willingness toward training perhaps elided willingness with narrated capacity in an attempt to mark some girls as pathological upon entry and determine who could be assimilated into the national order through training and who could not. The inspection notes that with the help of this bureau the school made a critical shift as an institution: "In 1941 the school has unquestionably come to a most momentous period in its history . . . marking the dividing line between the pioneering days of the school and the period during which it became a training school in the modern sense of the term."[101] The school was rendered modern and ushered into a professional and scientific future because of its new preoccupation with mental and psychological rehabilitation. In order to progress as an institution, some students had to be left behind as failures or pathological cases—these were students destined to institutionaliza-tion, sterilization, and/or pathologization because of their resistance to labor exploitation enacted through their sexual behavior and expression. The production of Black disabled, criminalized, queer childhood was in the service of trying to preserve the limited futures for such children.

The Future of Criminalized Black Girls

In March 2018 Netflix debuted *Girls Incarcerated*, an original documen-tary television series that followed adolescent girls sentenced to Madison Juvenile Correctional Facility in Madison, Indiana. In the opening of the first episode, one employee of the facility speaks with pride of Madison's success rate when compared with similar programs across the coun-try, and this success was marked by test scores in math and reading. Throughout the series, the girls refer to themselves as "prisoners" and "children in prison," while the staff members refer to them as "ladies" and "students." From eight in the morning to three thirty in the after-noon, girls at Madison attend "Promises," the facility's accredited school program, and the series also features a graduation ceremony from the high school program.[102]

The tension in the series between the role the institution sees itself performing and the experience of incarcerated girls manifests around the issue of education. Girls see themselves as imprisoned, while the in-stitution's agents rhetorically affirm them as properly gendered students by calling them "ladies" and "students." The name of the school program also codes these tensions. The "promises" of education at Madison are promises of futurity beyond the institution, which necessitates a present trust in institutionalization and confinement.

Madison Juvenile Correctional Facility and other similar facilities brand themselves as educational institutions with "promises" of a bet-ter future for institutionalized children, and they are part of a longer genealogy of correctional facilities that imagine and narrate themselves as schools instead of prisons. More than a rhetorical sleight of hand, the "school" component of "reform school" was integral to those who founded and funded these establishments in the nineteenth and twenti-eth centuries. Reform schools historically were total institutions whose purported mission was a complete education of mind, body, and morality, which included gender and sexuality. This purported mission was often at odds with children's experiences, characterized by violence, abuse, isolation, and lost opportunities. And yet these institutions persisted and continue to operate in the twenty-first-century United States.

The field of carceral studies, and especially recent work on carceral institutions for racialized populations, has done significant work on how reformatories were a way to extend the period of surveillance over marginalized populations, exploit labor, and deny these children entrance to the category of childhood because of their often-sexualized criminality. By taking seriously the gender and sexual component of the Virginia Industrial School's training program, I have illuminated the ways that Black girls' sexualities have been used as justification for their institutionalization and have been programmatically targeted in order to control their bodies, labors, and sexualities outside the institution. The production of Black criminalized queer childhood enables ongoing violence against and confinement of Black girls.

This history is important because Black girls continue to be criminalized, especially in educational institutions for "actions that deviate from social norms [that are] tired to a narrow, White middle-class definition of femininity."[103] Monique Morris critiques the term "school-to-prison pipeline" for obscuring the ways that Black girls are confined to various modes of institutional and domestic surveillance, including "detention centers, house arrest, electric monitoring, and other forms of social exclusion [that] allow us to see Black girls in trouble where they might otherwise be hidden."[104] She argues that when it comes to Black girls, we should be considering these broader "school-to-confinement pathways" that expand how we see the ways the state works to exclude Black girls from the social order and put their bodies and subjectivities under state control.[105] Morris looks to historical institutions for Black juvenile delinquent girls as sites where "the rehabilitative emphasis was not on making them more productive students, but rather on forming them into better servants for social elites" to contextualize the ways the state continues to criminalize Black girls and then fail them through institutionalizing them and calling it rehabilitation.[106] Education in carceral spaces remains "punitive. Though many operate with the intention or stated mission to be rehabilitative, the approach is often one that punishes children who have made mistakes."[107] The criminalization of Black girls in schools today orients them to spaces of confinement that impede their ability to enter the future. In the 2015 report "Black Girls Matter: Pushed Out, Overpoliced, and Underprotected," Kimberlé Crenshaw, Priscilla Ocen, and Jyoti Nanda articulate that these institutions lead girls of color toward "pathways that lead to underachievement and criminalization" and "direct girls of color down dead-end streets while obscuring their vulnerabilities."[108] Black girls are oriented toward these pathways in order to limit their futures. The promise of a future to Black girls obscures what's actually being promised to whom: when institutions promise Black girls a future, they are really promising to protect the white social order from Black girls. Until Black girls are given expansive possibilities for entering the future that aren't contingent on narrow, racialized gender and sexual norms, no promises are truly being offered to them.

2

Reforming Sexuality, Displacing Home

The Virginia Industrial School's materials tell the story of how Black girls' sexualities were criminalized and pathologized from the 1910s to the 1940s. While focused on a singular institution, the previous chapter's textured account of how narratives around racialized sexuality emerged and changed during this time period reflects larger trends in the legal domain and newly professionalizing fields of psychology and social work. Increasingly, institutions and their agents were interested in *treating* juvenile delinquency as a eugenically determined pathology, as opposed to reforming it through education: there were "shift[s] in authority over matters both criminological and sexual, from religious reformers to medical doctors, and later to psychologists, psychiatrists, and sociologists."[1] Julie Elman explains how "disability and adolescence had been intimately entangled disciplinary sites from the turn of the twentieth century onward," and political, social, legal, and medical authorities were preoccupied with "policing the sexuality, emotional expressiveness, embodiment, and behavior of teenagers" as it was "central to enforcing the normative social order and its ideals of democratic citizenship."[2]

This policing was more intense—and extended to the time before teenagehood—in the context of Black children. While family therapy emerged as a specialized subfield in the post–World War II era, removing criminalized Black children from their families was a strategy because their delinquency was seen as a consequence of "'disorganized, pathological families,' rather than being a direct consequence of structural inequalities, lack of resources, or discrimination."[3] In this era, reform schools' resemblance to hospitals and asylums increased, while their likeness to elite boarding schools decreased. This era also saw an increasing number of Black activists working to understand and upend narratives of Black children's pathology by considering how "the structural consequences of racism manifested themselves psychologically," a key concept in the work of activist-intellectuals like Drs. Kenneth and Mamie Phipps Clark.[4]

This chapter picks up in the 1940s and centers a literary text to both demonstrate this shift and consider how the text's literary form was leveraged to both pathologize and refute pathologization of Black children's sexuality. The text reveals at the granular level how one survivor of these institutions rendered and responded to his education. While the previous chapter focused on girls, this one focuses on boys. There are resonances in the ways both Black boys' and girls' sexualities were viewed as perverse and excessive. Both girls' and boys' displacement from home and kinship was as much about cutting ties from their families of origin as it was about preventing their roles as future parents. Criminalized girls' kinship displacement appears in the service of making them assimilable into another family's home via domestic service. Criminalized boys' kinship displacement appears more in the service of keeping them in a repetitious relationship with carceral institutions; they were viewed as less assimilable into subservient economic positions. Even repressive techniques like sterilization didn't extinguish the constructed threat of Black masculinity and sexuality.

Claude Brown's *Manchild in the Promised Land* (1965) is a first-person narrative of a young boy, Claude (also nicknamed Sonny), growing up in Harlem and passing through reform schools and other child welfare institutions in the 1940s and 1950s (for clarity purposes, when referring to the protagonist of the novel, I use Claude; when referring to the author, I use the surname Brown).[5] Childhood sexuality in the text is present before state intervention into Claude's life, and the narrative descriptions neither criminalize nor pathologize this sexuality: sexuality is a matter of fact for Claude and his peers. The reform schools that Claude attends attempt to pathologize sexuality in children through banning it *and* creating the threat of present and future homosexuality among children and their families—supposed deviant sexuality is one justification for institutionalizing children as well as the feared future that should discipline children. Specters of queer futures were invoked to regulate children into circumscribed futures. Claude does not internalize or subscribe to this sexual pathologization or implanted fear, so the institution orients him away from the future in other ways. The school attempts to supplant Claude's sense of home by making the institution home—a return to any space besides the institution is impossible, leaving the child in a liminal space; the only future available to the child would be another penal institution, thus directing him toward a circular, repetitive mode of being.

I understand this supplanting as a queering process because it is through these literal displacements and affective and ideological educations that Claude is positioned outside of reproductive futurity, sexual expression, and sociality. Claude and other Black children were institutionalized because they were queered by delinquency, as explored in the previous chapter. However, while Claude is orphaned by being removed from his family and placed under institutional care, he doesn't experience a bodily or sexual orphaning or, as Hartman put it, "mortification of the self." The institution's attempts to cut him off from sex fail across the text. Thus, the institution must find other ways to manage and mitigate Claude's entry into the future. The institution and its agents worked to make sites outside the institution uninhabitable so that Claude could inhabit and feel a sense of kinship only at school. Manufacturing this sense of home was the queering that the schools attempted. The schools approximated home through creating kinship structures where the institution and its agents parented children in a domestic setting. But this approximation didn't accomplish a normative end for students. Rather, it positioned students so that home and homemaking would be difficult to access or build outside the institution. A sense of home *could* be accessed through a return to an institution, which would guarantee the surveillance and management of children's bodies and sexualities over time. Claude and his classmates' sense of home, then, was eroticized to orient children toward futures with limited possibilities for relationships and sociality. Criminalized queer childhood in *Manchild in the Promised Land* is a temporal form that impedes Claude's ability to form attachments, relationships, and communities in adulthood; while he ultimately evades returning to an adult institution, his senses of isolation and displacement from the community of his youth are a function of enduring queer childhood. Sexuality might not be absent by the text's conclusion, but it has few outlets and no home.

Genre and Reading Method

The publisher's page of *Manchild in the Promised Land*, described on its 2012 reprint edition jacket as a "thinly fictionalized account of Claude Brown's childhood," confirms that "all the names in this book—with the exception of public figures, judges, staff members at the Wiltwyck School for Boys [the first reform school Claude attended] . . . are entirely fictitious, and any resemblance to the names of living persons is wholly coincidental."[6] This legal disclaimer is of note first because it refers only to the names—and not the story or the lives, words, and incidents of its characters—thus deviating from standard uses of this pretextual note; exactly which aspects of the novel are "entirely fictitious"?

The disclaimer takes on more weight when one considers the long-standing critical confusion about how to classify this text. The novel has been described elsewhere since its 1965 publication as "autobiographi-cal";[7] "autobiography";[8] "documentary autobiography";[9] "semiauto-biographical";[10] "autoethnography";[11] "not published as memoir [but] closely parallel[ing] Mr. Brown's life in virtually every detail";[12] "bil-dungsroman";[13] "another book by an angry young Negro";[14] a book that "can neither be rigidly classified as 'naturalistic' nor as an 'angry' auto-biography";[15] an example of "African Myths and Tales";[16] and, accord-ing to Henry Louis Gates Jr., a "rewr[iting of] *Black Boy* and Frederick Douglass's *Narrative*."[17] The "parallels" between *Manchild* and Claude Brown's life suggest that the text is a mediated record of institutional experiences, but the classifications of genre that qualify *Manchild*'s status as autobiography or fiction or even consider it "myth" permit the text to do more than memoir alone can accomplish.

Brown wrote *Manchild* after his journalism drew critical attention. Brown was born in Harlem in 1937, passed through a number of child welfare institutions and reform schools, and later attended Howard University and law school. While at Howard, he was approached by the former director of a reform school that he attended to write an article for *Dissent* magazine, a left-wing publication founded by a group of activists and intellectuals including Norman Mailer, Irving Howe, and Lewis Coser. The essay, "Harlem, My Harlem," recounts Brown's "skill at living in the street," glosses over his time in and out of institutions and ends with musings on how the misery of Harlem is "inspiring. . . .

Where else can one find so many people in such pain and so few crying about it?"[18] In the five-page sketch of his life, Brown devotes half of the first page to remembering an unbeknownst-to-him neighborhood sex worker who would talk to him "in a very sexy tone while she played with [his] ears" when he was nine.[19] Brown would have "discovered [she was a sex worker] sooner had it not been for my youth"—this claim confirms his subject position as child and shows that the Black child, while in proximity to sex, didn't yet comprehend it.[20] He isn't always already sexualized on account of his race; he carves out a temporal space for childhood.

The five-page story introduced many of the themes expanded in *Manchild*: childhood contact and interaction with sexuality, life in reform school, and displacement from but appreciation for the place he no longer calls home but still considers his: "my Harlem." "Harlem, My Harlem" attracted the attention of Collier Books (later acquired by Macmillan), and *Manchild* is the eventual product of a 1,537-page manuscript.[21] Its status as memoir-turned-fiction allows it to function as both a testament and an imagining. The text has retained autobiographical elements, but its "thinly fictionalized" status allows Brown to set the terms of his narrative: he creates the stories around and relations among Black youth sexuality, institutionalization, and survival. The story refuses the narrative of pathologization, criminalization, and unmitigated mourning or disposal of Black boys in Harlem. This refusal, however, doesn't repair or heal the narrator—nor does it outright condemn the institutions that pathologized him in the first place. The literary form enables the narrator to capture the ambivalent relationship children can develop to institutions—the harm they incur can occur alongside feelings of belonging and affection. It is precisely the manufacturing of these feelings that contributes to children's ultimate displacement from their communities of origin and from expansive future opportunities, but it is felt at the micro level in ways that complicate easy narratives of rejection or redemption.

Reading Brown's novel as a refusal goes somewhat against the grain of the reception of the text. *Manchild* was published at a moment when "the [so-called] urban crisis achieved general reception in its canonical form, as a ghetto-centered social and cultural upheaval organized under the rubric of race and its semi-synonymous subtopics of poverty,

REFORMING SEXUALITY, DISPLACING HOME | 79

crime, riots, and urban renewal."[22] The litany of possible ways to classify *Manchild* corresponds with confusion over how to read the text. The naturalist and straightforward tone of Brown's best-selling novel—what Houston Baker terms the "clinical realism in the narrator's technique of description"—was both shocking and captivating to its first generation of readers.[23] Brown's prose differed from "literary sophisticates like Baldwin, Hughes, and Jones . . . all of whom suddenly appeared to be out of touch with what was happening on the streets."[24] Many have read Brown's text as a sociological account of life in Harlem in the 1940s and 1950s that contains "critical objectivity."[25] For example, excerpts of the text were printed in various sociology, education, and criminology textbooks throughout the 1960s and 1970s, presented as evidence for what poverty and institutional life were like for urban-dwelling African Americans.[26] While readers might impose value on these excerpts, particularly if presented in a context that was framing the excerpt as evidence of deleterious effects of city life on Black youth, the text itself doesn't qualify or frame the experiences in that manner.[27] It takes on a neutral tone when describing sex, violence, and drugs.

Others have critiqued this sociological tone of Brown's work, citing the harm it causes to the Black community. For example, Albert Murray condemned the "pathological and degrading implication so common to the historical and sociological interpretations" of Black life.[28] He critiqued *Manchild* in particular for being "so full of the fashionable assumptions of the social sciences"; he was dismayed that it "is recommended all-around as if it were a profound, knowledgeable, and even comprehensive account of life in Harlem."[29] Murray's criticism pivoted, in part, on audience—*Manchild* would whet the appetites of white readers wanting to access some authentic Black experience, while Black readers "don't exist" among the imagined readers and would see how this one experience was being universalized in ways that increased stigma and stereotypes they faced.[30] Marta Sánchez builds on this point, noting that "[Brown's] Harlem audience expected . . . a Black Harlem writer to challenge the fundamental views dominant society held. . . . Brown was, in fact, a white people's 'boy': the successful exception that proved the mainstream expectation of black failure."[31] Sánchez captures the way that Brown's descriptions of his experiences and community felt like an exposure and betrayal to Black audiences, who were further demonized by this narrative. *Manchild* "confirmed the usual associations whites held of populations of color . . . poverty and crime, school truancy and lack of education, drugs and juvenile delinquency—everything . . . that the Moynihan report had helped to foment."[32]

Published in the same year as *Manchild*, the Moynihan Report condemned and criminalized Black families and invoked effects on the child to drive home these condemnations.[33] It stated that Black children were "constantly exposed to the pathology of the disturbed group and constantly in danger of being drawn into it . . . Negro youth are in *danger* of being caught up in the tangle of pathology that affects their world, and probably a majority are so entrapped."[34] This exposure is one factor, according to the report, in why Black youth experience a "disastrous delinquency and crime rate" and represent "a third of all youth in training schools for juvenile delinquents."[35] Carlo Rotella reads *Manchild*'s representation of juvenile delinquency as participating in a "new accrediting function for writers of Harlem like Brown, Malcolm X, and Piri Thomas, who cited their own delinquent careers . . . as markers of their intimate experience of ghetto pathology and its root causes."[36] While Black authors writing about delinquency in this period established authority in publishing on Black experiences, Brown's representation was read as confirming pathology that was ascribed to criminalized Black youth in the era—narratives that Black activists, intellectuals, and professionals were working hard to overturn, especially in medical, psychological, clinical, and legal settings. Brown did not endorse the Moynihan Report, however, and "attacked" it on the record when "testifying before a U.S. Senate subcommittee examining the Federal Role in Urban Problems."[37] He testified to the "war between us and them, the society which oppresses us, and we the oppressed. . . . A successful hustler drives a big Cadillac, because he is winning the war. If he gets busted, well, he is just prisoner of war . . . the only thing that has really brought any meaningful concessions from the white society into the Negro communities has been the riots."[38] Speaking because of the authority he established with *Manchild*, Brown here didn't endorse respectability politics or disavow criminalized activity; he observed how anything happening to Black youth had to be apprehended in a larger context of oppression.

I don't read Brown's text as confirming or representing pathology. Brown's descriptions, which I quote at length in the analyses to come, are both detailed and lacking in condemnation and judgment. These descriptions have, in part, prevented the text from being apprehended fully as a literary work of art. In his entry on Brown in *African American Autobiographers*, Emmanuel Nelson concludes based on a literature review that "as a sociological document, [it] is a valuable text. It offers a concerned insider's view of a community in crisis. As a work of art, however, it suffers from a lack of stylistic sophistication and aesthetic refinement."[39] Brown's descriptions, however, deployed in the literary form, enable the text to function as more than just a sociological document. Brown takes the same methods that have been used to pathologize and criminalize Black male masculinity and sexuality in order to depathologize and decriminalize them throughout the narrative. While social scientists have used the novel to support state-sanctioned narratives of racialized criminalized childhood—giving credence to Murray's critiques—they miss the ways Brown's novel employs the sociological field's methods of description in a literary context. Taking seriously the text's status as a novel reveals the ways that the text works to combat pathologization and criminalization precisely through its descriptions. In her descriptive reading of Toni Morrison's *Beloved*, Heather Love argues that Morrison's use of description "conveys the horrors of slavery not by voicing an explicit protest against it but by describing its effects. . . . Such moments in the novel draw us up short, turning our attention to the flatness, objectivity, and literalism in this famously 'deep' novel."[40] The novel "register[s] the losses of history rather than repairing them."[41] While *Manchild* is not a "famously deep" novel, it is infamously descriptive, and these descriptions are vital for providing a new lens into Brown's work that isn't about totalizing loss or totalizing resistance. Brown doesn't rebuke the institutions or agents with whom his protagonist interacted, nor the queering processes that he underwent that left him without a sense of home, kinship, or community. Brown's descriptions of Claude's experiences lay bare the effects of institutionalizing the child without qualifying these effects.

Several moments in the text suggest Brown is both aware of and engaging with the gaze of legal, sociological, and criminal authorities that scrutinize him. In one instance when Claude has to appear before a judge for criminal charges brought against him, he notices in the courtroom that there were "people there [who] just seemed to be visitors; they reminded me of the board at Wiltwyck [a reform school] that would come around and watch sometimes. They were all white people, in their forties, I guess, and they were just watching."[42] The judge says that he is going to give Claude "another chance"—he won't be sentenced to reform school this time.[43] Claude replies, "Man, you not givin' us another chance. You givin' us the same chance we had before."[44] Claude recognizes the white institutional gaze projected onto him, and he also notices how this gaze claims to be giving him "chances" when in actuality he's just being sentenced to repetition. He has not yet fully internalized the gaze; while he is in the "scene of instruction," he rejects their view and management of him and his future.[45] Scholar bell hooks has theorized about the "traumatic relationship to the gaze" that Black children have, especially in relation to parental figures.[46] These white adult authority figures are functioning to displace Black parents, and Claude is noting their gaze; and while in some ways disciplined by it—he must follow the court's orders—he is not silenced by it. He is beginning to realize the system destines him to a life in and out of state institutions. His response is a way to counter this gaze and reading of him, and it is also a way to begin finding pathways for living outside of institutions. Claude observes those observing him, and the text disrupts the gaze that tries to criminalize him under the flag of neutrality, objectivity, and observation.

Temporal and Spatial Displacement for the Manchild

The title *Manchild in the Promised Land* encapsulates some of the text's central dilemmas.[47] "Manchild" captures the competing temporalities mapped onto Black boys. On one hand, their age, physicality, and dependent status serve as evidence they are children; however, their race, experiences, and exposure to violence, sex, and drugs are justifications for state agencies to view and treat these boys as men, especially in legal settings and public discourse. Henry Giroux suggests that the use of the word "manchild" in the title is a "metaphor that indicts a society that is waging war on those children who are black and poor and who have been forced to grow up too quickly. The hybridized concept of manchild marked a space in which innocence was lost and childhood stolen."[48] Giroux picks up on some of the temporal problems embedded in the term: if childhood is the teleological precursor to adulthood,

Black boys do not get to follow the normative unfolding of this time-line. They are out of sync with the societal narrative paradoxically because "society"—or, more specifically, child welfare institutions and law enforcement agents—has stolen their childhood; their entrance to adulthood is both too soon and necessary to justify and maintain the "wag[ed] war."

Historically, "manchild" has been used in medieval, early modern, and biblical writing to describe the birth of a male child who is pre-sumably white.[49] In these instances, the child's future as a man was im-mediately projected onto and celebrated from his infancy; a white male child was not extricated from his future. Brown's use of "manchild" in the twentieth century rewrites this formula: Black male children are simultaneously denied childhood because they are viewed as adults, while also revealing that this ostensible adulthood is an ideological tool to deny Black boys the possibility of growing into men through literal or social death. "Manchild," then, marks an absence: Black boys aren't allowed to be children, nor are they guaranteed a future that allows them to grow up into men. The promise of futurity marked for the white man-child is an empty promise for the Black manchild.

This false promise of futurity is further conjured by the title's place-ment of the manchild "in the Promised Land." If "manchild" captures the temporalities that meet at the Black boy's body, "promised land" in-vokes the illusory space available to that body. In its biblical origins, it refers to the land of Canaan that God promised to Abraham and the Israelites; its contemporary secular meaning refers to "a place or situa-tion of expected happiness, *esp.* heaven" and is tied to suffering and exile in the present.[50] The promised land is a trope in both African American autobiography and prison literature, two of the genres in which *Manchild* most recognizably participates, especially during the Great Migra-tion. Its "promised" status marks it as meant for the future: it is not yet here, but one can imagine it on the horizon. In this way, the land might be queer in the sense that José Esteban Muñoz proposes in *Cruising Uto-pia*: a "horizon imbued with potentiality . . . distilled from the past and used to imagine a future."[51]

However, the "promise" must also be viewed with suspicion: who is doing the promising, and how does one know that the promise will be fulfilled? Is a perpetual horizon always productive, or can it help to subjugate populations forced to trust that the promise is not false, but possible? The participle "promised" to modify "land" obscures the agent who promises and thus who is responsible for any delays, deferrals, or denials of the promise. Sara Ahmed recognizes this as the elision of "'I promise you' . . . into 'the promise of,'" which shifts the focus to "how promises are distributed" and not who is doing the distributing.[52] Ahmed further notes that promises have an "end-oriented intentionality";[53] they "make the future into an object, into something that can be declared in advance of its arrival."[54] The promised land is a promise of futurity, which necessitates a present trust that the future is guaranteed and will arrive: "promises ground our expectations of what is to come."[55] But the title also suggests that the manchild is already *in* the promised land: the future is present, it has arrived, the child is here. Or is he? What is the future after promise?

The preface of the novel informs readers that this will be a story about children who are both out of time and out of place through questioning if Harlem is indeed the promised land for African Americans. Claude and his peers are the offspring of "a misplaced generation"; bodies and space are out of sync from the outset. Claude's parents and others like them came to New York after the Great Depression because they were told they could "establish their own place in America's greatest metropolis" where there were "unlimited opportunities for prosperity . . . [and] no 'color problem.' . . . To them, this was the 'promised land' that Mammy had been singing about in the cotton fields for many years."[56] However, "It seems that Cousin Willie, in his lying haste, had neglected to tell the folks down home about one of the most important aspects of the promised land: it was a slum ghetto."[57] Blaming "lying Cousin Willie" and Mammy is possible because of this slippage between who promises and what is promised; the erasure of the agent makes Black kin and ancestors culpable in the eyes of those who migrated to this new place, having invested in the circulation of their promise. Claude is one of "the children of these disillusioned colored pioneers [who] inherited the total lot of their parents—the disappointments, the anger. To add to their misery, they had little hope of deliverance. For where does one run to when he's already in the promised land?"[58] The promised land was a mirage that propelled African Americans to escape the conditions of the South, but upon arrival, the place was revealed to be an illusion. Here, the drive for the future is lost; there is "little hope" and just an affective "inherit[ance]" of "disappointment" and "anger."

The child who is supposed to simultaneously signify, inherit, and inhabit the future cannot because the promise of the future is left unfulfilled. Ahmed notes that happiness—a feature of the promised land, according to the *OED*—"involv[es] the logic of deferral: the parents defer their hope for happiness to the next generation . . . [which results in] the obligation of the child to be happy [as] a repaying of what the child owes, of what is due to the parents."[59] Here, children are the embodiment of their parents' deferred happiness. This generational formula for how promises work gets disrupted when the promised land is a lost object. Claude's parents "inherit[ed] the horizon" of the promised land and became gravely disappointed when the promised land turned out to be a fiction.[60] Claude cannot fulfill the cycle of intergenerational happiness because the promise was never delivered; his birth and generation mark the start of a new lineage, whose features are disappointment, anger, and displacement from futurity. He has nowhere to go.

Spatial displacement goes hand in hand with temporal displacement. After the preface, the text opens *in medias res*—thirteen-year-old Claude has been shot and "the only thing [he] knew was that [he] was going to die."[61] Claude survives and is taken to the hospital, but this declaration at the outset of the novel reveals that the future is already precarious for Claude; death seems inevitable. The potential withdrawal of the future looms throughout the text. After Claude is shot, "The neighborhood prophets began making prophecies about my lifespan. They all had me dead, buried, and forgotten before my twenty-first birthday";[62] his friends think Claude "would probably end up in jail before [he] was ten";[63] and his mother "asked [Claude] if [he] was ever going to be good or if [he] was planning to spend [his] whole life in jail, die in the electric chair, or let somebody kill [him] for stealing something."[64] Claude fears for his own future in the opening of the text, but he is also surrounded by others in his community who "prophesize" the available futures for him: death or prison. These narratives regarding the futures available to Black youth have been internalized and are repeated to Claude in an attempt to help him alter his course and disrupt feared inevitability.

However, the threats bounce off Claude. When his mother tries to get him to worry about going to reform school, he says, "Maybe I would die before I went, so it didn't make sense for me to worry about it."[65] When someone else suggests he could go to college one day, he thinks, "I couldn't tell her that I wasn't going anyplace but to jail or something like it."[66] The second statement suggests Claude has internalized the narrative of what futures are available to him, but the first indicates that this isn't a narrative that causes him anxiety—knowledge of his presumed fate gives him more freedom in the present. Indeed, when he gets angry at friends whom he "blame[s] . . . for [his] present fate," he pauses: "if they hadn't taught me how to steal, play hookey, make homemades [I wouldn't be here]. . . . Aw hell, it wasn't their fault—as a matter of fact, it was a whole lotta fun."[67] The acts that contribute to the prophecies of his shortened lifespan are also acts that give Claude pleasure ("a whole lotta fun"). Considering the link between pleasure and doom, J. Jack Halberstam suggests that when "the threat of no future hovers . . . the urgency of being also expands the potential of the moment and . . . squeezes new possibilities out of the time at hand."[68] The destiny of no future for Claude allows him to focus on sociality and pleasure in the present. As the text proceeds, sex becomes one of those pleasures that the child experiences and that the state tries to co-opt as it maintains the child's orientation to no future and no space.

Sexuality Outside the Institution: Straight, Gay, and Quotidian

Manchild portrays sexuality as present in and around the children of Harlem, but this portrayal is neither pathologized nor criminalized: it is part of the quotidian fabric of the lives of Claude and his peers. While Claude does survive being shot, his future is again questioned in the next scene. At the hospital, Claude's friends visit him, "mainly out of curiosity. The girls were all anxious to know where I had gotten shot. . . . The bolder ones . . . just snatched the cover off me and looked for themselves . . . [then] the word got around that I was in one piece."[69] This scene marks Claude's sexuality as a perceived target of violence and as something that is exposed. The possibility of him being shot in the groin causes "anxiety" among the girl visitors, signaling that they recognize the potential implications for Claude's sexuality. Their anxieties are alleviated when they realize Claude's potential as a sexual and even reproductive partner remains intact.

This heterosexuality present in the text's opening is also immediately followed by homosexual contact. Claude wakes up in the middle of the night to someone who introduces himself as a male nurse and speaks "in a very ladyish voice. . . . [He] ask[ed] me to rub his back. . . . While I rubbed his back above the beltline, he kept pushing my hand down and saying, 'Lower, like you are really grateful to me.' I told him that I was sleepy. . . . He asked me to pat his behind. After I had done this, he left."[70] Claude participates in a homosexual encounter enabled by minimal security in the hospital corridor at three o'clock in the morning, but he doesn't comment on whether he feels threatened, exposed, or in danger. What looks like a scene of violation is described with a notable calm and lack of condemnation. On one hand, this lack of registering the violation in the scene could be because Claude has been taught that his body and all racialized bodies are inherently open to violation; in the previous scene, the girls who quickly "snatched the cover off" to examine his body suggest that the Black male body is available for scrutiny and exposure to those who want to look. On the other hand, Claude's response suggests an amusement over the encounter. The next day, he tells his boy visitors "about my early-morning visitor. Dunny said he would like to meet him. Tito joked about being able to get a dose of clap in the hospital. The guy with the tired back never showed up again, so the fellows never got a chance to meet him. Some of them were disappointed."[71] The only threat that the encounter poses to Claude's friends is the possibility of venereal disease, but even this is presented as a joke. The hospital, another institution, becomes the setting for us to see how children are well versed in heterosexual and homosexual desires, and this knowledge isn't dangerous or repudiated.

While sex among children is often presented as evidence to deny them permission to be children in cultural narratives, Claude's renderings of his sexual encounters affirm his status as child.[72] Childhood sexuality isn't an oxymoron, and its existence isn't an impossibility in the text. Claude speaks with one of his female friends, Sugar, and tells her he doesn't want to fool around because he doesn't like her like that: "Sugar laughed and said that was just because I was young. . . . I laughed too and told her she was just as young as I. . . . Sugar said she was almost thirteen and that she knew I was only ten . . . one day I would be older than everybody. All I had to do was wait."[73] In this scene and others, Claude juxtaposes moments of sexual activity or discussion with reminders of his age. These reminders affirm that he is a child, resisting the narrative that sexuality excludes him from the category of childhood as well as the narrative that children must be asexual. Sexuality also doesn't stunt his growth: he imagines himself as able to grow up and become "older than everybody"—he sees his sexuality as present and projects it into his future. Sexuality becomes a means for accessing an imagined future denied to him elsewhere.[74]

Scenes of sexual activity among Claude and his friends are presented as ordinary: they aren't traumatic but rather a way to create and affirm social intimacy with one another. He visits his friend and sees the friend's older sister, Dixie: "By the time Dixie and I reached the front room, we were old friends. She took off her bloomers without giving it a thought . . . she didn't ask me to turn around or close my eyes while she took them off. This meant we were really good friends now."[75] Sex between Claude and Dixie isn't a romantic act but rather is about friendship; sex accelerates the path to intimacy. In another instance, he has sex with his friend, Jackie, who is thirteen; Claude "tried some of the things that I'd learned from [his friend] Johnny" and wonders if "maybe we just jugged because good friends were supposed to do that sort of thing . . . she taught me a whole lot of things."[76] Sexual activity is practiced between friends, and sexual knowledge is circulated among children in their social circle. The production of this sexual knowledge allows for the child to experience new kinds of sexual pleasure. Sexual pleasure and activity aren't disavowed or shameful; they are testament to community. Later, Claude recalls how, despite the experiences of sex between children, that it was still difficult for some of his friends to be perceived as sexual: "It was harder on the girls. . . . Dixie started tricking when she was thirteen. She was big for her age, and 'nice' ladies used to point at her and say, 'Oh, ain't that a shame.' But it wasn't. The shame of it was that she had to do it or starve. When she got hip and went out there on the street and started turning tricks, she started eating and she stopped starving. And I thought, Shit, it ain't no shame to stop starvin'. Hell no."[77] Claude reorients the adult view of children's sexuality away from the sex act and instead toward the system that produces it. Dixie's sex work isn't shameful in and of itself; what's shameful is that that's the only pathway available to her for a livable life and that she's starving in the first place. Her hunger should be a source of shame to others, not to Dixie.[78]

This reposition of shame is critical in relation to criminalized sexual children. Tavia Nyong'o discusses the role of shame in "sentencing" delinquent children to an afternoon in a state prison in the 1976 Oscar-winning documentary *Scared Straight!*: "Because [these children] do not respond to shame, they must instead be punked."[79] Nyong'o observes children who don't have the state-desired affective response regarding their behavior; since the state can't produce shame within them, they must be temporarily institutionalized so as to see what a shameless future can look like. Claude's refusal of sexual shame, which the state narrates as delinquent, paves the way for his institutionalization. He cannot be shamed away from his body or pleasures, so his body and pleasures must be monitored by the institution.

Sexuality in the Institution

Claude occupies multiple child welfare institutions throughout the text. When Claude is "staying away from home for weeks at a time" as a nine-year-old, he's often picked up and taken to Children's Centers.[80] When he wants to avoid being sent to reform school at age ten, he "cop[s] out on the nut . . . [and] was sent to Bellevue [a psychiatric hospital] . . . for at least twenty-eight days";[81] he avoids one institution by finding refuge in another. He goes to a Youth House when he's eleven and has "outgrown the Children's Center";[82] institutions begin marking the passage of time, becoming a way to track his development. And finally he attends two reform schools from the time he's eleven to sixteen: the Wiltwyck School for Boys and later the Warwick School for three stays.

The text portrays a historical moment when child savers "called for programs to revitalize Harlem by expanding the black community's access to public mental health resources . . . [and] recommended saturating those neighborhoods with psychiatric care."[83] These efforts attempted to solve community-level problems created by structural conditions and lack of resources through treating individuals, and they were part of a larger effort to bring professional psychological approaches and frameworks to bear on what was termed the urban crisis.[84] There was an increasing concern with the relationship between environment and mental health, and cities and their racialized communities were epicenters for exploring, diagnosing, and sensationalizing this link.

Children were of particular concern to these professionals and the government institutions they informed, and removing children from the environment was a strategy for treating them.[85] The Wiltwyck School for Boys in Upstate New York was a reform school that began as a private institution run by an Episcopalian organization in 1936 for Black boys ages eight to twelve and closed in 1981. In 1942, the school almost closed because of financial distress, but Eleanor Roosevelt's patronage allowed the school to remain open and reorganize its leadership.[86] At this time, the school began serving boys of all races, and in its early decades much of the school "staff was made up of black teachers and counselors from the South who wanted to work with these youth."[87] The school also lost its religious affiliation.

Roosevelt was part of a larger child savers movement that began in the Progressive Era; while most child-saving institutions were for white children, who were seen as capable of reform and worth saving more than their nonwhite peers, Roosevelt was part of a subgroup of white patrons supporting institutions for youth of color alongside patrons of color—Richard Wright and James Weldon Johnson were among the Black patrons of Wiltwyck.[88] Wright and Johnson's patronage accords with a shift in post-1945 institutions for Black children, which increasingly saw support and investment from Black intellectuals, activists, and professionals working to both study and respond to the effects of structural racism and inequities on Black youth in order to combat the pathologization of race itself. At the time Brown attended Wiltwyck, the institution learned it had a "recidivism rate among its graduates . . . at 50% since the school opened."[89] Wiltwyck responded by trying to provide more New York–based services to its former students, but the struggles to help these boys access futures outside of or not mitigated by the institution persisted.

While Brown attended Wiltwyck, a film was made about a fictional Black student attending the school in order to showcase its mission.[90] The Oscar-nominated film *The Quiet One*, written and directed by Sidney Meyers and distributed by Film Documents Inc. in 1948, is a quasi-documentary drama (the film "juxtaposes documentary footage and staged dramatic scenes").[91] The film introduces Wiltwyck via an expository intertitle that reads, "Wiltwyck is a school for boys of New York City who have reacted with grave disturbance of personality to neglect in their homes and in their community; and who, for various reasons of age, religion, race or special maladjustment, are not cared for by other agencies."[92] The film is narrated by a psychiatrist (whose commentary was written by James Agee and voiced by Gary Merrill) who says that while the boys on screen "seem like ordinary children . . . circumstances have deformed them."[93] Michele Wallace notes that the film "focussed on a universal male psyche from a psychiatric point of view . . . suggest[ing] that racial categories simply don't exist"—while the cast are predominantly Black children and adults, race is not acknowledged explicitly in the film.[94]

The environment from which the boys come is cast as that which has disabled them by making them feel neglected; but Wiltwyck "tr[ies] to show them they're wanted."[95] The film follows one boy, Donald, and depicts his life in Harlem as one of abuse and rejection by his grandmother and mother and abandonment by his father. The psychiatrist suggests this stunted Donald's growth; he says when Donald hears the word "baby," he relives these losses of kinship and "lives in [these memories] day and night," stuck in a temporal loop with no way forward.[96] This loop can get interrupted once the psychiatrist finally decides to tell Donald his mother "had disappeared" and implicitly won't be returning to him.[97] This ultimately enables Donald's healing, in the narrative structure: it's a "turning point" because he has "suffer[ed] the uprooting of the dearest thing you have known and try to transplant your affections, to go ahead rather than retreat—to put your need and your love once again in another's trust."[98]

This "transplant[ing]" of affect and trust is an act of supplanting; the institution has formalized the kinship disruption it began when it enrolled Donald, and now the institution and its agents are the people and structures in whom Donald should pledge allegiance. He forms an attachment with an older Black male counselor but gets jealous when he sees him around other boys and runs away. He walks along train tracks and has flashbacks to all of the familial rejection he has experienced, and "he began to see the home he'd broken his heart over for what it really was. And seeing that, accepting that, his own spirit began to come of age."[99] Donald's able to begin growing in the institution's eyes when he has fully rejected his family and any sense of "home" he had with them. The counselor finds him, and when they return to Wiltwyck "the baby in Donald began to die. The child was born" now that Donald can "accept his motherlessness, his homelessness, [and] this temporary home."[100] Wallace notes that "the institutionalization in the forties of a psychoanalytic/psychiatric discourse in the US was central to the formation of conventional notions of masculinity, sexual difference, family, and personality in dominant film practice."[101] The psychiatrist narrates Donald's proper acceptance of new kinship via moderated attachment to an adult male; he has been fully displaced from his home, and the film concludes by casting him as on the path to proper adult masculinity. Deborah Weinstein notes that "the Wiltwyck team [composed of psychiatrists, psychologists, and social workers] particularly bemoaned the fact that absent fathers could not serve as 'models for male identification' in son's development of culturally appropriate masculinity" in the 1950s and 1960s, and the film traces an earlier expression of this anxiety and its resolution.[102] The film exemplifies the promises that Wiltwyck made to children as well as to professionals, politicians, and law enforcement who feared these children and the communities from which they came: that reform school would treat them and extinguish the imagined threat (in the form of being present and future Black men) they posed to the social order.

In addition to Wiltwyck, Claude attends the Warwick School, also known as the New York State Training School for Boys, which was established in 1933 and was an experiment in taking juvenile delinquents under the age of sixteen from the city and moving them to the countryside. Claude describes Warwick as "jail in disguise":[103] "to someone passing by, Warwick looked just like a boy's camp. But everyone was under guard all the time."[104] Eleanor Roosevelt also invested in this school—which was built with the support of then–New York governor Franklin Roosevelt—and like other reform schools, the purpose was to train boys in skills that would allow them to be employable upon completing their time. In the era that Brown attended, Warwick was scrutinized for its mistreatment of Black students and faced "allegations of misconduct, rough discipline, corporal punishment, and racism," and the superintendent "regularly ignored the emotional needs of his largely black population."[105]

In *Manchild*, the schools function as totalizing spaces that alienate boys from their communities and (hetero)sexuality and control their bodies and labor. At school, "you had to do two years. For all that time, you weren't going to be back on the street, see any girls, go to the places you liked to go, or do the things you liked to do. They said the work was harder too."[106] Foucault suggests that in the nineteenth century boarding schools functioned as "heterotopias of crisis," sites where "manifestations of sexual virility were in fact supposed to take place 'elsewhere' than at home."[107] These sites shifted to "heterotopias of deviation" in the twentieth century, with places like hospitals, prisons, and retirement homes straddling the "borderline" between crisis and deviation.[108] The reform school of the early to mid-twentieth century also straddled this "borderline"—they were sites where sexuality had to be managed away from the home, but their status as schools invested in punishment and reform marked them as sites for deviant children. How were criminalized children's sexualities managed outside the home, and what could their sexuality—its expression and enactment—be when they left the institution?

Map of Claude's Institutional Life

Claude's youth spent in reform schools causes anxiety in his mother. When a judge commits Claude to reform school, the judge "said he thought I was a chronic liar and that he hoped I would be a better boy when I came out."[109] Claude's mother told the judge Claude "had already been to Wiltwyck School for Boys for two and a half years. And before that I had been away from my family too much; that was why I was always getting into trouble," to which the judge replies that "he knew what he was doing and that one day she would be grateful to him for doing it."[110] In this moment, the state intervenes in Black kinship and justifies this intervention through the rhetoric of reform and victim blaming. Claude's mother sees through this, pointing to the boy's displacement from home and family as the reason for his behavior. She recognizes the system that's entrapping Claude and disrupting her family, unable to deliver on the promises it preaches, but she has no legal grounds to do anything about it.

The mother reveals she also distrusts the state because of the way it has been producing sexual knowledge in the child. When Claude is in the Youth Center, his parents come to visit him; a boy comes over and accuses Claude of hitting him. Claude reacts:

> I jumped up, swung at him. . . . I called him a lying faggot. . . . Mama was looking scared about something. . . . "Boy, where you heard that word at. . . . Do everybody know what it means?"
>
> I thought I saw a way out with this question. So I said, "Yeah, it means he can't fight and lets everybody pick on him. That's what it means." . . . Tears started sneaking down Mama's face. . . . Dad started telling Mama it wasn't so bad, since I was only ten years old. . . . Mama started crying more and saying, "He'll be eleven years old soon, and he gittin' into that shit already."
>
> Dad said, "Can't nothin' real bad happen before he gits thirteen or fourteen."
>
> "Lord know I want that boy to be around some girls when he git that age."
>
> And Dad said, "No, Sugar, he'll be home then. . . ."
>
> I didn't say anything. It wasn't my place to say anything.[111]

Ten-year-old Claude's use of a sexual slur causes his mother to fear that the child is in close proximity with homosexuality *and* is able to name it. She fears that the institution has produced homosexual knowledge in her son; if it hasn't already produced homosexual behavior in him, it will if he remains there. She has witnessed how the state can easily remove her son from her home; despite her husband's optimism that Claude will "be home then," she knows that there is no guarantee. The child's future is in the hands of the parenting state, and she now realizes that her son's sexuality is also under the state's care. Contact with homosexuality, even in the form of knowledge, distances Claude from his family. This relationship has been already mediated because of the institution's strictures on visits and sending and receiving letters. Claude's silence in response to his mother heightens the descriptive tone of this passage—he doesn't assuage his mother's fear and provides no commentary or context for apprehending his mother's fear or his reaction to it. That it was "his place" to speak suggests that the child's displacement from his family though institutionalization means he lacks authority to comment on these matters; it might also capture his youth and how that doesn't position him to intervene.

The production of the fear of homosexuality reflects a larger cultural panic at the time around the contagion of homosexuality. The institution capitalizes on the "homophobic imagination" that "sodomy . . . is the 'situation beyond one's experience, impossible to anticipate,' and is associated with extreme forms of unfreedom like imprisonment, slavery, and rape."[112] In *Scared Straight!*, children are confronted with "the threat to 'do bodily harm to your asshole'" from the inmates, and Nyong'o reads this threat as setting up two poles with "lawless behavior" on one end and "lawful future lives of heterosexual domesticity" on the other.[113] The threat of homosexuality in Claude's case can only grow as his mother realizes that he has little chance for a "lawful future . . . of heterosexual domesticity" if he stays in the institution; the institution sets up an impossibility and she can't intervene. Nyong'o further observes that the threat of homosexuality "serve[s] not to produce queer subjectivities but to deter them at all costs. The efficacy of scaring straight . . . seems to come rather in the production of sodomy without sodomites."[114] Nyong'o points out that reform is always tied up with sexuality; straightening doesn't just indicate stepping off the wayward path but indeed means heterosexuality in penal institutions. Heterosexuality is contingent on the fear of homosexuality—children must be "scared straight," but homosexuality's role is just one of fear: there aren't supposed to be actual homosexual subjects in the institution. Their presence is imagined as a means to an end, but their actual presence would pose a disruption to the ostensibly desired heterosexual landscape of the institution. Claude doesn't seem to be scared straight; rather, his mother is.[115]

However, homosexual knowledge and activity don't incite the same response within Claude; he sees homosexuality as neither a threat nor a big deal. In fact, his proximity to homosexuality in the institution gives him a greater respect for homosexual boys; it is an unintended consequence of the institution. At Warwick, "one of the most interesting things I learned was about faggots. Before I went to Warwick, I used to look down on faggots like they were something dirty. But while I was up there, I met some faggots who were pretty nice guys. We didn't play around or anything like that, but I didn't look down on them anymore."[116] Claude recognizes his previous misconceptions around homosexuality. He is vigilant to demarcate the boundaries between others' homosexuality and his heterosexuality—"we didn't play around or anything like that"—but he now sees them as not inferior to him. This education explains his previous employment of the slur as well as his neutral encounter with the masquerading nurse in the hospital at thirteen; the institution has shifted his perspective from disdain to acceptance. "Faggots," once loaded with disgust, now takes on a neutral valence. The institution's attempt to produce a fear of homosexuality through proximity and contact with it has the opposite effect; he cannot be scared straight. His descriptions resist the institutionally desired effect of Black male youth contact with homosexuality in correctional facilities.

Claude is further fascinated with the openness of homosexuality in the institution. He says, "It was the first time I'd been around guys who weren't afraid of being faggots . . . some of them were so good with their hands, they had the man they wanted just because he couldn't beat him."[117] Interestingly, homosexuals' partners in the institution are described as "men" and not children: on one hand, this is affirming the cultural narrative that "queerness, for contemporary culture at large . . . is understood as bringing children and childhood to an end."[118] On the other hand, it is permitting the status of manhood to "queers [who have been regarded as] as temporally backward."[119] The simultaneous rendering of queer persons as childlike, but the impossibility for queerness and childhood to coincide, marks the homosexual child in reform school like the manchild: his childhood and his queerness both constitute and negate one another. At the same time, there is institutional space for these children: "At Warwick, there was even a cottage just for faggots. If a cat came up there acting girlish, they'd put him right in there. They had a lot of guys in there—Puerto Ricans, white, colored, everything— young cats, sixteen and under, who had made up their minds that they liked guys, and that's all there was to it."[120] The institution is intent on suppressing heterosexuality for the purpose of cutting off delinquents' reproductive capacities in one attempt to prevent them access to the future; the reform school reflects a Progressive Era eugenicist desire to "use the full range of state police powers to prevent the reproduction of criminality, deviancy, and dependency."[121] However, homosexuality isn't a threat to the future because of its non-reproductive sex. In fact, the institution finds a way to make use of homosexuality: it needs its presence to produce fear in children and their families. However, the fear doesn't work, at least in children. Claude even comes to "like" one of the boys, even if "that's just not my way, man."[122] The institution depends on homosexuality to queer straight boys, but it fails in its attempts to queer Claude through his proximity to homosexuality. While we don't get access to the homosexual boys' experiences in the cottages, the very existence of these cottages—a site of queer sex among differently racialized children—marks its potential as an unregulated space of possibilities within the institution. Marlon Ross notes that "segregation is the most efficient way to enforce categorical differences that otherwise might become insignificant as merely variable characteristics of a population."[123] On one hand, the cottage works to strengthen the distinction between heterosexuality and homosexuality, but on the other hand, it holds the potential to produce community within a policed space among a population perceived as deviant.

Later, Claude reveals one of the reasons why this attempt to queer him failed. When he is seventeen, he learns that one of his friends is gay. Claude doesn't "want anybody to think I was his man."[124] However, beyond maintaining the demarcation between his sexual identity and his friend's sexual identity, he isn't concerned because "faggots were an accepted part of life."[125] He further observes and remembers,

The people in the neighborhood were accustomed to faggots. Faggots were no big thing, neither were studs. . . . Some started at a young age. I remember once my little sister asked my mother, "Mama, is that a lady or a man?" It was a stud.

Mama just looked at her and said, "That's a bull-dagger, baby."

It was like somebody telling a child, "That's a horse." This was how the people accepted it in the community. Nobody could be shocked at people being faggots. Nobody thought there was anything so crazy about it. A lot of people, if their sons became faggots or their daughters became studs, were disappointed and hurt. At first you'd hear about people putting their sons out because they became faggots, and putting their daughters out because they started liking girls. But after a while, they always came back home. The family accepted it, the community accepted it, and everybody else accepted it.[126]

Claude undermines the expectation of fear that the institution is banking on: he reveals that all along homosexuality was "no big thing" and even "accepted . . . in the community."[127] His recollection of his sister's interaction with his mother at first seems inconsistent with the earlier scene where she fears that ten-year-old Claude knows what a "faggot" is. However, this scene solidifies that her fear isn't necessarily about homosexuality but more so about the institutional production of homosexuality and institutional control over her child's sexuality. While her fear might be tinged with homophobia—seeing a queer person on the street and accepting them is different than having to accept a queer person in your home and family—this scene reveals that she isn't invested in protecting her children from knowledge of homosexuality. She matter-of-factly lets her child know what she is seeing and doesn't qualify it with judgment. Homosexuality is a part of the community, sometimes repelled but always eventually reincorporated. Claude's rendering of how homosexuality in Harlem is perceived combats the institution's attempt to produce homosexuality as a threat and rewrites the cultural script that paradoxically aligns Black communities with both perverse sexuality and homophobia.

While homosexuality doesn't threaten Claude, it does work to unsettle some of the other boys' sense of gender. He says,

> The cats up there I really disliked as a group weren't the faggots but the guys who were afraid somebody might think they were. Warwick made everybody very conscious of his masculinity, and there were a lot of cute guys up there, guys who were real handsome. They were so handsome that if they weren't good with their hands, somebody was liable to try to make a girl out of them. So these guys used to be brutal, dirty. They used to do a whole lot of wicked stuff to cats. They would stab somebody in a mute or hit a cat in his head with something while he was sleeping. All that kind of stuff because they were afraid guys would think they weren't mean.[128]

Claude reveals that the threat of homosexuality does produce a hyper-masculinity among heterosexual students. In this way, the institution performs a self-fulfilling prophecy: state agencies and agents institutionalize boys whose delinquency is supposedly sexual, one symptom of which is hypermasculinity; they put these boys in proximity with gay and straight men; the boys react to this proximity through a heightened gender performance that is bound with violence. Ross notes that "straight white men are expected to protest, to over-protest, any proximity to homosexuality, especially in a situation where the gay man has an advantage over the straight one or is beholden to him."[129] The institution expects straight boys to "over-protest" the presence of homosexual boys by asserting their own heterosexuality through a hypergendered performance; the institution capitalizes on an anticipated reaction and creates the conditions for violence. The production of hypermasculinity is obscured and read as always already there. The institution relies on the presence of homosexuality to naturalize what it claims predates institutionalization. It also naturalizes violent reactions to homosexuality; both homosexuality and hypermasculinity are unsafe in the institution, and the presence of one relies on the other. The institution needs to justify the pathologization of children's sexuality routed through delinquency and so creates the conditions for it *after* institutionalization. So, while Claude himself is able to reject this pathologization, this is not a uniform reaction among his peers.[130]

Another way that the institution attempts to control children's sexuality is through banning it, or at least suspending its possibility while in the institution. The school's rules dictate that no sexual activity can occur. While the school seems to look the other way in terms of homosexual activity (at least based on Claude's rendering of the cottage for gay boys), there aren't opportunities for heterosexual interaction; masturbation is also restricted. To circumvent this rule, Claude's friend, K.B., sustains himself in school with an elaborate heterosexual fantasy. Before falling asleep at night, K.B. would ask Claude about the girls he knows and himself talk about Linda: "For the six months that my bed was next to K.B.'s, I went to sleep hearing about Linda. . . . K.B. said he had done it to her one time up on the roof."[131] Here, the imagining of sexual intercourse is a survival mechanism. It also creates a homosocial bond with Claude. In an institutional setting that attempts to pathologize and curtail sexuality in boys and hopes that those efforts will produce the pathologized symptoms they narrate the boys to have, K.B. and Claude participate in a heterosexual imaginary that solidifies a homosocial reality that gives both solace in the school.

The heterosexual fantasy also helps the boys to combat the ban on masturbation. One night, K.B. comes running into the dormitory announcing to the boys that he successfully ejaculated:

> K.B. came running into the dormitory with his dick in his hand and yelling, "Claude, I did it! I did it!" When he reached my bed and yelled out, "Man, I shot," all the beds in the dormitory started jumping, and everybody crowded around my bed with flashlights before K.B. stopped yelling. . . . Most of the guys said that . . . it was just dog water. I said that dog water was more than [one critical boy, Horse] ever made. Horse went heading for the bathroom saying he was going to show me what the real stuff looked like. Everybody followed Horse and watched and cheered him on while he tried for the real stuff. Horse only made dog water, just like K.B., but nobody paid much attention—everybody was trying to jerk off that night. It was a matter of life or death. After what seemed like hours of trying and wearing out my arm, I shot for the first time in my life. A lot of other guys did it for the first time too, but some cats just got tired arms.[132]

Masturbation is a communal activity. K.B.'s successful ejaculation, in defiance of the institution's restrictions on sexual activity, is cause for celebration. Some are impressed, while others contend that he didn't actually produce semen. One of these nonbelievers, in an attempt to prove what ejaculate actually looks like, masturbates in front of a crowd in the bathroom. While this act comes from a perhaps competitive masculinity, it produces community among the male students and incites further acts of communal resistance: "Everybody was trying to jerk off that night. It was a matter of life or death." Sexuality is critically linked to survival—an individual sexual act is scaled up to carry enormous weight in the context of this education. Making sexual activity public in the dormitory and the boys' witnessing of the possibility of sexuality in the institution inspire them to enact that which the institution has attempted to control and refuse. Some boys succeed, but some are just left with "tired arms." The outcome shows that there isn't an even distribution of success among the boys, but the universal attempt disrupts the institutional management of children's bodies and sexuality.

The final way that the school attempts to manage sexuality in the novel is through the prevention of heterosexual desire across racial lines. While Claude is at Wiltwyck, a group of girls from nearby Vassar begin to volunteer at the school. The girls' presence works initially to provide an outlet for heterosexual desire that has been able to exist only in the boys' imagination: when one boy, J.J., gets hurt on a bike, a Vassar girl holds him while she waits for help to arrive and "J.J. sneaked one eye open, looked up at those big breasts right over in his face, and started snuggling"; girls would play at the piano and "somebody was under there playing with her legs. . . . I never would have thought that white girls could be so nice. Cats could look up under their dresses and everything, and all they did was laugh."[133] While these moments could be perceived as violations against both parties involved—the college-aged girls are represented as participating in titillating activity with boys aged eleven to fifteen, and the boys are taking advantage of the girls' help by seeing it as an opportunity for intruding on their bodies—Claude's descriptions foreground the fun and pleasure of the interactions.

These interactions with the Vassar girls are permitted to continue because of three potential blind spots built into the panopticon of the institution: institutional agents either can't see children as capable of sexual agency and so don't see sexual interaction as a possibility, they can't imagine sexual desire crossing racial lines, and/or they can't imagine these women would be interested in these boys. This first possibility on one hand seems to undermine the vision of Black juvenile delinquents as sexual delinquents; however, it also suggests that the institution realizes this narrative, although one it enthusiastically subscribes to, isn't the reality of boys. Historically, there has been anxiety over "the problem of proximity between white female and black male bodies [which] was grounded in the possible threat to even one white woman's body."[134] That Wiltwyck isn't anxious about this proximity suggests that the circulation of the narrative of Black juvenile sexual delinquency is a myth deployed to justify managing their bodies, and so when childhood sexuality *is* realized, the school must intervene. The institution maintains these blind spots until one day one Wiltwyck student and one Vassar student disappear; they "came back, with smiles on their faces. They were happy, and I suppose everybody was happy—that is, everybody but . . . the staff. They were a little peeved. They wondered where in the world a n[*****] could be in a snowstorm with some pretty little Norwegian skiing teacher. That's not something to happen to people from poor Negro backgrounds."[135] The boys' age and youth aren't the problem for staff—it's that the boys are from the wrong class and racial backgrounds and must be kept separated from white bourgeois heterosexuality. As the Vassar students continue to work at Wiltwyck, the staff "found out that it wasn't working. The guys got used to the girls, and they started treating them like mothers and sisters . . . we were supposed to be glad to even be able to say hello to them."[136] The anxiety shifts from being about heterosexuality crossing racial and class lines to about the familiarity verging on kinship between the two groups. The boys are having inappropriate affect; the institution wants them to be grateful that white child savers are taking an interest in them—which simultaneously naturalizes the narrative that they are disposable and unworthy by virtue of their race and class—but the partnership between the institutions has an unexpected effect of intimacy.

The institution is intent on making sure the boys know that their only place is in punitive institutions where their bodies and sexualities can be managed. It is educating them to be unable to occupy any place outside the institution. The staff's bafflement that the boys are "supposed to be glad" to be interacting with white women and not desiring or growing close to them reveals an anxiety over the boys stepping out of their place and indicates why controlling their sexuality becomes all the more crucial. After the Vassar students leave when another is caught with a boy, Claude realizes he had been Wiltwyck for "two years, and there was nothing new about the place. We did the same things . . . Wiltwyck now seemed like a babyish sort of place."[137] Removing the Vassar students from Wiltwyck forecloses sexual possibilities and again orients the boys to a repetitive, circular institutional life. This possibility that gets taken away also makes Claude now feel the space is "babyish"—he recognizes that the repetitiveness embedded in Wiltwyck is also one that makes it impossible for him to grow up or move forward into a future, as a man or otherwise. Thus, being entrapped in space also entraps Claude in time—he is shut off from futurity and development. The presence and absence of white bourgeois heterosexuality, offered then made inaccessible to poor Black boys, makes visible the severance from linear, progressive futurity enabled in this institutional setting.

Queering Space within and beyond the Institution

Claude remains sexually active despite institutional attempts to restrict his sexual expression and exploration. Since the institution is unable to fully manage, make criminal, or make impotent his body and sexuality, it must find another way to orient his body away from the future. It attempts to do so by ensuring that Claude and other students will have no home to occupy outside the institution. The boys feel at home only within the institution and feel no sense of place once discharged; this maneuver works to guarantee the rotation of children in and out of state institutions, trapping them in a revolving door. In this way, schools queer the space outside of the institution by making the homes and communities from which boys came spaces that can't accommodate them. Failure to queer the boys in school leads to an attempt to queer the spaces available to their bodies to orient them to queer childhood: a time of displacement, both spatial and temporal.

The school works to make sure that the boys feel at home only in the institution: a site of punishment is importantly a site of feeling known and like one belongs. This is the twin promise of the educational institution that is a repressive and ideological state apparatus. When Claude gets a visit to see his family during his time at Wiltwyck, he realizes that "it seemed that everybody I used to hang out with before I went to Wiltwyck was in Warwick or someplace like it."[138] Claude's sense that his peers are all in reform school suggests a widespread state attempt to disrupt Black kinship through taking children away from Harlem. The result is isolation for the individual who does manage to secure a temporary release from the school. He realizes,

> I just wanted to get back to Wiltwyck and steal something and get into a lot of trouble. I never wanted to go back anyplace so bad in all my life. I wanted to be around K.B. and Horse and Tito and other cats like me. We could all get together up at Wiltwyck, raise a lot of hell, and show people that we weren't pigs and that we couldn't be fucked over but so much.

Simms and Claiborne and Nick and Papanek [Wiltwyck staff members]
and everybody else up at Wiltwyck knew I was somebody—even when
I wasn't getting into trouble. I couldn't wait to get back to where I wasn't
a pig.[139]

Claude's desire to return to Wiltwyck is stronger than anything he has
previously felt; his visit to Harlem is necessary to make him more distant from Harlem and more in need of the institution. The institution's
agents make him feel valuable. On one hand, this might point to a tension between the macro and micro levels—the state treats these boys as
disposable, while its agents make the boys feel known. However, making the boys feel known is necessary to solidify state power over their
subjectivity. The school functions as an ideological state apparatus that
interpellates Claude, attempting to produce an institutionally sanctioned
subjectivity in him while disguising that process of production. Feeling
known in this system is crucial in making him feel like there is no place
for him outside the system.

The institution's function as a site of both comfort and community
for Claude continues as he moves in and out of institutions. When he is
at Bellevue, he says, "I had a lot of fun in the nutbox and learned a lot of
new tricks. . . . I didn't know it at the time, but many of the boys I met in
Bellevue would also be with me at Wiltwyck and Warwick years later . . .
[it was] such a nice place that I was sad when Mama came to take me
home."[140] The psychiatric ward cultivates relationships with boys he will
continue to be with "years later"—in rotating targeted Black children in
and out of institutional spaces, the institutions disrupt the boys' familial
kinship and ties to their communities, but also produce new forms of
kinship and community among children. Claude marvels again at the
Youth House, noting, "I didn't know it then, but at the Youth House
I met a lot of guys I was going to see again and live with again in a lot
of places, white guys, Spanish guys, colored guys, all kinds of guys. . . .
Most of the guys in the Youth House were all right; some of them just
couldn't fight."[141] Claude recognizes that while these spaces are sites of
a range of racial identities and sexual orientations (marked by the eu-
phemistic boys "who couldn't fight"), that they're constantly living in
the same spaces over years creates some form of familiarity and kinship
among them.

Both moments are marked with the temporal gap between his initial encounters with these boys and the eventual familiarity of living with them over the years: "I didn't know it then." This marker reads as an odd narratorial intrusion missing elsewhere in the text: while this is written in the past tense and told from the perspective of an adult, that Claude reminds readers of his retrospective gaze here perhaps highlights the unexpectedness of this community formation and disrupts the repetitive, flat site of the institution—he "didn't know it then" because he couldn't have predicted it. The institution isn't a unidimensional space filled with controlled bodies; it is a dynamic site with children flowing in and out of the space and interacting with one another. The institution's power isn't top down; the boys constitute the space and influence its contours from the bottom up as well. Later, when Claude runs into a female friend, he learns that she too was sent to a reform school; she says that while there she "met some nice people," to which Claude responds, "Yeah, I usually met nice people too. That's how it goes. Sometimes you meet some of the nicest people in those places."[142] "People" may refer to the students, staff, or both. Regardless, Claude and his friend's recognition of the "nicest people" who constitute the institution suggests that while the institution is a site of social control and its agents are complicit in that project, intentionally or not, it allows for relationships and experiences that exceed a totalizing narrative of despair.

Exceeding this narrative is crucial for destabilizing solidified histories of state control over Black people and especially Black boys. Ross has noted the significance of these unexpected effects in the text, observing that "Brown is clearly concerned with recording the conditions which enable a sense of community even under the most degrading and threatening circumstances, and thus with indexing a common experience of a people whose lives have been increasingly represented reductively by the media in terms of violence, despair, and moral rootlessness."[143] Ross also picks up on these experiences that disrupt the one-dimensional and "reductive" narrative of pain and loss. While important to acknowledge the harm, abuse, and repression built into these spaces, it is also important to acknowledge these interruptions. The totalizing narrative erases moments of resistance, survival, and rejection—they naturalize and reinscribe state power, obscuring the ways that state power isn't monolithic and its moments of failure. Althusser famously described interpellation as being successful only "nine times out of ten"—these unexpected effects of institutional life and moments of resistance are interpellation's failure.[144] I point this out not to overappraise the value of these moments—but acknowledging them is important in complicating tidy narratives that erase attempts to assert humanity, pleasure, and connection. Even if these attempts don't *undo* the ultimate harm of these spaces, marking them is critical. To *not* acknowledge them is to bolster the state-sanctioned pathologizing and dehumanizing narratives.

The institution's response to community formation, however, might be exploitative. When Claude leaves Wiltwyck and gets into legal trouble again, he is sent to a different institution, Warwick. At Warwick, there were "guys from all over New York City. . . . And Warwick had real criminals. . . . There was so much to learn." Claude admits, "We all came out of Warwick better criminals . . . I learned a lot of things at Warwick."[145] The intimacy of the boys, then, translates to sharing knowledge among each other. And their knowledge contributes to them all becoming "better criminals" after leaving school. Their intimacy, then, on one hand helps the boys to survive while in the institution, but it also becomes part of a larger pattern to ensure the boys can be at home only in the institution: if they're "better criminals" upon leaving, that, combined with the policing of boys in Black communities, ensures their future in another penal institution. The school, then, doesn't appear intent on reform but rather must ensure the boys won't be able to reintegrate into the community outside the institution.

Claude reiterates that the only place he feels at home is in school. When he leaves Wiltwyck, he says, "I was thirteen . . . I was going through some kind of change. But I knew that more than anything in the world, I wanted to get back to Wiltwyck. Wiltwyck had become home, and I felt like a butterfly trying to go back into the cocoon."[146] Claude feels his displacement in Harlem has something to do with his age and not with the time he has spent already at Wiltwyck and other institutions. The institution hasn't stunted his growth in his eyes; he is going through a "change" and so sees himself and his subjectivity as dynamic and active. However, he wants to reject this growth and perceived momentum into the future by returning to Wiltwyck. Claude feels like he must choose between space and time: he can have a future with no home, or a home with no future. The Black child cannot have both.

Claude is sent back to reform school, but this time he is sentenced to Warwick, not Wiltwyck. He fears Warwick because it has a reputation for being tougher. However, at Warwick, "I was ready to stay there for a long time and live real good. . . . I'd had a place waiting for me long before I came. If I'd known that Warwick was going to be as good as it turned out to be, I would never have been so afraid. As a matter of fact, I might have gotten there a whole lot sooner."[147] Claude sees himself as fated to this institution—attending Warwick is inevitable. State-controlled institutions are the desired "place" for Black boys who have been narrated as dangerous and criminal. The school is intent on determining his future, but it also allows for comfort and pleasure while there ("to live real good"). After he leaves Warwick the first time, he goes home to Harlem, but "I just got fed up one day and went back to Warwick. . . . It was like coming home, a great reunion . . . there was a place for me."[148] Claude chooses to return to Warwick on his own accord. The institution has cultivated a desire within the child *for* the institution because of the way it has substituted and subsumed any previous home.

Feeling at home at school makes it increasingly impossible to feel at home outside of it. Every time Claude leaves an institution, he realizes that he is out of sync with the life and community he left behind in Harlem. He laments this feeling over the course of the text.[149] Claude says, "It was a bad time. It was a bad time for me because I was sick. I was sick of being at home. I was sick of the new Harlem, the Harlem I didn't know, the Harlem that I couldn't find my place in. . . . I didn't know this place. I didn't know what to do here. I was like a stranger. I longed to get back into Wiltwyck."[150] Removing Claude (and his peers) from Harlem makes it so that he can't settle this "promised land" and can't return to it after having left: in his absence, Harlem becomes unfamiliar and has no place for him. This alienation from home intensifies with each return and increases Claude's desire for the home of the institution. The reform school keeps Claude distanced from his community and under state control and surveillance.

When Claude leaves school for the last time, he recognizes the repetitive fate that awaits him but also sees an opportunity to defect. On "July 12, 1953, [he] went home for good."[151] Claude was "back on the Harlem scene now. I was sixteen years old, and I knew that I'd never be going back to Warwick. The next stop was Coxsackie, Woodburn, or Elmira."[152] Claude recognizes that his age, while legally still a child, would no longer permit him to attend reform school—his next stop would be adult prison. Claude reflects,

> I'd always been aware throughout my delinquent life of the age thing, and I knew that I didn't have a sheet yet. I knew that I didn't have a criminal record as long as I was sent to the Wiltwycks and Warwicks. But I also knew that since I was sixteen and out on my own, the next time I was busted, I'd be fingerprinted. I'd have a sheet on me for the rest of my life. I thought, Yeah, I could still make it, but, shit, what would I want to make it for? I knew I didn't want to go to school, because I would have been too dumb and way behind everybody. I hadn't been to school in so long.[153]

Claude recognizes that the "age thing" permits him to operate in a liminal space when he leaves Warwick for the last time. The institution has set him up to be a "better criminal," but there is a gap between his leaving the school and committing a crime that would guarantee a heightened level of state surveillance and management. The institutions' path seems circular and repetitive, but Claude realizes that there is an opportunity for a different mode of being outside of the institution. However, he realizes that that place isn't necessarily school—despite the way that these reform schools purport themselves to be educational institutions, Claude is "behind," capturing his temporal asynchronicity. Even if he can make it off this path, he doesn't know where he'll end up or what he can even do: "What would I want to make it for?" His previous desire to return to the institution is impossible because he can't return to Wiltwyck or Warwick; he is out of place in Harlem; and he doesn't want to end up in prison. He has survived the institution but doesn't have a way of being or place to occupy outside of it. Having no place makes him unable to imagine a future to "make it for."

Claude struggles to find a literal space to occupy. He moves to the East Village, and his mother says that "I shouldn't be leaving, I didn't have anybody outside. She said a boy of sixteen should still be living with him family."[154] What a boy "should" be doing at sixteen is impossible because of state intervention into Black kinship in Harlem. His mother affirms Claude is still a child who should be with his family. However, Claude "felt much older. I felt as though I was a grown man, and I had to go out and make my own life. This was what moving was all about, growing up and going out on my own."[155] Claude affirms his resistance to the institutional narratives that want to keep him infantilized under state care through casting him as an adult to deny him the ability to grow up and enter the future: he does not feel that the institution has prevented his growth. Growing up, however, comes at the cost of his community, family, and previous home. Yet his ability to grow up shows that his body has resisted the institutional induction into a chrononormative time meant to stunt him and orient him away from the future. Claude does move downtown, even though he "didn't have anybody on the outside." Exiled from the promised land, where and when can the manchild go?

Claude's inability to move elsewhere or forward is compounded by his isolation. While he was always surrounded by other boys in the institution from his neighborhood and elsewhere, he recognizes the fates that they've all met: "Most of the cats I came up with were in jail or dead or strung out on drugs."[156] The only futures available to Claude's friends are jail, death, and addiction.[157] The communities he had in the institution are absent outside of it: sociality in the school cannot translate back to the streets, and Claude witnesses the repercussions of isolation among his friends, living and dead.

Surviving Outside the Institution: Literature and Homosexuality

But why not Claude? How do we account for his inability to be fully interpellated or taken in by the institution or its allies? The novel demonstrates that institutions are often the only available spaces for children without futurity; Claude's failure to be interpellated makes us wonder what temporal possibilities are available for children without space. The novel offers two possibilities for survival: education and, surprisingly, homosexuality. Claude embodies the first possibility, while the figures who surround Claude in the latter part of the book reveal that homosexuality also becomes a way to escape the repetition and interpellation of institutional life, in part because of the way that it is practiced within and built into the institution.

While Claude is still in school, he is resigned to his nonfuture. One day, he is talking to one of the cottage's matrons, Mrs. Cohen: "She said that I could go to college if I wanted to. . . . I couldn't tell her that all cats like me ever did was smoke reefers and steal and fight and maybe eventually get killed. I couldn't tell her that I wasn't going anyplace but to jail or someplace like it."[158] Mrs. Cohen imagines a future for Claude in an academic institution, different from the other institutions to which Claude sees himself fated. However, "One day, Mrs. Cohen gave me a book. It was an autobiography of some woman by the name of Mary McLeod Bethune."[159] A contemporary of Janie Porter Barrett, the founder of the Virginia Industrial School in the previous chapter, Mary McLeod Bethune was an African American educator who founded an industrial school for Black girls in Daytona, Florida, in 1904, which has since evolved into Bethune-Cookman University. She dedicated her career to improving Black education and child welfare reform. She served as president of the National Association of Colored Women in 1924, and in 1935 President Roosevelt appointed her the director of the Division of Negro Affairs. In this position, Bethune advocated for "black supervision of black programs, to increase black participation in policy making, and to force [National Youth Administration] programs to train black youths for more rewarding services and occupations than were traditionally prescribed under Jim Crow."[160] Bethune's vision of education was one that expanded possibilities for Black children's existence and economic and political opportunities without reinscribing state desire for Black subjectivity and futurity. Bethune's autobiography helps Claude envision a future outside the institution. While he is not a benefactor of the educational model that Bethune put forth because of his status as a juvenile delinquent (Bethune's vision was implemented in industrial schools like those discussed in chapter 4, not reformatories), her vision for Black education nonetheless impels Claude to start imagining otherwise.

While Claude struggles to figure out what this otherwise might be, he eventually finds himself back in the classroom. First, he realizes that "I didn't have any kind of skill or trade, so the only kind of job I could get was doing some labor. This shit was beginning to bother me. I knew I didn't want to do this all my life."[161] While the schools preach reform through education and training the boys for economic opportunities, Claude's realization that he has no "skill or trade" and only has the option to do "some labor" reveals the rhetoric of the institution is out of sync with the reality of the boys who pass through it. This gap between mission and outcome solidifies the institution's desire to prepare boys only for a life that will have them back in the institution; the only other limited option is a life of hard labor. Claude begins attending night school and finds a job repairing watches. While working, he says, "For the first time in my life, I didn't have the feeling that I had to go to Coc-sackie, to Woodburn, and then to Sing Sing [all prisons]. . . . It seemed a little bit crazy, but I even had the feeling that if I wanted to become a doctor or something like that, I could go on and do it."[162] Claude is able to imagine a future for himself with the backdrop of normative, linear, future-moving time—he is literally working to fix time. His job materializes what he is attempting to do. Repairing time is indeed a per-haps impossible goal of boys who have passed through the institution and have not yet passed into another: how do they enter a future when they've been programmed to operate at a different pace, inhabit a dif-ferent rhythm? The attempt to repair time gives Claude the "crazy" idea that he could "become a doctor." Futurity comes at a cost: he is still feel-ing bereft from his family, community, and former home. However, even feeling like he has access to time itself opens possibilities for existing be-yond the state institution. Literature first enabled these imaginings, and later art offers another way to live them out. Claude decides to take up piano lessons and manages to acquire a piano. As he practices, "I could see the progress. For the first time in ages, I felt as though I was really doing things, learning new things. I felt that now I was going places and doing something. I was ready."[163] Artistry becomes the avenue for tem-poral ("progress") and spatial ("go[ing] places") possibilities. While he was previously unable to find a place, he can now both imagine a future and tie that future to space.

In portraying literature as enabling pathways to futurity not sanc-tioned by the institution, the text performs a metacommentary. *Man-child in the Promised Land* reveals why it must exist as a descriptive testament. The historical record and the state and institutions that au-thorize it permit only limited, pathologized narratives regarding Black youth and sexuality. *Manchild in the Promised Land*, with its descrip-tive style, is a counternarrative that expands the possibilities for Black futurity. It cannot entirely refuse or reverse erotics of education, but it describes how the eroticized body can inhabit modes of being beyond the institution, even if those inhabitations are unevenly accessible and enacted among children.

An unexpected way to survive the institution also comes through looking at the figures who surround Claude and aren't "in jail or dead or strung out on drugs."[164] He runs into several friends unexpectedly over the course of the text who are still alive by the end. When he moves downtown, he sees his friend Knoxie and learns that he is gay.[165] Shortly after this encounter, he runs into his friend Reno, who is with someone named Broadway Rose, "a faggot . . . [who] used to rule Rikers Island."[166] While Reno isn't named as gay, his familiarity and friendliness with Broadway Rose suggest he may be or is at least in proximity to homosexuality. He is not intent on maintaining the bounds between his sexuality and Broadway Rose's homosexuality. Reno is one of the final characters Claude interacts with in the text. He says to Claude that his time in prison "was college, man. . . . When I go to jail now, Sonny, I live, man. I'm right at home. That's the good part about it . . . when I went to Warwick, I made my own home. . . . Now when I go back to the joint, anywhere I go, I know some people. . . . It's almost like a family."[167] While Claude laments the future / no future that is available to the students of Warwick and Wiltwyck, Reno is content with this fate. He finds prisons to be sites of education, home, and family. Claude cannot accept Reno's submission to this fate: he wants to say, "'Look, man, we aren't destined.' . . . But I guess. . . . He'd just made his choice, and I'd made mine."[168] Reno's perception of the possibilities for living within the institution might have to do with his sexuality: as the text reveals in the reform school, while homosexuality is needed to inscribe the fiction of violent Black hypermasculinity, its place in the institution allows for an almost utopic community in the cottages. While Claude also found the institution to be a site of home and family, he cannot imagine jail to be the same as reform school, despite Reno's rendering of how the spaces function in the same way for him. Claude mourns Reno's rendering, almost vilifying Reno's "destiny" as a "choice," which runs counter to earlier instances of Claude pointing to the structural conditions that motivated individuals' decisions. It is also closer to judgment, thus diverging from the tone set across the text. Reducing the two fates to "choice" obscures the institutional production of these fates. Claude's "growing up" and making "progress" make him unable to see the possibilities of institutional life he left behind. Liberation for Claude is space outside of the institution and access to futurity; liberation for Reno is recognizing what the institution can give him that he can't access outside of it. Interpellation for Reno is not automatically linked with failure.

The tension between individual and community, choice and fate, survival through education and survival through homosexuality converges in one of the final scenes of the text, when Claude discusses with a friend, Danny, the fact that his younger brother has been incarcerated. Claude says that his brother "writes a lot of poetry in the joint" and earned his high school diploma there; their "Mama says he'll be a real fine young man when he comes out, provided he doesn't become a faggot."[169] Danny replies, "I think, man, with most cats, that stuff is all right in the joint. . . . You know. Taking other outlets, deviating from normalcy. As a matter of fact, that's a normal way of life there."[170] Claude notes the future that is made possible for his brother in prison through art and education: poetry and a diploma will allow his brother to properly inhabit adult masculinity. He sees this possibility for progress at odds with homosexuality. For Claude (and his mother), homosexuality cannot coexist with futurity. However, Danny's response that homosexuality is a "normal way of life" in this carceral space suggests that homosexuality is a survival mechanism in the institution. This final scene suggests that while Claude has found one path to futurity through literature, art, and education, there is an alternate path enabled by homosexuality. Queerness survives in the text. Homosexuality is an integral part of the institutional fabric. The state is so intent on criminalizing Black male heterosexuality that Black male homosexuality, while important in criminalizing heterosexuality, doesn't get targeted in the same way. Homosexuality can exist outside of the institution and is also a means for survival within it.

Through its descriptive mode, *Manchild* reveals the production of criminalized racialized queer childhoods for the text's incarcerated Black boys. Institutions and their agents attempt to sever boys from their sexual capacities and accompany this severance with an ideological understanding of their sexual deviance. Claude and his friends are not susceptible to these educations. They remain connected to their bodies and sexualities, and so the institution works to displace and disconnect them from their families and communities. They are trained to feel a sense of home at school so they won't feel home elsewhere. This spatial displacement functions as temporal displacement from an open, undetermined future. The boys are trained in a heteronormative affect—feeling at home—to orient them to a repetitious future in and out of carceral spaces and guarantee their inability to be part of heterosexual, reproductive home building and family making. Manchildhood is a liminal space of either isolation or suspension. Sexuality is not eradicated from these queer childhoods. However, reform schools determine the contours of sexuality's expression—or inexpression: either sexuality can be expressed within the confines of an institutional space, or sexuality can exist if it remains dormant and not acted upon outside of the institution.

3

Compulsory Sterilization

Sterilization through Ideology

Ruth Rodman Hayden's *Erma at Perkins* (1944) is the first-person narrative of a young girl, Ruth, who attends the Perkins Institution and Massachusetts School for the Blind from kindergarten through her graduation in 1913 (for clarity purposes, when referring to the author of the text, I use Hayden; when referring to the narrator of the text, I use Ruth). Although the text is based on Hayden's time in the school and includes real persons and events that populated and punctuated Perkins during this period, the titular Erma is a fictional invention whose experiences Hayden centers. Through Erma, Hayden most vividly explores the school's attempts to discipline behavior, gender, and sexuality to determine what avenues for economic and social possibilities are available to children after graduation.

Erma combats the school's attempts to discipline her body and desires, but Erma's ability to access a future outside of the institution depends on her capacity to accept and internalize this education in bodily, affective, and "sensorial discipline."[1] Erma must learn to renounce sexual desires, reproduction, and a future inclusive of either in order to successfully pass from girlhood to womanhood under Perkins's auspices. The institution teaches Erma to disavow sexual futures through training her to properly *appear* as a woman who can correctly inhabit domestic and public spaces. The assimilatory goal for blind children was to not disrupt the visual field by passing as unthreatening.[2] Erma—and through bearing witness to Erma, Ruth and her classmates—learns to renounce sexuality through an education in normativity to which she will never accede. Perkins trains her for a sexual future she can't access. Through Erma, the text demonstrates the production of disabled queer childhood through an education in gender norms and sexual disavowal.

Unlike at other boarding schools I explore, which promise children futures if they learn gender and sexual norms and whose promises were revealed as false upon exiting the institution, children at Perkins were educated in a heteronormativity they *knew* they would never fully inhabit. They were educated in multiple norms while at school, some of which they could replicate. For example, teachers "continually instructed [students] how to act like other people," modifying behavioral tics, "peculiarities," and "little habits [that can] make a blind child seem foolish."[3] Children were to become as "nearly normal as their limitations would permit."[4] The institution insisted that the limit of this normativity was sexuality. Heteronormativity—that is, life structured by heterosexual desire and participation in the reproductive order—was one norm the children were educated to renounce. Eugenic education taught students they could leave Perkins as neither sexual nor reproductive subjects. A successful education was one in which the children understood this gender and sexual normativity and also the fact that they could neither want it nor participate in it; they were taught they possessed inherent weakness of character that had manifested in their blindness, whether congenital or acquired. Children were taught their relationship to the norm would always be aslant.

Children were educated in heterosexual futurity but effectively sterilized by their education. I call this "compulsory sterilization," with sterilization functioning not as a metaphor but literally—children's education materialized in affects, habits, and perspectives that mitigated children's ability to access sexual and reproductive capacities outside of the institution. This education was occurring at the same time other institutions were medically sterilizing children with intellectual disabilities, diagnoses that were determined by race, class, and criminalized sexuality.[5] The ideological work of the school resulted in similar outcomes as the repressive techniques of contemporaneous medical and psychiatric institutions. Education "imposed asexuality" in order to, in Eunjung Kim's words, "disqualif[y them from] marriage or any sexual partnership and reproduction"—this process of "desexualization" was a desired outcome of the school.[6] And since, as Ela Przybylo argues, "asexuality is frequently framed as a marker of immaturity, closetedness, presexuality, or stunted development," arresting these children's sexual and reproductive capacities through imposed asexuality was a way to guarantee their position in a restricted temporal space that would keep them perceived as backward and childlike.[7]

Futurity existed beyond Perkins, but this future ideally had to be emptied of sexuality. Loss of sexuality entailed loss of other forms of intimacy and connection, limiting the possibilities for community, relationships, and sociality outside the institution. Children were positioned for economic futurity outside the institution; they could become laborers whose bodies posed no sexual or reproductive threat. In *Blind Rage*, Georgina Kleege addresses letters to Helen Keller, arguably the most famous alumna of Perkins (along with her teacher, Anne Sullivan). In one letter, Kleege describes one particular feature of the mythology surrounding Keller: "They say the reason you were always so prolific and tireless was that you sublimated or repressed your sexuality, and used the excess energy to power your work."[8] Kleege here captures a logic of erotic energy being harnessed and funneled toward economic productivity, epitomized by Perkins's utmost model of success. Disabled queer childhood produced at Perkins shaped how children could occupy the future: as economic contributors who were ever vigilant about expressing sexual desire because of the education they received in school. Their appearance as productive adult citizens obscures the compulsory sterilization they underwent.

This investigation contributes to conversations in queer and disability studies over the question of the future. As Alison Kafer argues in the introduction to *Feminist, Queer, Crip*, for disabled persons "everything from sterilization to institutionalization . . . has been justified on the grounds that such acts will lead to better futures for disabled persons and/or their communities."[9] Because disabled persons have been "figured as threats to futurity" and systemic and violent attempts have been made to deny them that future, "abandoning futurity altogether is not a viable option for crips or crip theory."[10] In other words, the future can be rejected by those who are already presumed to have access to it; for disabled persons—and many of the populations in this project—the future has never been a guarantee. This investigation of *Erma at Perkins* shows how claiming to prepare blind children for the future could be contingent on radical sexual dispossession—disavowal of sexual capacities is the price for entry into the future and requires painstaking monitoring of the self and internalization of eugenicist logics.

Sexual Immorality and the Perkins School for the Blind

Founded in 1829, Perkins was the first school for the blind established in the United States, serving as a model for other nineteenth- and twentieth-century schools that strove to educate and eventually integrate rather than institutionalize and segregate blind children.[11] Dr. Samuel Gridley Howe served as the school's first director, a position he held for forty years. He aimed to develop a curriculum that combined traditional subjects, like reading and writing, with training in trades so that students could be self-supporting and join the labor force after leaving the school. In 1837, the trustees described the daily schedule: "If we consider music as intellectual labor, and work as physical labor, then they devote eight hours daily to intellectual education, eight to physical education, and eight to sleep."[12] Perkins and other institutions wanted children to live independently outside the institution so that they wouldn't be dependent on state and private resources for the entirety of their lives. The goal was for them "to become members of general society, and not of a society of blind persons"—being in a blind community was a stepping stone toward becoming an assimilated individual.[13]

For Howe, this future outside the institution was not intended to include marriage or reproduction. Howe was preoccupied with heredity. He wanted to prevent blindness, and all of it was perceived to signify morally, from being transmitted from one generation to the next. In Perkins's *Sixteenth Annual Report* (1848), Howe argued that "diseased tendencies in parents, whether derived from their ancestors, or planted in their constitutions by intemperance or abuse . . . will reappear in a thousand forms: it may be blindness, it may be deafness, it may be white swelling, it maybe something else."[14] Howe condemned immoral behavior and "violat[ing a] law of nature," such as sexual acts like incest, adultery, promiscuity, and masturbation, for resulting in disabilities in children.[15] When one engages in sins of "sensual pleasures," he wrote, "there will appear in the far-off and shadowy future the beseeching forms of little children—some halt, or lame, or blind, or deformed, or decrepit—crying, in speechless accents, 'Forbear, for our sakes; for the arrows that turn aside from you are rankling in our flesh.'"[16] Here, Howe educated people in heredity by urging them to see their present sexual actions as accompanied by a "shadowy future" that takes the shape of a disabled child crying out in pain. Sexual impropriety occurs alongside and directly engages—and violates ("arrows . . . rankling in our flesh")—the child. In the temporal logics of this rationale, the disabled child is invoked to prevent its conception. Howe's image is a strange form of what Anna Mollow would call "rehabilitative futurism," or the future envisioned without disability.[17] A disabled future gets imagined precisely to prevent the realization of that future. The disabled child is granted a "shadowy future" to regulate and control the sexualities of people in the present perceived to have the capacity for transmitting immorality materially into in the future. Howe continued, writing that he hoped people would "resolutely keep aloof from any relations of life that might cause them to hand down bodily or mental infirmities upon the innocent ones of the coming generations."[18] The disabled child invoked here is an "innocent" child; however, once the child is born, its innocence would be erased because now that child also has the capacity to transmit sexual immorality in the form of blindness.

Thus, Howe was concerned with how to prevent blind children under the institution's charge from entering marriage or reproducing. He was convinced that intermarriage—that is, marriage between two blind people—was "to be deprecated [as] its consequences are almost always deplorable."[19] One solution for the problem of potential intermarriage was strict gender segregation on campus. In the *Seventeenth Annual Report* (1849), he wrote, "There must be a separation of the sexes. . . . In view of the various objections to intermarriage among blind persons, it seems to be an imperative necessity. . . . There is a stern moral duty to use every precaution against a perpetuation of such [hereditary] tendency through successive generations. Marriage in cases where one of the parties has such hereditary predisposition is generally unwise, often wrong; intermarriage between two persons so predisposed is always wrong, very wrong."[20] Separation was the school's "stern moral duty" and a direct attempt to prevent romantic intimacies that might result in marriage and offspring. Howe condemned any relation that a blind person might enter upon leaving the institution. Fear that blind persons might reproduce necessitated an attempt to eliminate all forms of intimacy, even with a nonblind person. This feature of Perkins was common to other institutions; Frances Koestler asserts that "schools for the blind went to extraordinary lengths to discourage even the most casual boy-girl social relations," and she notes the punishments that students were subject to if "found openly conversing with one of the opposite sex" because of the profound fear of passing on blindness.[21]

Howe was committed to this model of single-sex education despite the risks it carried. He admitted that single-sex communities "shall have all the evils which necessarily attend and follow so unnatural a condition of things."[22] Indeed, he struggled knowing his role in establishing and promoting this model even though it was "unnatural, undesirable, and very liable to abuse" because "the human family is the unit of society. . . . Communities in imitation of the natural family, especially those confined to one sex, are fertile of evil."[23] Here, Howe acknowledges that the school setup was opposed to the "natural family"—children's ability to form such families in the future would be severely impeded because of both the separation of the sexes and the lack of a model for what this unit should look like. Paradoxically, the sexual immorality that Howe was invested in preventing was going to be exacerbated by these conditions, suggesting that the school's claim to invest in moral training was a smokescreen—the school knew it was setting children up for perceived immoral behavior, but this immoral behavior was less threatening than literal reproduction.

Howe justified this paradox by claiming that "during the period of childhood and early youth, the advantages to be gained . . . outweigh the necessary evils attendant upon large boarding-schools."[24] Howe alludes to the "unnatural" relations, specifically same-sex desire and contact, that can emerge in single-sex institutions. These unnatural relations were the lesser of two evils—it was more important to prevent the possibility of reproduction than to stop homosexuality, perhaps because the latter did not risk transmission into the future.[25] Children had to learn what the "natural family" was but ideally not participate in natural family making themselves; potentially generating same-sex desires among students perhaps wasn't seen as contradictory to the mission of teaching heterosexuality since it, in fact, assisted in the prevention of *enacting* heterosexual reproduction. In this way, the tension between institutionally produced intimacies and heteronormative education was tolerable. Howe condemned institutions that didn't segregate the sexes; their model "presents various temptations and opportunities for acquaintances and friendships which lead to intermarriage; in other words, for breeding."²⁶ He continued that "this arrangement leads to constant trouble, care and expense. Attachments and intimacies are formed between the boys and girls which occupy their attention too much. . . . There is constant danger of impure purposes, and immoral relations creeping in."²⁷ Howe described impurity and immorality in passive terms—"danger" exists and "immoral relations creep" in—but he did not name the source of either. He had previously located danger in the body itself—disability, to him, was the result of perceived danger-ous behavior and proof of its capacity for both enacting and reproduc-ing dangerous behavior by the logic of heredity. Disability embodied past, present, and future danger. In this description, danger migrated outside the body and was seen as built into the very environment of the coeducational school. This concern reveals Howe's growing anxiety over how the institution itself could produce these unexpected effects in students—students would then be made responsible for what the in-stitution elicited (their disability was seen as making them weak and susceptible), but Howe acknowledged that the institution itself has a force that could exceed managerial intent.

Howe's convictions about the link between blindness and sexual im-morality in Perkins's early history impacted the rules, regulations, and architecture of the school into the twentieth century. In the *Eighty-First Annual Report* (1912), the new director, Dr. Edward Allen, wrote, "It is wise alike for economic and eugenic reasons to educate vitally handi-capped boys and girls strictly apart at all times and places. . . . Mak-ing each cottage of boys or of girls a family is especially desirable [and] wholesome. The doing of daily chores by all pupils can be made to have a profound educational effect; being contributory work it is moral; be-sides, it's practical training for life . . . it promotes the spirit of family in-terdependence."²⁸ Allen reinforced that the separation of boys and girls continue for "eugenic reasons"—that is, to prevent students from inter-marrying and having children. This logic was also "economic" because preventing the birth of potentially disabled children prevented expendi-ture of state funds on their education and care in the future. Thus, blind students were barred entry to a heterosexual future. However, their dorm life was supposed to be "wholesome" for them: it simulated "fam-ily" life and so served as "practical training." And yet the very separation of the sexes was supposed to guarantee that they would not have a family life in the future. These contradictory desires of their education reveal an impossibility: children were educated in norms they were not meant to access outside the institution. Training in family life was really just training in work so that students could join the labor force after graduation. This was the paradox at the heart of Perkins while Hayden attended and serves as the setting for *Erma at Perkins*.

The eugenics movement imagined a future without disability but had to deal with a present that included disabled persons. Many reformers whose work aligned with this movement proposed resolving this dilemma by institutionalizing and training disabled persons in menial labor. The eugenics movement operated on the grounds that "fortifying the health of the nation required institutional, systemic, and bodily interventions."[29] A hallmark of the movement was the institutionalization of people—immigrants, those criminalized as delinquents, the poor— who "might further contaminate society" through transmitting social ills through biological reproduction.[30] For example, men and women deemed feebleminded were routinely sterilized; even after extinguishing the threat of reproduction, institutions often required these persons to remain. Since Perkins and similar schools for the disabled intended for the majority of their students to graduate, enter the workforce, and not be dependent on the state, they worked to prove their students weren't a biological threat to the progress of the nation.

Schools had to figure out how to grant students economic futurity without reproductive futurity. The schools functioned as a site of what Nicole Markotić and Robert McRuer call "crip nationalism" because they tried to find a place for blind children in the economic order, ultimately bolstering the strength of the nation.[31] Crip nationalism can "generate other forms of dispossession," and one must undergo a form of sexual dispossession in *Erma at Perkins* in order to be incorporated into the labor force.[32] In the text, Ruth explains,

> The Massachusetts Division for the Blind was formally established about 1910, and its helpfulness was just beginning to be felt. . . . [We] were catching the first serious glimpses into the future. It was beginning to look like our own personal, very immediate future . . . but as yet we had very little knowledge and even less real skill or ability . . . our thought was taking a vocational, commercial, economic turn. We must not get through school,

until we had got something out of school that would sustain us and start us upon the road to self-support—the only road that leads to happiness.[33]

Ruth explains that students can't leave Perkins until they have work that will support them outside of it—economic self-support will "lead to happiness," a rescripting of the narrative that marriage will lead to happiness. Libidinal energies were to be directed toward labor for fulfillment. The school shifted its curriculum toward the end of Ruth's time at the school to include home economics and chair weaving. This Division for the Blind concerned itself with "prevention of blindness, education of the blind both young and old, the deaf-blind, the conservation of sight, home conditions and relief, employment, and legislation affecting or benefiting the blind."[34] "Prevention of blindness" included preventing reproduction of blind students. For students to access the future, they had to renounce reproductive capacities and learn a trade, becoming a part of the economic order and proving they would not be dependent on state resources for support.

Genre and Method

After graduating from Perkins in 1913, Hayden pursued a career as a teacher. She attended the Rhode Island State Normal School and attained her bachelor's and master's degrees from the Boston University School of Education and Graduate School. She was a teacher at the State Infirmary of Tewksbury in Massachusetts and later the Northern Colony and Training School in Wisconsin. Hayden was an active participant in conversations around the education of children with physical and intellectual disabilities, publishing articles and speaking at conferences throughout her career.[35] *Erma at Perkins* is the product of her master's thesis, written in 1941 and published in 1944 by Chapman & Grimes Press. Except for some reviews of the text in the 1940s, there is no extant literary criticism of this text.

While classified as a fictional text, *Erma at Perkins* straddles the boundary between fictional and nonfictional. In the text's dedication, Hayden declares that the work is the "true story of life at a school for the blind."[36] Some reviews overlooked the "true" elements of the story. Perkins's own publication described it as "a book which tells in fictional form the story of a girl all the way through her educational career at Perkins."[37] Other reviews delineate where real life and fiction brush up against one another, most notably in the invention of the eponymous Erma. In December 1944, a Massachusetts newspaper described it as a text that "combines a factual biography in fiction form with a history of the famous school. . . . Here is a boarding school story that is at once entertaining as well as authentic. . . . Except for the heroine, all the names in the book are real and will be recognized by many people hereabouts."[38] In February 1945, a reviewer for the *Christian Science Monitor* wrote that Hayden "records faithfully" her experiences in this "boarding school story": "Erma is a fictionalized character, but the other children and their teacher, and also the story of the great Perkins Institution from its early days, are actual fact."[39] Hayden's story is recognizable as a participant in the boarding school genre, whose features include female friendship, school traditions, fascination with teachers, pranks, punishment, and, as I'll explore later, erotically charged intimacies that must be disciplined. A comparison of the girls in Ruth's class, all named in a class song, with Hayden's graduating class recorded in Perkins's *Eighty-Second Annual Report* (1913) reveals one disparity: the latter lists seven students, whereas the former lists those seven plus one additional student—Erma.[40] This distinction suggests that Erma isn't a pseudonym for a classmate but a newly created character. The reviews may need to distance Erma from "fact" because it is most explicitly through Erma that the school's eugenicist desire to sterilize children of sexuality is revealed. As I will demonstrate, the school's sexual program and education shifts from implicit to explicit across the text. Reading Erma as anomalous and demarcated from the "facts" that surround her in the text overlooks the representativeness of her case. She is not exceptional but an exemplar of a system preoccupied with molding and restricting students' sexual and reproductive capacities.

The invention of Erma may allow the text to explore the disciplining of sexuality without discrediting anyone who could be "recognized by many people hereabouts" in the tale. Erma is constantly showing improper internalization of gender and heterosexual norms—"had it not been for Erma, the virtuousness of our class would have been somewhat about average."[41] The text's narrative form reflects a confusion over Erma's place in the institution. The story is told from Ruth's first-person perspective; narratorial intrusions reveal she is retrospectively remembering the story that unfolds. However, she closes most chapters by referring back to Erma. The narrative's imagined audience shifts across the text. At times, Ruth interrupts her narrative to address "my dear classmates."[42] At other times, she addresses Erma: "By the way, Erma; have you heard from Rosy?"[43] She later addresses Erma as if she's by her side: "Now, as I write and share these lines with Erma, she bursts into laughter and I ask what it is all about."[44] She also includes passages from letters written by the adult Erma recounting their school days. These interruptions to address Erma and then to explicitly include her in the production of the text invite the audience into a present that both Ruth and Erma occupy together. The production of the text is testament to the future that both Ruth and Erma can access outside the institution. This quasi-dialogue with present Erma comes after an anxiety-riddled homosexual episode (which I explore later), which was one of many times when Erma had to be isolated from other girls; this inclusion then affirms Erma's ability to grow up into a proper female subject devoid of improper sexual desire.

At the time of its publication, critics couldn't reach consensus over the intended audience for *Erma at Perkins*. While some reviews classified the text as a "boarding school story," placing it in a genre that includes children's and young adult literature, others were anxious to make clear that this story was for adults. A 1994 compilation of noteworthy texts for educators included the book in its "Education and Psychology" section and wrote that it "presents in a very clear, unemotional manner, a great many problems which confront the blind pupil. . . . Upon completing the reading of this book anyone should have a more sympathetic and understanding attitude toward the blind as individuals rather than as a class apart from other people."[45] This description of the text's supposed flat affect shows how the text diverged from nineteenth-century melodramas, where "blindness was the paragon of disabled difference for female characters . . . blindness [was] a source of their emotional excess, which st[ood] in contrast to the emotional control of their non-disabled counterparts."[46] Hayden's novel exhibits "emotional control" that makes it palatable to able-bodied readers. The 1945 *Christian Science Monitor*'s review agreed with the sentimental training the text was imagined to accomplish, noting, "It is a simple tale for those adults who will read it [and] should widen the public's understanding of the problems of the sightless child."[47] However, the review then shifted into a scathing critique, claiming, "It is weakened . . . by aiming too broadly at all ages of reader."[48] The text's only aim should be to "widen the public's understanding" of blind children, with the "public" being synonymous with "adults." Appealing to a wider audience dilutes and "weaken[s]" this intent. The text itself deploys "weakness" throughout to describe moral failings that are perceived as bound with blindness, which echoes Howe's language across the reports.[49] This review's redeployment of "weak[ness]" to describe the form's failures reasserts that binding. The need to prevent children from reading the text was perhaps born out of a desire to protect children from the sexual content it contains. The text's sexual content isn't mentioned in the reviews, but it's perhaps coded in these calls for protection.

In the following analysis, I trace the ways that the school produced disabled queer childhood through educating children in the rhythms of heteronormativity through inducting them into institutional time where the institution serves as home and family for students; the moments it reveals children are meant to learn these rhythms with the knowledge they themselves will never fully inhabit them; and finally the way these lessons become centered in—and ultimately internalized by—Erma through preoccupation with disciplining her body, gender, and sexual desires.

Institutional Time at Perkins

In the text, Perkins inducts its students into institutional time. When Ruth arrives at school as a kindergartener at the age of seven, she "felt that something new and different was about to begin at once— something that would not end for a very long time."[50] Arriving at Perkins marks her entry into a distinct institutional temporality. As she goes through her first day at the school, she notes that each transition in the schedule is marked by a bell. Bells punctuate her day: "the bell rang and class was dismissed";[51] "This freedom was enjoyed for about ten minutes, then a bell rang, all the children stopped their play";[52] "That's the singing bell";[53] "It seemed a long time before the bell rang";[54] "We children played house with a doll and a dog between us until the bell rang for supper";[55] "Mrs. Hill tinkled a grace bell and all was quiet";[56] "soon the bed-bell rang";[57] "At six-thirty next morning the rising-bell rang";[58] and then "breakfast bell rang."[59] Syncing children to move with the bells was something Perkins instilled in students from its founding years: the *Annual Report* from Perkins's third year, 1835, remarks on how "the pupils are accustomed to move at the stroke of a bell," capturing how children's bodies were temporally regulated.[60] Scholars like E. P. Thompson and Mark Smith have argued that the emergence of technologies to regulate time in the industrial era determined which bodies could keep up with labor production.[61] Foucault also argues that the timetable created the "obedient subject," and "authority . . . function[ed] automatically in him" through his compliance with the clock. Bells at Perkins are part of a larger attempt to discipline children's bodies to enter the economic order and submit to the institution.[62]

Institutional time has a far reach in Ruth's world. Ruth takes pride in the fact that Perkins students go home for the summer because this is one feature that distinguishes them as students at a school and not patients in an asylum.[63] However, the end of each school year is marked with a longing to return: upon leaving for the summer, "we were dreaming of the big things we would do next year, when school would re-open and things would go forward again."[64] There is never mention of this time between school years, and here Ruth reveals that time outside the institution is oriented back toward it. Students cannot inhabit temporality outside the institution until they have completed their time at Perkins. Institutional time is the *only* time.

Institutional time is complemented and enforced by the school's approximation of kinship and home for students. Ruth "learned the rules and customs of that well-regulated household. But one day I found my place in a large and happy family, and slipped into it quite easily."[65] The institution's disciplinary tactics mark an affective transition for Ruth from being a part of a "household" to being a part of the "family." Regulation of the mind and body is a condition of being a part of the family; "slipping" into this family erases the institution's manufacturing of those rules for kinship formation. Learning to be a part of a family is a vital part of her education: "We each had a reasonable share of the general housework to do. . . . This is a fundamental rule at Perkins . . . each person comes to feel herself a responsible member of the family, upon whom depends in part the welfare of the whole"; as a result, "there is scarcely ever any friction in the domestic life and the Perkins barometer nearly always registers wholesome activity and peaceful goodwill."[66] One must "come to feel" a sense of kinship for the operation of Perkins to work. Describing the outcomes of approximating kinship as "wholesome" suggests that this home life is contributing to the physical and moral health of the girls. Ruth explains that the school uses the Cottage System, which "is intended to develop (as far as possible) a normal family group . . . the family group is made broad and resourceful and, except in size, is much like a normal family anywhere."[67] The point of Perkins's kinship structures is to *look* "like a normal family." Qualifying that one can only approximate normality "as far as possible" suggests there is a limit to normality; the gender and sexual normality coded in family life being strived for in the school is an unreachable goal. Describing family in these terms permits Perkins to produce an alternative version of kinship that trains students in knowing about kinship norms without inhabiting them fully. Students only need to know what a "normal family" is *like*—they don't need to reproduce it in school since they themselves are not intended to actually have families outside of school.

Education in a Heterosexual Imaginary

In addition to the school's temporal and household arrangements, other features of the school invite students to learn gender and sexual norms. Ruth describes the space outside where they have play time:

> Three of the alcoves were empty; in the fourth was a good sized and very beautiful dollhouse. It was an exceptional dollhouse not just there to be played with. It was designed, furnished, and equipped as a typical American home. A little blind child may not know what a chimney looks like or where the ridgepole is or how the platerail runs around the room. Some children talk of andirons, art squares and chandeliers, while other children have never heard of these things. But there they were in the dollhouse—object lessons for our inquiring need.[68]

"Empty" spaces for imagination are adjacent to domesticity and heteronormativity—these norms, then, may in fact be influencing the imagination permitted in the "empty" spaces. The dollhouse isn't just a space for "play" but a pedagogical site for inculcating within student "American" norms. Melanie Dawson has argued that dollhouses trained girls in the nineteenth century to understand white middle-class values of usefulness and the "impending duties of womanhood."[69] The Perkins dollhouse trains blind children in a future that is not supposed to be "impending" for them. These norms are materialized in the dollhouse through architecture and furniture. Knowledge of space and objects allows students access to understandings of proper homemaking and nationally sanctioned domesticity. Gender and sexuality are located in and apprehended through the environment. Foucault suggests that architecture and material space refer to the "sexuality of children" without naming it and reflect an anxiety over managing it.[70] This scene unsettles that formulation because children refer to architecture to learn about sexuality that the institution does not want located in their bodies. That Ruth describes this education as one "for our inquiring need" erases the institutional manufacturing of students' needs and desires.

Children are also educated in heterosexual norms through their teachers, who provide both appropriate and deviant models for heterosexuality. The narrative first introduces its villainous teacher, Miss Lane, for whom "a personal description will explain her better than any attempt at character analysis. She was tall, thin, flat-chested, with bright red hair, long athletic arms and legs and tongue. She was the primary teacher but her disciplinary ability made us acquainted long before Erma's group was eligible to her classes."[71] Miss Lane's personal descriptions are physical characteristics that reveal her body's failure to exhibit the proper female figure. Miss Lane's "disciplinary ability" and her role as enemy to the students get conflated with gender impropriety. This gender impropriety becomes a sexual impropriety when Miss Lane is compared to another teacher, Miss Church, whose classroom "was not nearly so gloomy as the one occupied by Miss Lane. Perhaps the difference arose from the happy circumstance that Miss Church was in love."[72] Children are learning to link typically positive affects with heterosexuality and typically negative affects with non-femininity and non-heterosexual partnership. The school needs both types of teachers to teach children to recognize and differentiate between appropriate and inappropriate heterosexual norms.

As the text proceeds, we learn that this education that Erma and her classmates are receiving in heterosexual and gender norms is one they are learning, but not for the purpose of replicating in the future. Ruth describes school dances, where

> no boys attended; so far as my associates were conversational on the subject, boys were neither missed nor even thought of. In our day, co-education among the blind was most highly disapproved. . . . From kindergarten days we have lived and played with girls only, and it was, for us, the pleasant, normal, natural way of life. As our class approached High School it began to be more permissible for the older girls . . . to invite acceptable young men, especially to the senior dance. In our Junior year there may have been four or five boys to thirty or forty girls. But in our memorable Hallowe'en dance, there were no boys, no silly notions, just a jolly good time for healthy, happy girls.[73]

Ruth reveals that girls are educated in a "normal, natural way of life" that excludes interaction with or "thought of" the opposite sex. When girls are given the option to interact with members of the opposite sex, they still prefer not to, instead opting for single-sex experiences that are a "good time for healthy, happy girls." This description suggests that heterosexuality is never a false promise to students; their inability to participate in it is transparent from the outset. To approach being "normal," "healthy," and "natural"—categories from which their blindness excludes them, according to the institution—girls must renounce sexuality. The institution tests them by giving them the option to invite members of the opposite sex when they're older, and most girls don't. These students have properly internalized the school's education.

Ruth reveals that this education is reinforced by students' growing fascination with and comprehension of reproduction and heredity. She says, "We were getting old enough to notice that blindness was inherited . . . [and] things that 'ran in families.'"[74] Even blindness that "would be laid to accident" could actually be recast as "the consequence of willful and repeated disobedience."[75] Students are taught to link their blindness with innate negative qualities that have the potential to be passed on through biological reproduction. Even one girl whose blindness was acquired through an accident says, "I have no one but myself to blame for my fate."[76] Blindness is considered a block to normalcy, which the school educates them to believe is the ultimate goal; students regularly hold "public performance[s]" where they "showed the public what we could do and what our school was accomplishing."[77] What the school hopes to "accomplish" is to produce students who can perform normalcy in the form of behaviors and labor. Performing normalcy for the public doesn't require performing normalcy in private—norms that dictate domestic and sexual life need only be learned, not achieved. Students learn that blindness will always pose an obstacle to accessing sexual norms because of the risk of reproduction.

Students, thus, come to understand that sexual reproduction isn't for them. The cottage system allows them to "get a general idea of domesticity, from housemaid and mothers' helper, to home-maker, wife, or mother. Well!—maybe not mother."[78] Children are educated in norms that they are allowed to be in proximity to but that they cannot enact themselves—they can be a "mothers' helper," but "not mother." Training in domesticity allows students to *approach* normalcy in the future. Their blindness presents a barrier to normalcy and health only when they try to be sexual or reproductive subjects. Ruth wonders, "Were we different from other girls, that we didn't need high-balls and boy-friends to help us have a good time? Possibly not. Yet, perhaps, not having the boy-friends made some of us grow up different. One of our most successful graduates said that every time she had to talk to a man—even a bus driver or a store clerk—the shivers ran up and down her spine, for years after she had left school."[79] That the student who cannot "talk to a man" is "one of [Perkins's] most successful graduates" reveals that one is successful when one has passed through the school learning heterosexual norms without acting on them. Ruth also reveals that at Perkins, some blind girls must "grow up different," and this difference reveals itself around present lack of need for heterosexual interaction and future inability to interact with the opposite sex. But "growing up different" might also mean growing in some deviant way—not "up" but aslant to institutional desires. Sexuality is a "stumbling block" to institutionally sanctioned developmental trajectories that must be managed.[80] Erma is one such girl who "grows up differently" at Perkins, and the institution becomes preoccupied with how to alter the course of her growth toward a heterosexual future without sex. She must grow "up" toward a future determined by the institution.

The text does include mention of some girls who do have access to heterosexuality after Perkins, but their mentions serve to show that they are anomalous. Ruth describes one classmate, Nora, who was "unusually normal—not blindish. She was one of the very few blind girls whose smile was a thing of graciousness . . . blind children need to be taught to smile. . . . That Nora was afterwards happily married may be only a coincidence, or it may be a consequence of the habit and ability to smile."[81] Ruth speculates that Nora gets access to heterosexuality because she actually can achieve some form of gender "normal[cy]" that the others' blindness prevents. In another instance, Ruth describes a classmate, Elsie, who "was a very lady-like girl, who has since married and gone to live in Newport, R.I.—a greater claim to society than any the rest of us can boast."[82] Elsie gets access to a future—marriage—that most of the others do not. Elsie's only descriptor is that she "very lady-like," suggesting an epitomizing of gender propriety—replicating this norm so properly grants her a future not accessed by the others. That Ruth describes marriage as giving Elsie a "greater claim to society than any of the rest of us" suggests first that "the rest of us" don't get married and that they understand marriage as a great achievement (a "claim"). Students understand heteronormativity and the value it holds in society, and they also understand they cannot access it because their blindness prevents them from fully inhabiting gender and sexual norms. Thus, girls aspire for other futures in the workforce, which the institution teaches them is what will make them valuable and self-sufficient. Ruth explains that among her class, "Jessie and Johanna were helping in the office and in the industrial department of the Connecticut School for the Blind. A few of the girls were having extra housework with a view of becoming mothers' helpers."[83] Futurity sanctioned by the institution is accessed in another institution as a teacher or being of service in a domestic setting.

Erma's Body and Desires at Perkins

The control and regulation of Erma's body begins the moment she arrives at Perkins. She has "beautiful long curls," but "short hair was the requirement . . . the school barber despoiled the rebellious Erma of her great glory. There were tears, shrieks, and it was said a kick or two; but the curls were sacrificed [sic] to the cause of independence and cleanliness."[84] Erma is left with "a becoming boyish bob that any little girl could comb without help."[85] The description of Erma's haircut participates in this motif of haircutting as an act that violates bodies in an attempt to regulate subjectivity.[86] She is "despoiled" of her curls, suggesting a violent removal; historically, "despoil" can mean to both seize possessions and sexually assault women, emphasizing the present and foreshadowing future violations of Erma's gendered and sexual body.[87] The haircut is the first step in disciplining Erma's "rebellious[ness]," materialized physically on her body. The narrative dilutes Erma's fight against this disciplining, writing, "There were tears, shrieks, and it was said a kick or two"—these acts of resistance are described passively instead of giving agency to Erma. It is further tempered with "it was said," which adds a layer of uncertainty to Erma's acts, filtering them through hearsay. In these attempts to mitigate Erma's resistance, the narrative is complicit with the institution's attempts to discipline Erma. There may be an unexpected effect of her haircut though—Erma is left with a "boyish bob." This haircut supposedly enables the hygiene and self-sufficiency the institution prides itself on valuing, but also perhaps opens the door for Erma's rebelliousness to be enacted through gender impropriety or "boyish[ness]."

Indeed, Erma must be disciplined in gender and sexual norms over the course of the text. In one instance, a teacher finds Erma and a classmate, Catherine, while they "were playing house": "Catherine was the child, Erma the mother. Catherine had misbehaved and Erma was spanking her . . . sitting on the footboard of the low bed with Catherine across her knees."[88] Miss Lane (as a reminder, the evil proto-lesbian teacher) catches them and "for the rest of the week Erma had to spend the study hour down the schoolroom 'away from all the other little girls.'"[89] The school is training Erma in heteronormativity and domesticity, but she "play[s] house" improperly—perhaps there is fear of the erotic component of Erma's play with Catherine. Another reason this is improper is perhaps because in actuality Erma is supposed to only *know* what a mother does—by the end of her time in Perkins, she should know that she herself can never fulfill the role of mother. The classmate escapes punishment; it is Erma who must be kept "away from all the other little girls." The institution's agent fears that Erma's gender and sexual impropriety could contaminate the others; she is separated to prevent others from replicating her.

Erma continues to demonstrate that she is unable to properly internalize the heteronormative education she's receiving. Later, while her class is learning a hymn, one of the lyrics describes the Lord holding the "perverse and foolish" narrator home on His shoulder; this image reminds Erma of "a story [Miss Church had been reading] in which a girl fell down a ledge and her sweetheart carried her home, with her broken leg dangling down his back."[90] Ruth narrates, "Erma laughed. . . . Nowadays when so many youngsters are being sent to school for the feeble-minded we thank our lucky stars that the custom was not so prevalent a quarter century ago."[91] Erma confuses a lesson in spirituality with a lesson in heterosexual romance—she conflates two institutions, exchanging the Lord for the "sweetheart" and the "perverse and foolish" narrator with the girl. Her misunderstanding over proper sexuality results in Ruth expressing gratitude that this is the 1900s and not a few decades later—if the latter, Erma might have been classified as "feebleminded." In this moment, Ruth reveals how feeblemindedness functions as a capacious category to capture improper sexual and gender understanding. Since this moment predates this categorization of pathology (this moment takes place in the first decade of the twentieth century), it remains Perkins's job to properly educate Erma.

Renouncing Sexualities at Perkins

A turning point in Erma's education is when her friendship with a girl, Genevra, is deemed suspicious by their teachers. Fascinatingly, the institution's fear of homosexuality actually produces it in Erma; Erma is *made to believe* that her friendship is improper, and the resulting separation adds a romantic and erotic charge to her desire to be reunited with her friend. Erma experiences institutionally produced queerness, and this queerness contributes to her discipline: the school harnesses this queerness in the service of Erma's heterosexual education, which entails compulsory sterilization. Making Erma aware of a constructed homosexuality permits the school to educate her to renounce it. Renouncing homosexuality is the first step in educating Erma to renounce all of her sexual capacities, including reproductive. The institution believes that blindness is the manifestation of moral weakness, and students must repent through a commitment to a future free of sexual activity. Making Erma aware of her institutionally recognized homosexuality disciplines Erma out of *all* sexuality so she'll never come close to engaging in romantic or physical intimacy again. The novel then fully resolves this newly emergent homosexuality by killing Erma's love interest and migrating that love interest to a male body, whom Erma then must refuse in order to graduate Perkins. The fears that Howe held about the same-sex intimacies generated in these institutions are extinguished in *Erma at Perkins*—the text shows how these intimacies are not at odds with children's heterosexual education but in fact can contribute to disabled children's supposedly proper internalization of heterosexuality—understanding it but not expressing it.

Ruth opens the chapter by reflecting on cases of "hysterics" in the school, noting that of the few cases, "one case was attributed to a 'crush' on one of the teachers."[92] However, in each case of the hysterical girl pathologically obsessing over her teacher, "after a few 'scenes' . . . [they] came back to normal and settled down to be self-contained and self-supporting alumnae"—"in every case . . . a normal and well balanced mental poise developed."[93] Erma reveals that one need not have anxiety over girls' "crush[es]" and the sexual impropriety they must suggest because sexual impropriety can be resolved: in each case, girls "came back to normal." Where girls go so that they are able to "come back" is left ambiguous—do they "go" away to a physical space (whether that be a hospital or isolated place in the school), or is it an interior space in which they temporarily dwell, only to become "normal" and "self-contained"? If they "come back to normal," that suggests they were normal at one time already—does being cured of potential homosexuality through self-containment retroactively construct normalcy? Ruth includes their status as economically independent graduates to ensure that homosexuality in the school is resolved for the future. To become an alumna is to become a proper sexual subject—which, in the case of Perkins alumnae, is a nonsexual subject.

Ruth's discussion of the hysteric is the prelude to her introducing the problem of Erma's friendship. Ruth explains that "there were (besides the cases of hysterics) a few square pegs in round holes—misfits either in school life or cottage life . . . there were the inevitable 'crushes' that spring up among people who live too much with their own sex. The sad phase of this juvenile experience is that many a genuine and valuable friendship is ridiculed as a crush. Upon this reef Erma's fine friendship with Genevra very nearly went to destruction." Ruth distinguishes crushes that get pathologized as hysterical and crushes that make one a "misfit." Her description of how these crushes come about—an "inevitable" outcome of "liv[ing] too much with [one's] own sex"—suggests that these "misfits" are experiencing situational homosexuality, which is also emphasized by the description of this as a "phase," as a temporary mode of desire on the way to proper sexuality.[94] The very arrangement of the school has produced and amplified these desires, and while it is not an entirely unexpected effect of that situation, it must be vehemently disciplined.[95] That said, Ruth maintains that Erma is *not* experiencing any "misfit" desires—she affirms this is a "genuine and valuable friendship." Nonetheless, Erma's friendship with Genevra comes under scrutiny.

Erma is one of several girls made aware of her perceived inappropriate desire. One of her teachers, Miss Lilley, "came upon two girls standing in the open hallway with their arms about each other[. S]he said, 'Girls! Your conduct is disgusting.' And when the girls expressed honest and innocent perplexity . . . she added, 'Well! It looks very suspicious.'"[96] Whether or not the girls are actually acting on homosexual desire is unimportant to Miss Lilley—since the school is a site for teaching girls how to perform norms in behavior and appearance, even "looking" outside the norm is deviant, regardless of the desire (or lack thereof) accompanying it. Ruth says that forbidding girls' behavior without explaining it is dangerous because "without telling or showing [them] why . . . it is the best way of making [them] find out [them]selves."[97] In making students self-conscious of physical intimacy without explaining why it's suspicious, the institution opens the door for students to actually explore homosexuality—for the ultimate purpose of renouncing it.[98]

But before girls can explore homosexuality, they have to figure out what it is—and the school also provides this roadmap. Ruth explains that at first, "we girls honestly did not know. We had read a few decent love stories. . . . We had also read and been taught of beautiful friend-

ships [that] existed. . . . We saw in our very midst . . . the more conspicuous devotion between Miss Marrett and Miss Lilley herself. Of what,
then, was she suspicious?"[99] As Ruth and the others try to imagine what
was "suspicious," they grasp the models of intimacies that the school has
provided: literature and the "conspicuous devotion" between two of their
teachers—one of the very teachers who raised the initial "suspicion."
That their relationship is described as one of "devotion" might suggest an
erotic dimension to their connection. Devotion in the text is deployed
to describe excessive affect that seems at odds with the institution: Ruth
notes that "devotion to some form of beauty offers the only escape from
the humdrum toil of daily life," suggesting that devotion disrupts institutional rhythms;[100] one of their classmates, Alice, "adored Miss Lilley
almost as devoutly as she adored the saints and angels—she has since
entered a convent," suggesting potentially erotic "adoration" must be
funneled into an institutionally sanctioned form of adoration;[101] and
Erma writes a song about one of the only nonwhite students at Perkins,
Mary, with the lyric, "Flowers of affection we scatter around her— / what
shall we choose our devotion to prove?" suggesting devotion for someone who represents a group of people often left out at Perkins in this
era.[102] Devotion has a coded meaning in the text, signifying erotics in
the way it operates aslant to institutional desires.

The teachers are looked to as models to figure out what is "suspicious"
about physical intimacy between girls. From Miss Lilley and Miss Marrett students "had learned not just subject matter, but how to live."[103]
Ruth explains that Miss Lilley

> was not merely looked up to as a teacher, but she was justly admired
> by everyone who was in school. Miss Marrett was envied both for hav-
> ing Miss Lilley's friendship, and for being so worthy of it—as everybody
> knew she was. Young as we were, we consciously studied their charac-
> ters as much as we did the subjects they taught. . . . For thirty years at
> least, each has been the other's first choice for companionship. . . . Their
> friendship—as they enjoyed it and we observed it—is one of the finest
> fruits of Perkins life.[104]

The description of the teachers' "companionship" and "devotion" to one
another suggests a rejection of heterosexuality in favor of, at the very

least, friendship and, at the most, a romantic relationship. These teachers are teaching heterosexuality without experiencing it themselves: in this way, they are the perfect models for students because students are supposed to know about heterosexuality without enacting it themselves in the future while also being productive workers. Indeed, the relationship is an object lesson—students pore over and "observe" it to the same extent as their lessons. The teachers may also inadvertently provide an alternate future in the model of their "companionship." That girls have "envy" over their relationship suggests a desire to access the intimacy they are witnessing.

Miss Lilley and Miss Marrett incite what Kathryn Kent calls "disciplinary intimacy," which captures the ways that normalization can constitute queerness.[105] Disciplinary intimacy is the "intense maternal pedagogical system that compelled young girls to internalize the mandates of bourgeois motherhood, [and] ended up inciting in them other, less normative desire and identifications."[106] The teachers act as parental figures to the girls, educating them in the "mandates of bourgeois motherhood" despite the fact that neither they nor the students have accessed or will access it. A future outside of motherhood, then, is one queer effect of disciplinary intimacy enacted in the school. Kent explains that "the subject-forming project at the heart of disciplinary intimacy threatens to queer, even as it regulates, the female subject"—in other words, attempts to produce girls as proper gender and sexual subjects often have queer effects, especially in the form of desire toward the very person(s) managing their subjectivity.[107] Students oscillate between wanting their teachers and wanting *to be* their teachers, a slippage between desire and imitation.

Erma's desire to replicate her teachers' friendship with Gen makes her teachers anxious. Ruth says, "What wonder that those [students] who called themselves special friends looked to these two [teachers] as their ideal. Certainly it was so with Erma and Genevra."[108] After Miss Lilley observes other girls' "disgusting" behavior, several dyads of friends are selected to be separated, and Erma and Gen form one of them. They "were told to avoid each other as though one of each pair had the smallpox," an analogy that codes the fear of the contagion of homosexuality.[109] Since these girls' friendships are known throughout the school, their separation is also performing important public work: other stu-

dents are supposed to see their separation and learn that their friendship is inappropriate. The school attempts to cure feared homosexuality
through public shaming without naming what it is that they fear, exem-
plifying Foucault's claims in *History of Sexuality*: without naming sexuality, these rules and regulations at Perkins pivot on sexual discipline.[110]
After this punishment, Erma says, "Gen and I spend all our recesses
together . . . but I can't see any harm in that. We never go to each other's
room, nor off the grounds. . . . Why shouldn't we be good friends?"[111]
Erma doesn't understand what she has done wrong, and her naming of
the things she and Gen haven't done together suggests that they haven't
actually engaged in homosexual behavior. Ruth speculates that the head
matron who doles out this punishment, Miss Bennett, didn't quite know
why she was separating the girls: "Probably she had read, or perhaps
observed, that some schoolgirl friendships degenerate into sham love
affairs that weaken characters that are already weak, and corrupt the
morals of the strong."[112] Ruth reveals that it is specifically a fear of sexual
capacity among blind persons that drives the institutions' fear of its existence. The use of "degenerate" and "weak" demonstrates that sexual
relationships are imagined to deteriorate the very constitution of these
children, already marked as inferior by virtue of their blindness. Even
though homosexuality is non-reproductive, it is still a threat. Sexuality
ultimately cannot be a part of the institutional goals of health and normalcy in the context of Perkins students. Health and normalcy without
sex, heterosexuality without sex: this is what the institution desires for
its students' futures.

The separation of students exhibiting potentially homosexual behavior has the effect of actually producing homoerotically charged intimacy
between them. In the case of Erma and Gen,

> when this "separation" was laid upon them, without warning and without
> explanation, natural conduct was blocked, and sought expression in ways
> that were not natural. Wholesome school-girl friendships took on a ro-
> mantic and sentimental twist they had not known before. At once those
> girls began to think of themselves as being like the heroines in books who
> were forbidden to see their sweethearts. What was more natural than for
> them to turn to letters and secret meetings? . . . Letters were easy . . . they
> soon fell into the most sentimental love notes.[113]

In trying to prevent homosexuality, the school enables it. The institution's rules alter what is "natural" for the girls, and their interactions take on an energy of desire. Through describing this shift as still "natural" and not resorting to pathological language, the text might be doing one of two things. On one hand, the text is resisting participating in the demonization of this attachment and intimacy between the girls. Ruth notes, "Across the yard . . . we occasionally saw the boys. They also walked with their arms about each other. And if they carried locks of each other's hair, and if Tommy wrote sonnets to John—what of it? Romance is as human an instinct as religion or self-preservation, and will find expression. Wouldn't it be wiser to provide or allow a natural outlet, than to create false barriers and force a secret outlet?"[114] Ruth contests that even if what was initially happening between Erma and Gen was homosexual, it should have been allowed to have a "natural outlet" and not be forced to secrecy, which intensified the relations. On the other hand, describing their shift toward romance as still "natural" might be a way to show how the institution is producing homosexuality for pedagogical purposes. If it's perceived as natural, then it has a place in the school and is serving a purpose. Same-sex intimacy is a site of discipline into sexual renunciation. The production of homosexuality through an attempt to prevent it must occur in order for the school to teach children to repudiate all sexuality.

The text resolves Erma's homosexuality through removing her love object. Prior to their separation, Gen had a "gentle influence over Erma . . . [and was] the most ennobling influence of her life . . . one day she saw Genevra playing for chapel, and had an impulse to wait outside and walk over to the cottage with her."[115] After this encounter, their connection "blossomed into friendship, and soon bore fruit."[116] Like the friendship between their teachers that was "one of the finest fruits of Perkins life," Erma and Gen's connection "bore fruit." Perhaps "bearing fruit" is what's dangerous to Perkins—it suggests a reproductive capacity. While the school has produced these teachers, Erma and Gen's friendship is engendering something in excess of the institution. The school fears production of intimacy for fear of what else it could produce. Yet, through spending time with Gen, "Erma began to speak softly and correctly . . . she was learning, learning from Genevra. The softening, chastening influence was also exhilarating."[117] Far from a "sham love affair," the friendship between Gen and Erma was actually didactic for Erma. Gen was helping to induct Erma into proper femininity and, through "chastening," tempering potential extraneous sexual energy. That the school interferes with these lessons from Gen, which it also has been trying so hard to impart to Erma, suggests that the need to educate Erma in sexual renunciation takes precedence. By causing Erma to question what is suspicious about her friendship with Gen, the school is making Erma fearful of *any* connection, sexual or otherwise, with a person. Through making their relationship take on a romantic dimension *precisely through its prevention*, the school makes this the "natural" course of things, proving what they produced and making it off-limits to Erma. If this was "natural[ly]" what happened with Gen, it could happen with any friendship, so Erma must withdraw from future intimacies.

Gen is ultimately made off-limits through her sudden death. One teacher speaks to Erma privately and tells her that "if two people are together a great deal, one is apt to sap the strength of the other—the stronger one drawing from the weaker one."[118] Erma sees this as the first rational explanation she's been given for why she and Gen must be separated. This explanation, however, primes Erma to perhaps see herself responsible for the "tragedy" that was to come: "Dainty, delicate Genevra was in very truth too good for this hard world. After only four days' illness, she slipped peacefully away in her matron's arms. . . . Erma had been allowed to visit her . . . afterward Erma felt she had received the first blessing of a new-born angel."[119] After doing the work of "softening and chastening" Erma, and then being a pawn in the institutional project to properly discipline Erma, Gen passes away. Her death has elements of little Eva's death in *Uncle Tom's Cabin*—she is "too good for this hard world," sent to "soften" those around her before dying peacefully and angelically. After her death, Erma goes to her room and tells Ruth, "Instead of the usual evening prayers, I just sat on the floor with my head on the bed, and thought for a long, long time."[120] Erma responds to the loss of Gen by breaking with institutional time. This break is small, but that she tells Ruth she "thought for a long, long time" without revealing the content of her thoughts suggests it was a break that allowed her access to a private interior denied elsewhere by the institution. The death of Gen functions both to eliminate the improper love object and to make Erma withdraw and surrender to the institution's power over her body and desires.

Renouncing Reproductive Futurity

Erma's complete internalization of the institution's desires for her comes in the text's penultimate chapter. Perkins is a coed campus, but the boys and girls are separated for their education with the exception of public performances and, later, morning assemblies. A newly blinded student, David Vincent, wanders onto the girls' campus and Erma, now a teenager, helps to redirect him. Their brief encounter makes Erma think "perhaps life might be worthwhile again, sometime; there might be more to it than just earning a living; there might be friends—not to take Gen's place, but just to keep one from feeling empty and acting useless."[121] While David doesn't replace Gen, meeting him makes Erma think he might be able to provide her with some of the affective and social needs she's been missing since being separated from Gen. She wants more than the guarantee of economic futurity.

However, Erma is careful to curb the social connection she wants with David. When David tries to talk to her again, Erma cries, "Heavens! Don't you know we aren't allowed to meet or speak to each other? They'd have the girls and boys at opposite ends of the state if they could afford it."[122] Erma reveals that even though she is interested only in friendship with David, she knows that the institution could easily misconstrue friendship as a romantic relationship (or transform the former into the latter). She realizes the risk in even talking with David, demonstrating her internalization of her education. She also reaffirms the institution's desires for children to have no interaction with the opposite sex, for fear of romance that could lead to reproduction. This is something the institution has invested in and that Erma imagines they'd make even more extravagant investments in if they had the proper resources.

However, these desires are not yet *completely* internalized by Erma. She sneaks around with David, and as David spends more time with Erma, one of his friends says to him, "She's a peach . . . but it's dangerous, you know—we're blind."[123] As a new student, David does not yet understand why their blindness makes this friendship risky. He is annoyed by the rules restricting gender interaction, which force him and Erma to arrange secret rendezvous for limited times. As his affection for Erma grows romantic, David says, "I think I am going crazy! How can a healthy, strong man endure to be blind? Helpless? Bound by the foolish, inhuman rules that take what little is left of normal life away from us?"[124] David finds these rules around gender interaction and sex dehumanizing. For him, these interactions contribute to "normal life," and he doesn't understand why his blindness precludes him from the sexual and intimate aspects of "normal life." Because he has experienced life outside the institution, he has been inducted into heteronormativity that, up until he was blinded, he expected to inhabit. The institution cannot accomplish its goals with David because it has not been able to educate him from a young age. The production of disabled queer childhood is difficult in someone who experienced a duration of youth outside the institution.

David's resistance to the institution's desire to bar him from sexual normativity serves as a test to Erma. He confesses his love to Erma, and Erma replies, "We mustn't. You don't understand. . . . Not because you are blind, David, but because I am blind, too. If you had been here at school longer, if you knew all the pupils who have blind brothers and sisters, blind cousins, and even blind parents, then you would understand why we mustn't. We couldn't—ever. . . . We couldn't ever have children, it wouldn't be fair—to them."[125] Erma argues that David doesn't understand *yet* why they can't be together because he hasn't been at the school long enough. Her objection to their partnership pivots on their inability to reproduce. Not participating in the reproductive order is seen as an act of justice. Like the "shadowy" disabled child invoked by Howe, here Erma invokes a disabled future child to prevent its conception.

Perkins's education is a sterilization program that students willingly undertake. Erma holds steadfast to this belief despite the fact that both her blindness and David's were acquired. David argues that "our blindness wouldn't be inherited," to which Erma replies, "A weakness has to begin somewhere. It isn't because you are blind, but because I am blind, also. It isn't right for blind people to intermarry. We couldn't ever live a normal life . . . we would have to give up so many things that are necessary for a normal, active life. . . . Neither of us could drive a car, or read our mail, or get the ants out of the baby's stockings."[126] In 1913, Erma echoes the eugenicist sentiments of Dr. Howe in the 1840s. Since her blindness wasn't congenital, she believes it "beg[an] somewhere" in her and so could be passed on. Her first objection was about the fact they couldn't reproduce; she adds to the objection by saying they "couldn't ever live a normal life." Part of that "normal life" is the ability to reproduce and parent. But the only reason Erma hold this belief is because Perkins has educated her to understand blindness as a barrier to a sexual or reproductive future. Perkins traps her in a logic where reproduction and normalcy are interchangeable, and she understands her limits in accessing both. As Julian Carter argues in *Heart of Whiteness*, normalcy is attained only through white heterosexuality.[127] Erma and her classmates can never access the institution's idea of normalcy because they must renounce sexuality. She can strive for it in all other ways, perhaps because of her whiteness. Perkins has taught Erma that normalcy rules above all, and they have worked to help her and other students appear normal so they can seamlessly integrate into the workforce after graduation. The promise of something approaching a normal life comes on the condition of repudiating sexuality. Students can have a future outside of Perkins, but Erma reveals that that futurity is contingent on denouncing sexual and reproductive capacities. In this way, Perkins works to sterilize its students and ensure control over their bodies and sexualities even after they leave the institution.

Erma's ability to take on David's challenges proves that she has successfully internalized Perkins's education. When David argues, "Other people have done it," Erma snaps, "'Not the kind of people we want to be!' . . . She was quite herself again. Her fear of being caught, even the thrill of being alone with him had passed. Again, for the moment at least, she was a level-headed young lady at the verge of Commencement."[128] David's objection here suggests that not all persons who are blind subscribe to this model. But Perkins has taught Erma that there is only one model for citizenship to aspire to, and this model does not include sexuality or reproduction. Proving that she has internalized Perkins's education makes Erma "herself again"—she has become the institutionally sanctioned, gender-appropriate subject that the institution has been trying to discipline. She is now ready to graduate because she has proven she can enter the future that Perkins desires for her. She will be disciplined by her internalized disabled queer childhood. The institution's monitoring and disciplining of the expression and exploration of intimacies, desires, and connections will continue even after she has left.

In the text's final chapter, Ruth affirms that she, Erma, and their classmates successfully leave Perkins. She says that as graduation approaches "there was a sadness mingled with our joy, a growing-up feeling that we must weigh our words and acts so as to make life come out the way we wanted it to be."[129] The school manufactured the girls' "growing-up feeling" in order for their affects to be synced with life beyond Perkins. Girls feel that life will unfold "the way we wanted it to be," occluding that what they "want" is a desire sanctioned and produced by the institution. Erma writes a song for graduation: "O'er us is arching an uncertain future, / Purple or golden, what prophet may tell? / Dearly we love thee, old home of our girlhood, / Fondly, yet sadly, we bid thee farewell."[130] These lyrics are the final lines in the novel. However, the incorporation of adult Erma throughout the text reveals no "uncertain future" for her: she has passed into an institutionally sanctioned future devoid of sexuality. She calls Perkins "old home of our girlhood"—this formulation casts Perkins as the site ("home") for a temporal experience ("girlhood"). That girlhood gets a "home" at Perkins perhaps suggests that girlhood doesn't actually end upon graduating. Perkins made itself home to girls, acting as a material anchor for affect (a sense of home) that allowed it to indoctrinate the girls into an institutional time that synced their minds, bodies, and interior worlds with the institution. While the girls leave Perkins, their girlhood remains there. Exiting the institution is not truly exiting it since they remain tied to it. That is why they have a "growing-up feeling" instead of actually "growing up"—just as they approach normativity without experiencing it fully, they will "feel" like growing up without actually doing it. Perkins is able to continue to control girls' bodies and sexualities beyond the institution. Girls can leave once they have successfully internalized an education in normativity and fully understand the sexual limits of that normativity.

This reading of *Erma at Perkins* positions reproduction and heterosexuality as two means of accessing futurity that the institution denies. I do not mean to cast reproduction and heterosexuality as the only means for accessing futurity or make them synonymous with it. Rather, the institution constructs these as the ideal ways to access futurity, and girls are supposed to understand they will never reach that ideal yet strive for it anyway. Contemporary artist Riva Lehrer articulates the conflict over lamenting disabled girls being barred entry to modes of gender and sexual norms that, if they did access them, would be restrictive and oppressive: "Outside of 'special' school, I saw the normal girls being prepared for womanhood. . . . Women's studies has taught us to see the damage caused by rigid gendering. But there is a different kind of confusion caused by its absence, when it's clear that you're not being included because you've been disqualified."[131] Blindness "disqualifie[s]" Erma and her classmates from full entry into heterosexual womanhood, but the institution also works to ensure that alternate modes of gender and sexual expression won't be explored or experienced. They are given glimpses of what alternate futures could look like outside of bourgeois womanhood through their queer teachers, but replicating these models can result in even stricter disciplining of their intimacies and affects. Students are disciplined out of growing sideways and instead can only be on an institutionally sanctioned trajectory of growing up, even if they will not fully grow up. Students are not given the choice to reject these norms, but they are coerced into believing they must aspire to replicate them with the full knowledge they will never succeed in this project. Students are left in a queer temporality where heteronormativity is always on the horizon, their subjectivities are bound to the institution, and their bodies can perform labor without posing a sexual threat. They can leave the world of Perkins trained to be mothers' helpers—but "maybe not mothers."

4

Cleansing and Contaminating Sexuality

Cleansing African American Labor of Sexuality

About midway through Raoul Peck's 2016 Oscar-nominated documentary *I Am Not Your Negro*, a 1960s Chiquita banana advertisement featuring Godfrey Cambridge plays.[1] As Cambridge emerges from a giant banana and dances on screen singing the brand's theme song ("I am the top banana . . ."), Samuel L. Jackson narrates James Baldwin's words from a 1968 *Look* magazine profile of Sidney Poitier: "In spite of the fabulous myths proliferating in this country concerning the sexuality of Black people, Black men are still used, in the popular culture, as though they had no sexual equipment at all. Sidney Poitier, as a Black artist, and a man, is also up against the infantile, furtive sexuality of this country. Both he and Harry Belafonte, for example, are sex symbols, though no one dares admit that, still less to use them as any of the Hollywood he-men are used."[2] Pairing this text with this clip is ironic because it's hard to read Cambridge's performance as anything other than sexually suggestive, and homosexual at that—he is a closeted gay man emerging from a giant phallus singing and dancing an effeminate anthem. This pairing drives home Baldwin's point that even when sexuality is apparent, it must be denied to Black men in the artistic sphere. The film then cuts to a clip of Sidney Poitier in *Guess Who's Coming to Dinner*, and Jackson continues, "Black men have been robbed of everything in this country, and they don't want to be robbed of their artists."[3] Even after Black men have been robbed of their "sexuality" in the cultural sphere, their artistry survives this loss—how can Black men preserve their artistry under conditions that entail desexualization?

I Am Not Your Negro has been criticized for erasing Baldwin's sexuality. The documentary uses text from Baldwin's unfinished manuscript *Remember This House* and other published writings to address racism in the past and present as well as activist movements that recognize and combat the dehumanization and devaluation of Black life in the United States. Scholars including Dagmawi Woubshet have written that except for a passing reference to the FBI's classification of Baldwin as a possible homosexual, Baldwin's sexuality isn't mentioned in the film, which is a failure in representing how the "experience of race and sexuality were closely intertwined for Baldwin."[4]

By including Baldwin's critiques of how Black sexuality is viewed and "infantil[ized]" in the United States, the film paradoxically reveals how it participates in the very erasures that Baldwin recognized in his lifetime. More than that, it updates Baldwin's twentieth-century critique to suggest that today it is specifically Black homosexuality that is incompatible with the representation and consumption of Black artistic labor. In an essay in *No Tea, No Shade: New Writings in Black Queer Studies*, Kaila Adia Story remarks that today "white queers and black straights continue to silence our [Black queer] voices and/or sanitize our images in an attempt to make our lived experiences more palatable or respectable to the larger public."[5] The 2017 documentary "sanitizes" sexuality from Baldwin's social, political, and cultural work, just as Baldwin argued that the country at large "used" African American men for their artistic production as if "they had no sexual equipment at all." Baldwin can serve as a contemporary hero for critiques of state violence against Black people as long as he is represented strictly as a Black man. To be a Black gay man would have "complicate[d] its audience's views of Baldwin," making him less "palatable or respectable."[6] Metaphorically cleansing Baldwin's work of his sexuality enables its transmission into the cultural sphere.[7]

This limitation of Baldwin's representation is especially important given the constitution of the audience to whom he has now been rendered respectable. As scholars of Baldwin note, white liberal readers composed a large share of his audience.[8] Likewise, critics have noted that the documentary is pitched toward a white liberal audience, making visible on screen what many Black viewers have already known intimately about racism, state violence, and race relations in the United States.[9] The absence of Baldwin's sexuality suggests Black artistry is less palatable to white consumers when it's produced by a Black gay man. Story asserts that "popular culture . . . is a site where some of the most pernicious forms of respectability politics flourish," not only because it is a site where heterosexuality is asserted but because homosexuality is demonized in that process.[10] The directorial choice to erase Baldwin's homosexuality is a compromise to preserve and extend a sanitized version of Baldwin's legacy to a wider audience.

Baldwin's critique captures a dynamic at play in the twentieth-century and contemporary United States among Black labor, Black sexuality, and white consumption of that labor. On one hand, there is a "fabulous myth" that Black sexuality is perverse, rampant, and excessive—in short, pathological; on the other hand, when Black persons, and particularly Black men, enter "popular culture" as artists, they are often rendered impotent or seen as asexual.[11] Black men cannot be "admit[ted]" as sexual subjects by a straight white audience doing the consumption—even if the desire exists as an open secret, it must be denied. This dynamic is a version of what Eric Lott describes as "love and theft," where white consumers must "rob" Black artists of their sexuality in order to take pleasure from their artistry. This robbing is a way to control and manage Black cultural work.[12]

The act of theft occurs because of simultaneous fear and desire—despite the myths of Black male sexuality as pathologized, there is still a desire for it. This desire is resolved through sanitization of Black male sexuality.[13] At the turn of the twentieth century, there was fear that Black cultural forms, such as jazz, were disrupting the social order by transmitting "traits thought to be essentially African American."[14] As Black artists were able to begin gaining some entry into white-dominated cultural spheres as the twentieth century progressed, white consumers still worried that this cultural labor would contaminate white audiences since this labor was produced by persons viewed as pathological. White consumers could in part enjoy Black cultural labor through denying Black sexuality.

In this way, consumers of Black labor were also managers of Black sexuality in the cultural sphere. Scholar bell hooks writes how Black artists might respond to this dynamic: "marginalized groups, deemed Other, who have been ignored, rendered invisible, can be seduced by the emphasis on Otherness, by its commodification, because it offers the promise of recognition and reconciliation"—in other words, when one has been denied entry into the cultural sphere, one can be taken by "the promise of recognition and reconciliation" that consumption offers, especially when that promise and recognition come with mate-rial resources that make life more livable.[15] But bell hooks explains that this is a fantasy of progress, veering into the postracial, that results in a "nostalgic evocation of a 'glorious' past."[16] Promises of entry into the cultural sphere through sanitizing sexuality—rendering it invisible or packaging it to accord with white middle-class respectability—is a way for white culture to continue to control Black bodies and labor, as they have done for centuries. Thus, Black artists have an "over-riding fear . . . that cultural, ethnic, and racial differences will be continually commodi-fied and offered up as new dishes to enhance the white palate—that the Other will be eaten, consumed, and forgotten."[17] Black artists have been stuck in a framework where the value and circulation of their labor have been determined in part by white audiences, who sanitize Black sexual-ity through consumption.

The film follows Baldwin's commentary about sexuality immediately with his words on the fear that African Americans will have their Black artists stolen from them, lost to mainstreaming, whitewashing, and ex-ploitation. These selected sentences from the 1968 Look article have been rearranged—in the article, this sentiment about losing Black artists ap-pears earlier and apart from Baldwin's words on sexuality. By framing the "robbing" of the Black community of their Black artists with the voiding of those artists' sexuality, the documentary shows how the loss of Black sexuality in artistic production amplifies the threat of losing Black artistic production, as well as the stakes in preserving what can survive after being "robbed." If the presence of sexuality risks the loss of art, then artists must adhere to white gender and sexual norms—sanitize sexuality—in an effort to preserve and retain some ownership over their work. Adherence is a path to survival that maintains gender and sexual codes in the public sphere that "perpetuate the myth that black sexuality and identity is inherently pathological."[18]

The documentary shares Baldwin's 1968 words to show that he is sub-ject to this same treatment in 2017; his words provide a longer genealogy to the sexual sanitization of Black cultural labor. The film, then, might be participating in the erasure of Baldwin's sexuality in order to illustrate that, in addition to its larger project of revealing that our world is not postracial in 2017, it also is not post-queer—and it is especially not post-racialized queerness. A pressing question that remains is if there have been any shifts in the role of sexuality in Black artistry since 1968: is it that Black men are cleansed of sexuality in the social, political, and cultural spheres today, or is it specifically Black homosexuality that remains subject to erasure, policing, and management?

Institutional Cleansing of Black Labor

This chapter focuses on the role that educational institutions for Black children have played in perpetuating and deconstructing "fabulous myths" about Black sexuality. Educational institutions for African Americans in the late nineteenth and twentieth centuries stipulated that Black labor, both cultural and manual, had to be perceived as devoid of sexuality through an embodiment of sexual respectability in order to be consumed by a white ruling class. The schools achieved this perception and adoption of respectability through policing sexuality in institutions—this was a top-down mandate from those who controlled the institutions' financial resources, often white benefactors, and carried out within the institution by administrators, teachers, and students alike.

These mandates functioned to *cleanse* students of their perceived pathological sexuality in exchange for ostensible entry into the economic, political, and cultural spheres. The discourse surrounding hygiene in these schools reveals a slippage between literal and metaphorical (that is, bodily and moral) concerns over Black students' cleanliness, and especially their actual bodies' capacities for literal and metaphorical contamination. I explore the schools' preoccupation with cleanliness in order to trace how gender and sexual norms were taught, maintained, and disciplined in these schools; hygienic practices were the means through which the school educated children in erotics.[19] I examine hygiene programs in combination with other tactics for bodily management and surveillance to consider their effects on Black sexuality, especially Black homosexuality, in educational and cultural institutions, in the twentieth-century and contemporary United States.

Reconstruction-era educational institutions emerged to train a newly emancipated population of African Americans in industry, trades, and domesticity. Booker T. Washington, founder of the Tuskegee Institute, has been critiqued for advocating industrial education. Opponents argued that training African Americans in skills would keep them subject to and subjugated by a white ruling class, a hierarchy essentially codified by the 1895 Atlanta Compromise.[20] These schools emerged at a time of great debate regarding the education of children, especially newly emancipated African American children. John Dewey, a prominent educational reformer, argued for student-centered pedagogy that encouraged hands-on learning.[21] Dewey's philosophies were interpreted differently by persons on opposite ends of the political spectrum. More left-leaning reformers used his ideas to institute field trips, small classroom sizes, and experiential learning; Tova Cooper argues that both Richard Henry Pratt (the founder of the first Native American boarding school, explored in the next chapter) and Washington were "conservative educators" who interpreted Dewey to "emphasize manual training, physical education, and instruction in personal hygiene" in their schools.[22] This program would "train laborers for maximum efficiency in the capitalist marketplace."[23] Dewey himself approved of this application of his philosophy—he "sanctioned efforts to train students for optimum efficiency in the capitalist workforce," revealing how educational philosophy and pedagogy were racialized in the late nineteenth and early twentieth century.[24]

According to Roderick Ferguson, these schools operated by a "logic" that "industry would play a crucial part in reforming the black subject from degenerate and immoral primitive to the normative citizen-subject of the United States."[25] In other words, industrial education was proposed as the mechanism through which Black subjects could be transformed into moral citizens. Ferguson argues that industrial education was an "alliance between sexual normativity and citizenship."[26] Industrial training was not just education in and management of labor but also training in gender and sexual norms, where "sexual normativity claimed to be able to draft African Americans into citizenship and humanity."[27] Learning gender and sexual norms was necessary in order to access the American promises of "citizenship and humanity." This line of thinking resonates with Siobhan Somerville's central claim in *Queering the Color Line*, in which she argues that the classification, maintenance, and policing of the boundaries between Black and white were not parallel to but deeply connected with the classification, maintenance, and policing of the boundaries between heterosexuality and homosexuality at the turn of the twentieth century.[28] In other words, postbellum educational institutions for African Americans helped constitute a heterosexual Black subject. In this way, Ferguson sees African Americans as the "original model minority" in the United States, and this status emerged because of the intimate, inextricable link between educational training and heterosexuality.[29] Schools and the norms that they purported conferred what Chandan Reddy might call "freedom with violence," or when "socially and institutionally produced forms of emancipation remain regulatively and constitutively tied to the nation-state form."[30] In order for African Americans to advance (and survive, in the eyes of these educational institutions), state-sanctioned gender and sexual norms had to be learned and perceived sexual or gender deviance had to be punished.

W. E. B. Du Bois is the most famous critic of Washington's approach to education, arguing it would never lead to full social, economic, and political equality for African Americans. He instead advocated for a liberal arts approach to education to cultivate an intellectual elite who could lead the fight for racial justice. Washington's model would reproduce the working class; Du Bois's model saw some possibilities for economic advancement. With the decline of the Washington model of industrial education in the 1920s and 1930s, there was a rise in elite educational institutions for African Americans; colleges founded in the Du Bois spirit had primary and secondary counterparts throughout the United States.[31] These schools transitioned from preparing students strictly for manual labor to training them for cultural labor through artistic, aesthetic, and intellectual productions. The schools expanded the economic possibilities for students by diversifying the labor they could engage in beyond the institution, but this potential future was contingent on gender and sexual propriety.

Ferguson urges scholars to expand the conversation around African American education in the late nineteenth and twentieth centuries; viewing education as solely a debate between Washington and Du Bois "assumes a dichotomy between industrial education and humanistic training, never knowing that this dichotomy might have been fictitious because of shared moral and normative investments."[32] In other words, while different educational models and goals may have guided the institutions for which Washington and Du Bois advocated, ultimately both types of institutions were invested in helping students enter the social and political orders as proper gender and sexual subjects. These institutions reveal "power's manifestation through the racialized compulsion to gender and sexual normativity"—schools were a way to manage the Black population and control Black sexuality, labor, and reproduction.[33] Both types of institutions produced Black populations capable of and invested in reproducing normativity and regulating gender and sexual impropriety within their communities. Schools advocated for a "self-discipline and policing" that Saidiya Hartman argues demonstrates "the displacement of the whip. . . . The whip was not abandoned; rather it was to be internalized."[34] This policing of self becomes a policing of one another, so that Black labor was already perceived as cleansed of pathological sexuality by the time it entered the public sphere.

The manual labor for which industrial schools had trained students required a commitment to sexual propriety; to be a laborer was to embody and enact respectability, which was coded as heterosexual. Paying attention to hygiene programs and other tactics for bodily management in industrial schools reveals how schools educated children to experience their bodies and sexualities as dirty and shameful—schools had to educate students in the racist, eugenicist discourse about their supposed pathology in order to alienate students from their bodies and sexualities. This alienation worked to ensure their ability to be racialized heterosexual laboring subjects outside the institution. Children's sexualities were viewed as contaminated by virtue of their race, and this metaphorical contamination translated to strict hygienic practices and regimens in the school. Schools indoctrinated students in this perception of their bodies, but the antidote to dirtiness and shame—strict hygiene—was often impossible given the poor material conditions resulting from lack of funding and overcrowded facilities. In other words, schools could not always provide children with the facilities that would enable them to carry out these hygienic regimens. Norms were enforced, even when material conditions made them impossible to achieve. Students were trained in norms they could not enact in order to cultivate shame toward their bodies.

I examine materials from the Manassas Industrial School, a private boarding school that educated Black children in traditional academic subjects, industrial trades, and domestic training to show how, in the words of an early annual report, "personal cleanliness" was a matter both "moral and physical."[35] I've selected Manassas for my case study because it was long running and considered a model for the successful education of Black students. It operated as a private residential school for almost fifty years, before being taken over by the state; during those fifty years, Theodore Roosevelt took an interest in the school and Andrew Carnegie served as a generous benefactor. The school's program made it an attractive investment for white political leaders and philanthropists.

While students did marry and reproduce after leaving this institution and others like it, their ability to be laborers was intertwined with their ability to occupy a narrow sexual subject position. To embrace or explore sexual capacities, especially beyond the heterosexual and reproductive, was to put one's position as a laborer and citizen at risk and be "a direct liability to both the community and State."[36] Students were educated that the narrative about their pathologized sexuality was reality and that in order to access a future outside the institution, they had to accept this narrative and demonstrate gender and sexual propriety. They were permitted heterosexuality as long as it remained tacit and confined and didn't interfere with their ability to work. The school cleansed students of potential deviant sexualities so that by the time they entered the social, economic, and political spheres as racialized laborers, their sexuality was already controlled, their labor ready to be consumed. Black queer childhood in these schools was an internalization of the bourgeois mandates for sexual cleanliness.

These imposed narratives that limited expression of sexuality continue to permeate African American education and especially cultural production. I trace the echoes of industrial education and its mandate for gender and sexual propriety (i.e., heterosexuality) in *Choir Boy* (2015), a contemporary play by Oscar-winner Tarell Alvin McCraney.[37] *Choir Boy* explores how the management of Black queer sexuality and artistic production are intimately, even violently connected in a contemporary African American boys' boarding school. The play contains portals to industrial education through invocations of hygiene, cleanliness, and industrial work, with the school's showers serving as a site where artistic labor, homosexual desire, and the management of sexuality converge and confront one another. The play engages with the film *I Am Not Your Negro*'s provocations about Black sexuality by ultimately arguing that Black cultural labor for white consumption has room for heterosexuality, but not homosexuality. The school violently cleanses students of sexual im-

propriety, which is synonymous with homosexuality, so they will be recognized and received as citizens and laborers outside the institution. A
focus on hygiene encodes a preoccupation with sexuality in the historical
record and archival materials; *Choir Boy*'s aesthetic account reveals that
this preoccupation is explicitly about the sexuality of students' bodies.
Choir Boy bridges the Washington and Du Bois models of education by
revealing how Black labor is incompatible with homosexuality. This policing within the institution is based on perceptions of Black sexual deviance created by a white ruling class. These perceptions pass as reality and
determine the conditions under which a racialized subject can enter and
operate within the economic, social, and political spheres.

Moral and Physical Cleanliness in the Manassas Industrial School

While Tuskegee and the Hampton Institute are the most famous African American educational institutions, a number of industrial schools,
including boarding schools for primary and secondary education, were
established throughout the United States during and after Reconstruction.[38] In this section, I examine materials from the Manassas Industrial
School to demonstrate the school's preoccupation with sexuality. The
biographer of Jennie Dean, founder of Manassas, remarked that Dean
"buil[t] the foundation for another miniature Hampton or Tuskegee,"
and each of these institutions was invested in training students in
respectability through developing habits of the body that were imagined
to help instantiate morals especially around sexual behavior.[39] Historians have documented the relationship between literal hygiene and social
hygiene (i.e., eugenicist) programs in late nineteenth-century institutions, seeing the latter metaphorized in the former.[40] I take seriously
the role of literal hygiene practices and regimens regarding cleanliness,
bathing, and grooming to consider how they account for and resolve
perceptions of sexual deviance in order to produce Black heterosexual
laborers. More than just slippages, the literal and metaphorical consolidate and inform one another so that the focus on literal cleanliness
becomes what Lauren Berlant terms a "dead metaphor," when "by repetition, the unlikeness risked in the analogy the metaphor makes becomes
so conventionalized as to no longer seem figural, no longer open to
history."[41] In other words, focus on literal hygiene in the school as an

avenue for moral cleanliness wasn't taken as "figural" but was imple-mented as reality—maintaining the body's cleanliness *was* maintaining the body's gender and sexual propriety. Berlant argues inhabitants of the United States are "dead citizens," where heterosexuality constitutive of citizenship is "dead, frozen, fixed, or at rest," a repetition of a sanitized past to preserve the nation for a fetishized, figural Child.[42] In the case of industrial schools, institutions taught Black children to clean themselves so that they could inhabit the economic sphere and remain subject to a white ruling class outside the institution. Citizenship was contingent on this cleanliness—these students were always already excluded from gathering under the banner of the fetishized, figural Child and instead had to sanitize their sexualities, rendering them dead to access citizen-ship in a nation never oriented toward protecting them or their future.

A focus on hygiene shows how the institution was invested in manag-ing Black children in their quotidian practices and habits—management of the population occurred through mandating these intimate, micro-level routines of the body. A 1905 school publication states that some of objectives of the school include "to train in habits of usefulness those committed to its care, by developing them mentally, morally, and physi-cally," "to teach the dignity and importance of labor and by means of trades to perform it skillfully and with pride," and "to make its students self-reliant, careful thinkers, thorough in their work, manly and wom-anly in their bearing and to cultivate habits of industry."[43] These objec-tives reveal that the school imagined itself to be responsible for the care of students' minds, morals, and bodies. Synchronizing the three so that students could find "pride" and "dignity" in physical labor allowed the school to create properly laboring heterosexual subjects: students would be "manly and womanly in their bearing" as they "cultivate[d] habits of industry." Black girls and boys could become "manly and womanly" only through development of physical and moral habits, but they were barred full entry into the categories of men and women because these categories are always already white in the United States.

Manassas's focus on hygiene resonates with both Washington's and Du Bois's investments in gender and sexual propriety through preoc-cupation with cleanliness and hygienic habits. In *Scenes of Subjection*, Saidiya Hartman looks at Reconstruction and post-Reconstruction edu-cational institutions as sites where the violence and control over Black bodies, labor, and subjectivities were carried out under the guise of care. She argues that "issues of prosperity and hygiene are central to the regulatory efforts of the state . . . since cleanliness and domestic order are confluent with social stability, economic health, and the eradication of idleness," explaining why looking toward these institutions' investment in students' cleanliness reveals collusion with state-determined parameters for entry into the categories of citizenship and humanity.[44] Both Washington and Du Bois wrote conduct books that were tools for cultivating habits of the body that were considered crucial for respectability and racial uplift.[45] Hartman explains that these handbooks promised "the full privileges of citizenship . . . [to] those who realized the importance of proper conduct and applied the principles of good management to all aspects of their lives, from personal hygiene to household expenditures."[46] Handbooks cultivated proper management of the body and home, which would give students access to citizenship. Nazera Sadiq Wright argues that these manuals were part of a genre in the early twentieth century in which Black activists produced literature that "sought to manage black girls [and children] in the public sphere by correcting behavioral traits, relying on religious beliefs, and promoting education as paths to good citizenship."[47] These books were "written mainly to protect African Americans against systemic, racialized violence in the form of lynching and rape"—in other words, adherence to white norms for gender and sexual conduct may have had the effect of controlling and limiting Black subjectivities, but encouraging this adherence was an effort to "protect" African Americans from violence that they would be susceptible to if they didn't enact these norms.[48] Survival was contingent on acquiescing to this racialized management of bodies, genders, and sexualities.

Washington's vision "emphasiz[ed] black girls' domestic education and hygiene," and he further details his investments in cleanliness in his 1902 autobiography *Up from Slavery*.[49] Prior to attending the Hampton Institute, Washington was a domestic servant for a woman who showed him "the importance of cleanliness, orderliness, and system among upper-class Victorian whites."[50] Washington was trained in white upperclass norms as a requirement for performing labor, and Hampton further developed these values. He writes that the "most valuable lesson I got at the Hampton Institute was in the use and value of the bath . . . not only in keeping the body healthy, but in inspiring self-respect and promoting virtue."[51] Washington was trained to believe both within and outside the school that physical hygiene would lead to "self-respect"—hygiene was the route toward racial uplift, and he carried these values to Tuskegee. At Tuskegee, Washington "insisted that everywhere there should be absolutely cleanliness . . . people would excuse us for our poverty . . . [but] they would never excuse us for our dirt" and "absolute cleanliness of the body has been insisted upon from the first."[52] Washington reveals that white norms regarding the body determined quotidian practices and habits around the body at Tuskegee. Students were clean not just for their own sake but so that they could not give white benefactors or skeptics a reason to stop believing in the value of this institution. Washington writes that "the school will always be supported in proportion as the inside of the institution is kept clean and wholesome and pure."[53] This slippage between the cleanliness of the institution and the cleanliness of students' bodies suggests that if students were to forgo their hygiene routines, the survival of the institution, now seen as unclean and impure, would be at stake.[54] The students' bodily practices impacted the social and moral perception of the school and helped the institution reproduce itself through guaranteeing continued support and patronage.

The Manassas Industrial School for the Training of Colored Youth was founded in 1893 by Jennie Dean, a formerly enslaved woman, with the financial backing of Jane Thompson, a white benefactor. In a December 1908 letter from Thompson to William Loeb, secretary of President Theodore Roosevelt, Thompson petitioned for financial support from the president: "I have been Jennie Dean's friend and helper since 1888, twenty years, and know her very soul. She is clean, upright, and unselfish."[55] The first attribute Thompson noted was Dean's "clean[liness]," suggesting that Dean and her institution were worth investing in because they were combating the assumed pathologies of their race. Later, Thompson noted that "Jennie Dean, like Mr. Roosevelt, is a believer in marriage among young people. She is a born match-maker among her own people, and takes delight in pairing them off, and as soon as [they are] married starts them to buy an acre of land and build a home."[56] In addition to being "clean and upright," Dean demonstrated a commitment to sexual propriety. She created heterosexual unions, showing that in her institution she could successfully manage "unruly" rampant

Black sexuality and constrain it into proper and propertied marriages. Thompson offered cleanliness and sexual propriety as reasons to support the school—it was managing Black sexuality through education.

Frederick Douglass was among those who spoke at the school's 1894 dedication, and during its operation the school garnered the support and attention of high-profile philanthropists and politicians. So while a private institution, the school was invested in by persons whose interests aligned with the state.[57] The school's status as private did not protect it from the influence and rule of those who wanted to control Black labor. In February 1906, President Roosevelt invited Dean and some teachers and students from the school to visit the White House. In his address to them, he said, "No body of our fellow-citizens can have a greater claim to being received at the White House than a body like this, which stands for the fundamental duty of American citizenship, the duty of self-education. . . . I think we can accept this school as typical—not as exceptional, but as typical."[58] Roosevelt suggests that Manassas was "not exceptional" but an exemplar of what African American educational institutions should look like in the United States. By training students in "self-education," Manassas established itself as a model after which other primary and secondary industrial schools could fashion themselves. Roosevelt continued that this education was a way for students to perform their "duty to themselves, their duty to their neighbors, [and] their duty to the State at large."[59] In being educated, students are fulfilling a patriotic "duty," but students wouldn't be able to complete their ultimate duties to the state until they were laboring citizens outside the institution. This elision between duty to and labor for the state obscures how this obligation for self-edification was harnessed and directed toward the state.

Roosevelt amplified this flattened temporality of current training and future service when he proclaimed that "any such school as this is increased tenfold when the school is founded . . . by a colored man or colored woman to help the colored boys and colored girls of to-day to make the best type of self-respecting, self-supporting American citizens of the future."[60] Roosevelt suggested that when these schools have Black leadership, they are in more of a position to create "American citizens of the future." That these "citizens of the future" will be "self-respecting" codes the sexual propriety required to enter the economic sphere. "Self-respect" codes an individual pathology that must be resolved, obscuring how it is really respect of the white ruling class that is being catered to through this gender and sexual training. Black students were not guaranteed entry to citizenship until they completed their education—this is why they were framed as "citizens of the future." Citizenship was a promise that mandated sexual propriety, and Roosevelt's praise of Black leadership shows how these mandates were carried out by Black leaders and teachers within the school. Students were trained in sexual norms before entering the economic sphere so that their labor would be consumable. Education of the labor force and consumption of that labor enabled each other. The state's close surveillance over and support of the school, via the president, reveals why Manassas is a particularly apt site for considering institutional cleansing of the student body.[61]

The school's materials reiterate that education and cleanliness were necessary in order for students to attain citizenship. A 1908 report asks potential benefactors, "Is it not worth while that you should have some share, however small, in helping the negro to win his freedom—the freedom of economic independence and sterling character that comes with a trained mind and hand? Is it not worth while in a democracy like ours that even the humblest children of the republic should have a chance to become useful citizens?"[62] This report suggests that education would have the effect of cleaning students (giving them "sterling character"). This cleanliness would give students the "chance to become useful citizens"—education and cleanliness were not guarantors of citizenship but merely increased the odds. A 1910 report reiterated that while citizenship was a promise, it was not a guarantee: the school was "daily saving Negro boys and girls from the dreadful clutches of ignorance, unthrift, poverty, and sin, and converting them by the most careful training and discipline into active, self-supporting men and women worthy of citizenship in the great republic."[63] Making students "worthy of citizenship" did not necessarily result in admission to the category. This description also affirms the school's role in monitoring gender development in children—they "discipline[d]" their passage from childhood to adulthood to ensure they could properly enter the social and political orders as laboring citizens cleansed of perceived pathology. This monitoring of gender was emphasized in an April 1921 advertisement for the school in the *Crisis*, the publication of the NAACP founded by

Du Bois, which stated that the school has "high moral standards" and "prepares boys and girls to become useful men and women."[64] The goal from childhood to adulthood at Manassas was to become "useful"—training in gender and sexual propriety potentially granted one access to an economic future.

The school's annual reports reflect the intimate connection between hygiene and discipline. The *1915–1916 Annual Report* states, "The discipline of the school seeks to stimulate in the student body the co-operative spirit. . . . Each student is taught that the success of the whole school depends, in a measure, upon him—upon the cleanliness of his personal habits . . . and honest performance of all his duties."[65] In order to be a "co-operative" member of the student body, one has to be clean. The school continued to reveal an emphasis on cleanliness; for example, "rooms and wardrobes are inspected daily by officials, and cleanliness and neatness are at all times demanded."[66] Institutional agents carefully monitored students' cleanliness, which was both literal and metaphorical. The same report states, "The essential qualities of manly and womanly character—energy of spirit, attentiveness, application, seriousness of purpose, and personal cleanliness, moral and physical—receive careful consideration throughout each and every course."[67] To be an "essential" man or woman at Manassas was to practice "personal cleanliness, both moral and physical." The school curriculum imagined that literal hygiene and moral education would contribute to developing gender and sexual propriety among its students.[68] Clean bodies and clean morality—that is, virtues that align with sexual propriety—were linked in the school's discourses. Part of the binary thinking about the Washington and Du Bois models of educations has to do with their perceived divergent views of approaching the Black subject—the Washington model focuses on Black subjects as physical laborers, while the Du Bois model focuses on Black subjects as intellectual laborers. The Manassas School's materials help to further disrupt this binary by showing how manual labor was deeply intertwined with intellectual and moral development—the body was a vessel for both modes of educational progress.

In addition to subjects like literature, history and civics, domestic science, blacksmithing, geography, music, carpentry, music, and agriculture, the school also had a program in physiology and hygiene. This subject was "of great importance in view of the inattention of the masses to it. Its importance in the rural community cannot be overestimated and every effort is made to stress the necessity of giving proper care and attention to the body as well as the home in general."[69] The school's commitment to hygiene was first an attempt to educate students in habits they were presumed to not have prior to the school. The school assumed students were coming to them inherently dirty and with no knowledge of hygiene by virtue of their race, class, and geographical position. Students were to give "proper care and attention to the body as well as the home in general"—there is an elision here between the students' body and the homes they will one day care for as domestic servants. This slippage suggests that care for the body was in the service of future labor in white homes.

The primer the school used reinforced these lessons in bodily care for the purpose of future labor. The annual reports suggest that John Ritchie and Joseph Caldwell's *Primer of Hygiene* was the primary text for transmitting this education.[70] The primer accompanied lessons in physiology and hygiene with images and illustrations of white children; incorporating this text into the African American industrial education curriculum was intended to teach Black children that to be clean was to be white. They could aspire to proper hygiene, but they would never be fully clean by virtue of their race. The text, then, reveals how the school participated in training children for an aspirational future that would always be unreachable.[71]

This primer stressed the relationship between hygiene, happiness, and work: "Every person who comes into this world has a work to do. . . . The member of a family or of a school who is not trying to help the group to which he belongs is unhappy, because he knows he is failing to do his share of the work. . . . When our bodies are strong and well we rejoice in them. . . . Hygiene [is] important because it teaches how to care for the body."[72] The primer's tone suggests a universal view of human development and physiology, but in the context of industrial education, the racial composition of the student body would impact the reception of these assertions. This introduction to the primer tells Black students that they are born to labor and will derive pleasure from it by virtue of working in the service of the community. Students could "rejoice" in their bodies when they were cared for and oriented toward labor. In this way, pleasure was linked not to bodily affects, sensations, or sexuality but strictly to habits that positioned the body to do work. The primer's lessons included details on how bodily organs like the heart, kidneys, and digestive system worked as well as how diseases like tuberculosis, diphtheria, and trachoma spread. Absent from their lessons were mentions of sexual organs or sexual disease. The preoccupation with cleanliness was a preoccupation with sexuality, but sexuality could not be named. It instead was coded in these concerns over bodily hygiene and health.

The primer's unit on bodily habit formation delineates the link between bodily maintenance and identity formation: "We do know that in the movement of the muscles, in the training of the mind, and in the building of the character, nothing has so great an influence as the habits we have formed," and "as we form habits of the body, so we form habits of the mind."[73] The primer suggests that the way habit formation occurs in the body is analogous to how it forms in the mind and character. Students "should form habits that will carry you on in the road to health, and to respected, truthful, successful manhood and womanhood."[74] Habit formation, both physical and moral, was constitutive of proper "manhood and womanhood." Students had to clean and maintain their bodies so that they could leave the school as proper gender and sexual subjects who could enter the workforce. Hygiene routines formed habits that were meant to build up the health of the students but also the health of the nation through their labor.

A concluding chapter of the primer that reinforces the link between bodily and moral development reveals why the stakes of acquiring these habits were so high for Black students:

> Sanitation comes from a Latin word (*sanitas*) that means wholeness, or health. It is the science of how to preserve the health, especially the public health. . . . It is of interest to note that from the same Latin word from which *sanitation* comes, we get also our words *sanity* and *saneness* (soundness of mind), and *insanity* (unsoundness of mind). *Sanity* and *sanitation* mean the same in their origin, and we might conclude that to practise sanitation is to act sanely and sensibly, while not to practise it is to act in a way that indicates either a lack of knowledge or a lack of wisdom.[75]

The primer argues that to be clean is to be sensible, knowledgeable, and respectable. Sanitation was a sign not only of education but also of psychological well-being. There is a veiled threat in this comparison between sanitation and sanity: if students did not develop these bodily habits and become proper men and women, they risked further institutionalization to treat their pathology. To read this lesson as a threat isn't a leap. At the same time institutions were educating Black youth for future labor, they were also incarcerating Black youth in reform schools for their criminalized sexuality—the difference among these student bodies is that while they were all viewed as capable of sexual deviance, the students in reform school had, in the state's eyes, acted upon it and so posed an especial threat. As the first chapter demonstrates, insanity in the form of a feebleminded diagnosis was used to explain Black juvenile delinquents who continued to engage in criminalized sexual behavior even after leaving the school. The institution considered their bodies and moral habits unclean, and they declared them unsound in order to exert the ultimate cleansing of these children's sexualities through medical sterilization. Not far from the Manassas Industrial School in the state of Virginia was the Industrial Home School for Colored Girls of chapter 1. Several girls were transferred from the Virginia School to Manassas between 1915 and 1927.[76] Several girls were also transferred during this time from the Virginia School to the Petersburg State Colony, a hospital where at least some of them were medically sterilized. This transfer of Black students among institutions that had purportedly different missions suggests that the risk of being displaced for violating school codes regarding cleanliness was real. In an era when insanity was so inflected by race and sexuality (and racialized sexuality), the stakes of committing to hygiene programs that were a sign of sanity were high. Manassas students had to commit to the hygiene program, a guarantor of gender and sexual propriety, in order to ensure they would have access to some future, even if a limited economic future in which they could occupy only a narrow sexual subject position and not risk further institutionalization. The primer reveals the stakes of this education for Black youth in the early twentieth century.

Despite the school's reported investment in hygiene, habits in hygiene could not be enacted given the material conditions of the school. The 1907 report notes, "A not less urgent need is that of better bathing facilities for both boys and girls. . . . It is difficult to teach effectively the lesson of cleanliness without bathing conveniences."[77] The school was preoccupied with cleanliness and urged students to see the connection between their physical and moral cleanliness but could not provide them with the facilities that would allow them to practice these principles. The effect of this gap between lessons and material realities may have been shame—if students were taught that being physically unclean was immoral and backward, to have to sometimes inhabit that condition would be shame-inducing.

The school continued to perpetuate this gap between lessons and conditions. In 1912, the *Manassas Bulletin* reported,

> All of the industrial departments are at present over crowded and embarrassed by the lack of facilities. The boys' dormitory is overrun, and boys are now rooming in what used to be the store house. The girls' dormitory is also full. . . . It is not the purpose of this school to become a large institution. A small school providing close and steady contact between teacher and pupil, and doing *thoroughly* the work which it undertakes— this is the aim at Manassas. It will be impossible to realize this aim without the facilities which we are struggling now to secure.[78]

The report reveals that the school was overcrowded, which was undermining the ability to carry out the mission of the school. The institution desired for there to be "close contact between teacher and pupil," and this was literally a risk—the same report details recent outbreaks of diphtheria and tonsillitis in the school. The school wanted to train their students in hygiene and clean habits but could not provide the conditions for this to happen.

In Jennifer Opager Baughn's investigation of materials that circulated to institutions in the early twentieth century about best practices for maintaining their grounds and facilities, she notes that these publications "emphasized hygiene—a broad term encompassing all aspects of the school's physical environment."[79] Opager Baughn explains that "as defined by Progressive Era school planners, 'hygiene' included both the building and grounds of the school and the physical well-being of students," and they were linked—for example, poor ventilation in the dormitories would increase the likelihood of spreading illness in confined quarters.[80] Thus, the hygiene of the institution and the hygiene of the student body (and students' bodies) were inextricably bound. Yet

Opager Baughn shows how even when the physical plants of schools were to blame for students' ill-health, schools blamed the students for not abiding by their hygiene regimens. Students were striving to maintain bodily habits that the architecture disallowed, and so neglecting maintenance of the institution was "a problem of both moral as well as physical dimensions."[81] The institution's health took precedence over students' health, and students were blamed for exerting a negative force on the institution when their bodies were unhealthy or unclean. Effects of external conditions were blamed on individual pathologies.

This investigation of the Manassas Industrial School reveals how the body and its hygiene were a preoccupation of the institution, and this preoccupation enabled the production of Black queer childhood as a mode of self-policing. Without naming sexuality, concerns for the physical body reveal concerns with its moral and sexual capacity.

I pair this analysis now with *Choir Boy*, a play that explores how hygiene and cleanliness violently eroticize the body, while also imagining if erotics can exist in school beyond this education. While *Choir Boy* depicts a (fictional) contemporary institution educating an elite class of boys, its preoccupation with institutional and bodily hygiene resonates with the mission of industrial education. Like industrial schools, the boarding school of *Choir Boy* works to align labor with a version of white middle-class sexual respectability; sexual expression beyond that risks one's future economic opportunities or access to cultural, social, and political capital. As a play concerned with the legacy of industrial education, it functions, in the words of performance studies scholar Diana Taylor, as an "archive" and "repertoire," imagining the relationship between the institution's official record and the embodied practices, gestures, and affects that exist because or in spite of this record.[82] The boarding school in *Choir Boy* is an institutional offspring of the industrial school that tracks how sexuality and labor remain intimately connected in African American education. The play creatively imagines if and how they might coexist.

Cleansing Artistic Labor and Homosexuality in Tarell Alvin McCraney's *Choir Boy* (2015)

Playwright Tarell Alvin McCraney's *Choir Boy* (2015) is set in the present day and explores the drama and ultimate violence within the choir at Charles R. Drew Preparatory School, a fictional boarding school for Black boys. First performed in 2012 at the Royal Court Theatre in London, the play had several productions in the United States, its most recent on Broadway in 2018–19. In a 2019 interview, McCraney describes the school as "mythical," capturing how it is an imaginary setting in a world that doesn't invest in the futures of Black boys.[83] To set the play at an elite, fictional boarding school exclusively for Black boys in the contemporary moment produces a counternarrative because these institutions have become almost extinct over the course of the twentieth century. In the early twentieth century, there were close to a hundred African American boarding schools operating in the United States.[84] As of 2014, that number stands at four, although there are ongoing efforts to establish others.[85] The rest lost their institutional identity during desegregation or dissolved due to lack of funds.[86] Historically Black institutions have struggled to stay open, especially at the primary and secondary levels, since they need to justify their existence in a nation that desires to be postracial. McCraney's play asserts the existence of one such secondary institution without romanticizing it—Drew Prep is a site for both community formation and self-discipline, Black identity and assimilationist impulses. The play imagines what an institution needs to do to survive the conditions of a present that sees Black boys as disposable and their sexuality as threatening.

That the school is named after Charles Richard Drew immediately captures its concerns with cleanliness and contamination. Drew was a Black surgeon who during World War II invented a method of blood preservation that helped to develop the first blood blanks. His method prevented the contamination of donated blood and was a lifesaving technology that allowed American donations to be transmitted overseas to hospitals treating soldiers. At the same time, the American Red Cross banned Black blood donations, citing unscientifically supported concerns over mixing blood across racial lines. Eventually, African Americans were allowed to donate blood during World War II, but their donations were still segregated, a practice that continued until 1950.[87] Fears of metaphorical contamination melded with fears of literal con- tamination, linking Drew Prep to national fears over how to manage, control, and contain Black bodies. As an institution, it is poised to do all three.

Set in the present, the play considers the legacy of industrial educa- tion in contemporary educational institutions for African Americans. The play explores the cultural labor force that Drew is expected to pro- duce and what presence, if any, sexuality can have in the bodies per- forming that labor. At Drew, students are anxious to police each other's perceived class status and sexuality, which reflects the "Drew men" they are expected to become.[88] The institution both produces this anxiety and resolves it through designing a system in which students are informants about each other's infractions that would impede their ability to become self-supporting, heterosexual Drew men. The school's honor code cre- ates a system of surveillance that distracts students from this produc- tion; they internalize the institutional panopticon, looking at each other to find and report infractions. In this way, students help to manage and police each other's passages from boyhood to manhood, which is a pas- sage into normative sexuality. The shower is a key site in the play for the management and policing of gender and sexuality, revealing how hygiene enables the monitoring of Black sexuality.

The play centers on the choir leader, Pharus, "an effeminate young man of color," who incites the anger of the headmaster's nephew, Bobby, and his friends because of Pharus's perceived homosexuality and the leadership role he has been granted.[89] For Bobby, the former should dis- count the latter. But for Pharus, being a Drew man is to be in possession of a tacit sexuality. In other words, as long as he does not act on his homosexuality, he is a credit to the institution and can successfully pass through it. These competing narratives invite audiences to consider the place of sexuality in cultural labor performed by Black bodies: When does Black sexuality have a future, and when must it be curtailed? Who aligns Black labor with white-determined respectable sexuality—the managers of Black labor, the consumers of Black labor, and/or the la- borers themselves? The play considers how sexuality makes itself present in an all-boys boarding school, how it must be disciplined, and how it is permitted to be expressed.

The play's opening scene introduces its thematic concern with Black masculinity and sexuality. The play begins at Drew's Forty-Ninth Commencement Exercises, where junior Pharus has been selected to sing the school song, "Trust and Obey," a coveted and prestigious solo.[90] As Pharus nears the end of the first stanza, Bobby, standing behind him among the other choir members, interjects, "Sissy," then "dis sissy," and finally, as Pharus is singing the final line of the song, "This faggot-ass n[****]."[91] Pharus stops, disrupting his performance—the last word of the song, "obey," remains unuttered. Bobby punctuates a song about being submissive to God with racialized homophobic slurs. His interruption suggests that spiritual service is incompatible with homosexuality. Being called a slur that invokes his sexuality *and* race disrupts Pharus's concentration. Sexuality isn't the entirety of the issue at Drew; it's racialized sexuality—transitioning from a Black boy into a Drew man mandates sexual propriety. At Drew, students "know the rule: 'A Drew man doesn't tell on his brother . . . he allows him the honor to confess himself.'"[92] While this is the rule as it applies to vertical authority—Drew men do not tell on each other to teachers and headmasters—the "honor to confess himself" is a pressure to succumb to horizontal policing. In other words, students know and monitor each other's behavior, and students who are out of line must turn themselves in, which is considered an "honor"—external monitoring is internalized policing transformed into a noble characteristic, which preserves the community.[93] Bobby must call out Pharus. To call out his racialized sexuality at graduation suggests he doesn't want Pharus to have a future at Drew: it must be stopped now.

Because Pharus didn't complete the song, he must go to the headmaster's office; his mistake invites the institution to subject him to greater scrutiny. The headmaster explains to Pharus that the board of trustees was displeased that he was picked to perform the solo. While the race(s) of the board of trustees are unknown, the board acts as an entity that monitors the school's cultural production and determines the distribution of resources among students and the institution. At the graduation reception, the board members "were already passing, whispering . . . 'Why him [Pharus]? Why *that* one,'" and the headmaster replies, "Well you heard him, he's the best regardless of the . . . ,'" before trailing off.[94] These comments imply that Pharus stands out and apart from his classmates; the board sees him as a poor representative of Drew. Pharus's effeminacy and the sexuality it is presumed to suggest remain unnamed; the headmaster knows his sexuality is the issue but cannot articulate it— Pharus's sexuality is an absent presence in the ellipse. The headmaster advocates for Pharus as "the best"—his musical talents, when not disruptive, bring honor to the school. His artistic contributions outweigh the reality of his sexuality.

However, because he disrupted the ritual, Pharus's talents are now void. The board and headmaster can now name and act on a priori homophobic impulses. The board wants to revoke Pharus's scholarship, which would virtually expel Pharus from the school. Pharus is able to avoid expulsion by promising the headmaster he has not and will not act on his sexuality: "There is nothing I want to do more than be and act as a Drew man should. I try to conduct my behavior by the book. I do not lie . . . and I don't snitch."[95] Pharus confirms to the headmaster that he wouldn't commit any infraction that would impact his standing as a Drew man. He has committed to enacting the gender and sexual propriety conduct books mandate. Pharus pledges to the headmaster that he is not acting on the homosexuality everyone presumes of him. He upholds the unwritten code of the school—not "snitch[ing]"—a rule that allows students to govern each other's behavior.

Pharus assures the headmaster that he has fully internalized this rule and its effect—the policing that he has experienced has enabled him to police himself. The headmaster presses, and while Pharus alludes to the fact that he was called a derogatory name, he says, "I heard that whisper and I didn't answer back[,] I just kept on singing."[96] Pharus suggests that while Bobby was hailing him as a racialized homosexual subject, he did not answer the call. His refusal to "answer back" rejects the ways that the student body monitors and categorizes his body and sexuality. Pharus wants to prove that he is successfully policing himself. He believes his sexual practices (or, as it is, lack thereof) should permit him to be a Drew man even if his sexual identity is a barrier to that. He curtails his sexuality in order to be a cultural laborer for the institution.

Pharus's voice supports the image of Drew as a school that molds young men of tomorrow, while his gestures undermine the strength of that masculine image in the institution's eyes. In other words, his body betrays his words. However, the legacy of the choir mandates this tension. The headmaster reminds Pharus of the importance of the choir; he starts, "The choir means a lot to this school. We've relied on its support since—" and Pharus cuts him off to complete the narrative.[97] As if by rote, Pharus recites, "Founded by the second headmaster who heard a group of boys singing in the showers, and decided to use a choir to gain attention and financial support for the Little All Boys School That Could. Why the headmaster was close enough to hear them boys singing in the shower I'll never know. . . . But that was the olden times, people was just more close then, I guess."[98] This origin story, drummed into the student body, suggests homosociality, possibly homosexuality, and a voyeurism bordering on violation at the heart of the choir. The choir was founded because a headmaster decided to capitalize on boys' talents to fund the school. This is a rewriting of the Blackface minstrelsy scene; Lott argues that in the nineteenth century, the widely figured first Blackface performer, T. D. Rice, was "confronted one day with the dazzling spectacle of black singing, [and] the story goes, Rice saw his 'opportunity' and determined to take advantage of his talent for mimicry."[99] Taylor writes that these "scenarios of discovery . . . [are] never for the first time," and so this white "discovery" of Black talent accompanied by the impulse to make it a financial opportunity is part of a larger genealogy of white spectators exploiting Black labor.[100] In the nineteenth century, this was done through white persons donning Blackface; in this contemporary institution, it is accomplished through controlling the output of Black labor supposedly to benefit Black students. But importantly, the choir would bring accolades and monetary gains to the *school* and not to the boys themselves, at least directly—the priority is the institution that can educate and manage Black boys and develop them into proper laboring heterosexual subjects. The students' talents are exploited to fund an institution that will further exploit them. While the institution talks of Drew men, the origin story refers to a "Little All Boys School." This is a subtle admission that while the school claims to make boys into Drew men, it is in fact containing Black masculinity and sexuality in order to funnel these boys toward futures where they and their labor can be controlled. They will always be boys—rendered childish, backward, and immature by virtue of their race.

The site of the shower as the site for recognizing the cultural labor that these boys can perform is crucial to this origin story. The shower is, in Hartman's formulation, a scene of subjection. Industrial education's emphasis on hygiene reflects their desire to prove that Black bodies could achieve respectability and sexual propriety that would allow them to enter the labor force. The shower is a portal that shows how clean bodies and sexualities are a preoccupation in Drew as well. While Drew is a private African American boys school, it is still producing a labor force contingent on sexual propriety. The difference between the late nineteenth- and twentieth-century industrial schools and private schools and contemporary schools is that the white-dominated political and social orders have expanded the kinds of labor they will accept from Black persons. The cultural labor of Black people has value, but that value is still contingent on respectability and heterosexuality. The origin story of the choir reveals both the valuation and exploitation of Black cultural labor and the deeply intertwined relationship between hygiene and sexuality that underpins the production of this labor.

In this narrative of the origin of the choir, homosexuality is a veiled secret at its heart; for Pharus, his homosexuality is legible on his body, and the institution cannot ignore it. After Pharus proclaims this origin story to the headmaster, the stage directions read, "*Pharus's wrist goes limp. The Headmaster corrects Pharus's limp wrist*," and the headmaster says, "Tighten up."[101] Pharus's talents are undermined by his "limp wrist." The headmaster is a stand-in for the institution, "correct[ing]" his body in an attempt to discipline his sexuality; until he "tighten[s] up," his cultural labor cannot be accepted by those who fund his education, who see their investments in managing Black bodies and sexualities failing in Pharus.

The play's treatment of class also reveals how the school is negotiating the legacy of industrial education. While Pharus didn't snitch on his classmates, the headmaster deduces that his nephew, Bobby, and Bobby's friend, Jr, were responsible for distracting Pharus. In the fall semester, the headmaster punishes them with "quad duty," which means cleaning up trash around the school.[102] Bobby fumes, "[The headmaster] got me out there Booker T. Washingtonin' that quad. That's for scholarship boys to earn they keep."[103] Bobby scorns the fact that he has to perform manual labor at the school. Manual labor is the "Booker T. Washington" view of Black education and, in his eyes, only to be performed by poor Black students. For Bobby, his status as a non-scholarship student permits him to focus strictly on other forms of labor, such as the cultural labor of choir. Even though most industrial schools closed in the early to mid-twentieth century with the shift from the Washington model to the Du Bois model of education—that is, the shift from producing a Black working class to producing a Black middle and elite intellectual class— this moment reveals that the legacy of industrial education lives on in the latter. There is still room for manual labor in the institution, but it is a form of punishment: you are explicitly punished for breaking a rule or implicitly punished for being poor (when you do manual labor to "earn [your] keep"). That Pharus is one such scholarship student expected to clean the institution suggests perhaps a mimetic relationship between the work he does and the work of the institution: the institution must clean him of his deviant sexuality, and he must clean the institution in an appeal to "earn" his spot. The school promotes a version of Black advancement that is contingent on stratifying the aspiring Black artistic class by class and sexuality. Those who have more material resources and those who are heterosexual are better positioned to access "citizenship and humanity" outside the institution. Drew wants to imagine the distinctions between the Washington and Du Bois approaches to education to obscure their shared missions: both are contingent on policing and controlling Black male bodies, sexualities, and labor.

Bobby blames Pharus for his current predicament and takes issue with Pharus's sexuality, the privileges it isn't discounting, and its perceived effects on the sanctity of a Drew education. At the first choir rehearsal of the school year, he accuses Pharus of snitching on him to the headmaster, running off "faster than your little heels could click."[104] Bobby sees this alleged infraction (snitching) as tied with Pharus's homosexuality. When the other choir members ask what they're talking about, Pharus explains, "While serving my duty as tenor in the choir . . . Brother Bobby and his homie Jr decided they were going to cuss me like street trash."[105] Before, Bobby was scoffing at the fact that he had to pick up trash during quad duty, a labor he saw reserved for the scholarship students; Pharus's claim suggests that Bobby and Jr's cussing rendered him "street trash" and simultaneously attempted to cleanse the school of that trash. The division of the school's labor becomes clearer. Students deemed lesser, by virtue of their class and/or sexuality, are to clean up the school's literal trash, performing the manual labor required to maintain the school; this is considered menial labor, necessary but disdained. Students better positioned to enter the artistic class are oriented to perform a metaphorical cleaning through their policing of the student body; this cleaning is lauded and cruelly enjoyed. Literal and metaphorical cleanliness are a preoccupation of this institution, and students are differently trained to perform the tasks of cleaning. Some are cleansed, some do the cleansing.

Pharus tries to convince his classmates that he is monitoring himself, effectively cleaning the body they see as dirty and impure. The institution, however, is fearful of Pharus's capacity for contagion. Pharus removed Bobby from the choir, and he is disciplined by the headmaster. Pharus is supposed to be policed, not police others. The headmaster uses this occasion to remind Pharus of his sexuality: "I thought I asked you to tighten up," echoing his earlier call to Pharus to "tighten up" his limp wrist.[106] He tells him he cannot lead the choir, but Pharus doesn't accept this punishment and attempts to name what the institution refuses to acknowledge. He asks, "What am I gonna tell my mama? . . . That you took me off lead because your nephew called me a racial and a homophobic slur?"[107] He pushes further, asking how to appeal the headmaster's decision: "Should I talk to the board of the school about it?"[108] While the board already knows about Pharus's homosexuality, his threat to explicitly share the calling out of his racialized sexuality would be to name that which the institution refuses; it would make his sexuality present and therefore reflect the failure of the school. Pharus tells the headmaster he just wants to lead the choir "without being called out my name . . . ," and the headmaster interrupts, "Pharus, your wrist!"[109] Pharus responds, "I'm sorry. . . . Is my wrist the reason why I am being. . . ."[110] In this interaction, Pharus explicitly calls out the "racial and homophobic slur"—the absent presence of his racialized sexuality is invoked in order to return to a position where it can be unnamed. He tries to convince the headmaster that he is holding up his part of the contract of being a Drew man—he is leading well and doing what he can to prevent his sexuality from interfering with his work in the choir.

In this way, Pharus's cultural labor is cleansed of perceived deviant sexuality by Pharus himself—instigated by the institution and his peers, to be sure, but ultimately something that Pharus enacts upon himself. In the original encounter, Bobby, not Pharus, names racialized sexuality and thus breaks with institutional codes. Pharus has to call out Bobby now in order to return to the silence around his sexuality. But this silence is not and never will be enough for the school; the moment he utters his commitment to a silent homosexuality the headmaster calls out "your wrist!"—a reminder that his body betrays him in the eyes of the institution. Pharus is confused; he doesn't understand how his character can be impugned by his gestures. The headmaster yields and lets Pharus resume his leadership position but with the knowledge that he is oriented toward failure. Pharus cannot correct his body and so cannot fully become a Drew man. As long as he inhabits a Black, homosexual body, he will fail. He is being trained for a future as a Drew man that will never be fully available to him. But the school needs his cultural labor in the present, so it allows him to continue as a student there.

Cleaning the Body and Mind

Institutional mechanisms mark the passage of time at Drew. For example, the headmaster makes announcements through the school's PA system at the end of each day. In one such announcement, he notes an infraction committed in the school science lab and declares, "Let us be honorable Drew men, those responsible should come forward now."[111] He concludes by wishing students to have "a great first week to kick off our fiftieth year anniversary, all schedules kept, all rooms clean. Keep your minds clear, and your hands in prayer. Five minutes and lights out."[112] The school's code to not snitch on each other doesn't exist in a vacuum; the headmaster urges students to come forward, revealing the self-policing for which the institution advocates. Policing each other is really about internalizing the school's rules. This internalization is effected through external forces—the institution is constantly maintaining its surveillance, but it disguises external forces as internal features of character—features that make a Drew man. This exhortation for self-monitoring is joined with wishes for routine and hygiene. Like the internalization of institutional management, here the cleanliness of students' environments is linked with cleanliness and morality of mind and body.

In another announcement at the end of the day, the boys are preparing to shower. The headmaster announces, "There is a season for all things. We enter now into the middle [of the semester] . . . it can get heavy. Look to your fellow Drew . . . remember who you are. We are Charles R. Drew Prep, Proving Men for Tomorrow. Showers then quiet hour."[113] The scene of the shower is the scene for subject formation and affirmation. And the subject is "Charles R. Drew Prep"—individual identity *is* the institution. Students are not just the institution but its promise and mission for the future; they are "proving" the value of Black labor for the future. This elision between the identities of the subject and institution suggests that the boundaries between them are blurred— both mutually constitute each other, and the shower is the site where these bounds are drawn and maintained. The shower is also the site of unexpected effects—the boys are preparing to shower and told to "look to your fellow Drew"; this imperative could be understood as a solicitation to elicit homoerotic glances.

Pharus continues to affirm his commitment to the school's hygiene routine. Pharus gives a presentation on spirituals to his classmates, and he argues that the songs didn't contain coded messages for freedom. As Pharus's classmates critique him, Pharus responds by considering his argument in the larger context of African American education. He says, "Black people were told in classrooms like this . . . [that] our history, American or not, was shameful and ugly and anyone trying to rewrite themselves[,] trying to come up from all that ugly would file together, rub together any piece of anything that might be true to make it over, to make it better."[114] Pharus is trying to say that the spirituals in and of themselves don't need to be made better and that their affective content is enough to make them worthy—acknowledging this undoes the "shameful and ugly" histories that educational institutions have taught to generations of Black students. That Pharus calls this act of rewriting the spirituals an act of "fil[ing] together" and "rub[bing] together" pieces of knowledge is significant. The etymological root of *file* is "foul," and as a verb it means "to render (materially) foul, filthy, or dirty . . . to destroy the cleanness or purity of."[115] Similarly, while rub as a verb implies physical contact (the valence of which depends on its usage: the *OED* notes that rub can be slang for masturbate or can be used to mean cleaning an object), its noun form implies waste and detritus (think "rubbish").[116] Pharus affirms his alignment with the institution. He considers this rewriting that others have done an act that desecrates Black artistic production. He argues instead for what he understands to be a cleanliness of Black artistic production. Pharus wants to participate in this hygiene program.

While Pharus has mitigated his sexuality elsewhere in the institution, the shower is a space where he permits himself to be a sexual subject. This site of institutional disciplining fails—Pharus cleanses his body while asserting the existence of his sexuality in the shower. Pharus defies the school's insistence on the mandate that personal hygiene will lead to state-sanctioned sexual propriety by expressing homosexual desire in the shower. The first instance of this happening is a friendly teasing with his roommate A.J.—he comments on the size of A.J.'s penis and speculates on his sexual performance. They continue bantering until David comes in and tells them they're being "inappropriate."[117] While Pharus stops because of institutional policing carried out by students, the fact that his sexual being can be present in the shower, in this instance, resists complete institutional control of his body and sexuality. That the shower is also a site where the boys sing also means that the shower is a site where Black artistic expression and sexuality can coexist.

The next time that Pharus expresses his sexual desire in the shower, however, it has dire consequences. He invites an unseen student to act on his sexual desires: "Same Pharus, I'm still here. Where are you? Can't you show up and be here too? It can't all be bad and if it is then use what you know, tell me to go on then, tell me to go away."[118] The unseen student remains in the shower, and the stage directions say, *"Pharus walks into the shower stalls until he is unseen by us. The sound of a door opening. Jr reenters the shower. The sound of a punch hitting a face. Pharus falls onto the floor, now back into view, holding his face."*[119] The audience later finds out that Pharus was speaking to David; David enters the shower but attacks Pharus when he "thought [he] heard somebody come in."[120] We do not know if they engage in sexual activity in the brief time before Jr enters—the action remains unseen. The monologue suggests that he and David have already been having a relationship. Their relationship, up until now, has never been seen or acknowledged in the play, and even here when it is acknowledged only Pharus is visible. Homosexuality can be expressed in the shower, but it cannot be enacted. Pharus's veiled invitation for David to come out—"show up"—is violently rebuked. David is closeted and has directed his body and future toward God; he plans to become a priest, which gives him a respectable path toward (homo)sexual renunciation. In the shower, he is confronted with the reality of his sexuality and the possibility to act on it. His attack on Pharus is an ultimate siding with the institution and manifesting the violent homophobia that the institution's codes and rules have been expressing this whole time.

Pharus's response to this violence reveals that he recognizes that there is no space for his sexuality at Drew. The headmaster tries to get Pharus to tell him who committed this assault. Pharus says it "wasn't a fight . . . fight mean you put hands up and fight back. I just . . . just took it. . . . Everybody round you always telling you, showing you that you ain't nothing, that they don't want to be nothing, what you fight for then? . . . I fell in the showers."[121] Pharus has internalized the school's mission. He believes he deserved this assault. He has tried to live "by the book" in the institution by not acting on his sexuality—but the ultimate site of discipline is a site where he refuses to fully acquiesce to the school's control over his body. When he is assaulted for that, instead of seeing it as an injustice, he sees it as his due punishment. He revises the narrative, telling the headmaster he fell; he takes responsibility for his injuries. The headmaster accuses him of lying, and Pharus says, "Pharus is a Drew man . . . he lives in the Drew way . . . he follows the Drew rules."[122] Pharus not only blames himself for his assault but uses it to assert that he is the ultimate Drew subject and will not tell on a fellow student. That he slips into third person when speaking about the incident suggests an attempt to dissociate who he is as a sexual subject from who he is as an institutional subject; he must self-alienate in order to be a Drew man. The headmaster is astounded: "That rule [about snitching] was made up amongst students. This is a real matter."[123] The headmaster busts the illusion of the school honor code, but it is too late—Pharus has already internalized it. This moment reveals that the force of the institution and institutional time can outweigh micro-level attempts toward justice. The headmaster wants to get justice for Pharus to make clear that assault is not tolerated at Drew. But policing of sexuality is tolerated, and that is synonymous with assault in this instance. Pharus is willing to take the blame in order to gain entrance into the subject position of a "Drew man" and the future it affords.

The headmaster is astounded because this incident forces him to acknowledge homosexuality within the institution. He talks to a white teacher who taught at Drew decades earlier, Mr. Pendleton, about the institution, asking, "Was it this hard in your day?"[124] Pendleton recounts what he can of the occasional violence students would experience off campus, and the headmaster replies, "Huh. That's not in the annals."[125] The headmaster suggests that his understanding of the institution comes solely from its annual reports. Because of what escapes this record—in this scene, histories of violence that students experience from the neighboring white community—he cannot connect the present violence with any history. His word for the annual reports—annals—is somewhat of a homophone of "anals," connecting the absence of recorded violence with an encapsulating material presence of homosexuality. Pendleton is surprised that the headmaster has turned to the annals for accuracy: "Do they ever read right? Is there anything in there that really . . . are you really surprised? . . . This has been an all-male school for forty-nine [years]. . . . And you never thought once . . . once that there could be. . . ."[126] For Pendleton, the fact that the historical record could reflect total reality is preposterous. He can be shocked because as a white person he has the luxury of being a part of a race that has shaped the historical record in the United States. But the headmaster is a Black man who has worked with the history and education he has been given—to question its completeness or authenticity would be out of line. In this moment, the play also critiques the limits of historical knowledge, especially of marginalized populations, thus making the case for aesthetic representations that imagine and explore what the record disallows.

The institutional memory is scrubbed of sexuality, which puts the institution at risk of reproducing itself as a violent entity against anyone perceived to be sexually deviant. Pendleton continues to be baffled at the headmaster's surprise over a homosexual relationship in the school. While he can't name it—homosexuality is again encoded in an ellipse—he tries to get the headmaster to see why this was to be expected. Pendleton continues, "Fifty years of this school, in the records or not, this is not the first time 'love' found this form. Won't be the last. You plan on staying Headmaster, I'd prepare for that."[127] Pendleton suggests that homosexuality has been and will continue to be part of the institutional makeup, even if it's left out of the official record. The headmaster's "shock" seems incompatible with the preoccupation he has had over Pharus's sexuality up until this point.[128] From correcting his limp wrist (twice) to defending

Pharus to the board, all signs have pointed to the headmaster knowing of Pharus's homosexuality and abiding by a "don't ask, don't tell" policy. His shock, then, is about the fact that this homosexuality isn't an identity but a practice in the school. He is shocked because he was able to police Pharus's sexuality since it seemed visible on his body through his mannerisms. He didn't suspect there was another gay student at the school. The reality of their relationship reveals that the institution cannot see and therefore police all sexual deviance—gender expression isn't indicative of sexuality, and Pharus and David's relationship reveals the failure of the institution. David is expelled for fighting, and Pharus's role as leader of the choir is rescinded. The play ends with Bobby singing the school song. That Bobby is granted this role even after the headmaster learns of a recent sexual encounter he had with a girl off campus reveals a recommitment to focusing strictly on homosexuality. Learning about David makes the headmaster realize homosexuality could exist within any student, and that is more threatening than heterosexual impropriety. Cultural labor is united with heterosexuality in the end. Homosexuality has no visible place in the institution or artistic production.

Cleanliness and Contamination in Black Queer Studies

In Baldwin's *Giovanni's Room* (1956), American expatriate David and Italian Giovanni begin an affair, and when David says that he is leaving to return to his girlfriend, Giovanni yells,

> You do not . . . love anyone! . . . You love your purity, you love your mirror—you are just like a little virgin, you walk around with your hands in front of you as though you had some precious metal, gold, silver, rubies, maybe diamonds down there between your legs! You will never let anybody touch it—man or woman. You want to be clean. You think you came here covered with soap and you think you will go out covered with soap—and you do not want to stink, not even for five minutes, in the meantime. . . . You want to leave Giovanni because he makes you stink. You want to despise Giovanni because he is not afraid of the stink of love.[129]

Giovanni accuses David of being sexless ("a little virgin") while preserving his sexuality as a highly valuable commodity ("precious metal, gold, silver," etc.). To be in possession of sexuality but not let anyone come in contact with it is "to be clean." David, in this projection, hasn't lost his sexuality but instead controls it through adherence to cleanliness, not wanting to be contaminated by "stink." Giovanni tries to reveal that this self-perception is an illusion; David only "thinks" he entered and is leaving "covered with soap." He tries to convince David that trusting the promise of cleanliness is just a way to become sterile and in love with his own "purity."

Dwight McBride analyzes this scene as an important critique by Baldwin because it makes clear his embrace of sexuality deemed deviant and unclean. McBride writes,

> The very thing that Baldwin extols here in Giovanni in contrast to David (i.e., David's obsession with being pure and clean—rendered, by association, as a very American desire complicated by his nationality in the novel) is what characterizes the topoi of Baldwin's work and art. He did not care for purity. Rather, he wallowed in the dirt of the unclean parts of the psyche, the cluttered rooms where life, for him, really happened. David—not unlike the representations of an institutionalized African American studies—represents the pitfalls and suffering of a life lived in observance of the rules about what we should be, how we should love, indeed, what we should feel.[130]

McBride argues that Baldwin's writing did not adhere to the politics of respectability, especially around sexual respectability—his writing was "impur[e]," "unclean," and "dirty." McBride scales the dynamic between Giovanni and David—unclean and clean—up to the state of the field of Black studies. He argues that adherence to propriety regarding subjects and objects of study imposes strictures that could keep practitioners of this scholarship unhappy, "suffering a life lived in observance of the rules" that dictate narrow conditions for entry into the academy where they can produce intellectual labor. José Esteban Muñoz argues that queer studies also dictates narrow conditions for entry into the field from scholars of color in the introduction to *Cruising Utopia*. He writes that he was disillusioned with the antirelational thesis that, at the time, was dominating queer theory because he interpreted it as a move on theorists' part to "distanc[e] queerness from . . . the contamination of race, gender, or other particularities that taint the purity of sexuality as a singular trope of difference."[131] Muñoz observed a desire on the part of white queer theorists to keep the field clean from perceived "contamination" of race; Muñoz experienced the field as a hostile environment for scholars attempting to study racialized queerness.

E. Patrick Johnson echoes this concern in the field of Black studies in the introduction to *No Tea, No Shade: New Writings in Black Queer Studies*. He reflects on the time that has elapsed between the 2005 publication of *Black Queer Studies: A Critical Anthology* and the 2016 printing of *No Tea, No Shade*, which amounts to a generation in institutional time. He observes that previously, though Black queer sexuality had been written about in explicit terms, it was "usually in the realm of fiction or poetry and was published by trade presses."[132] It's not that Black queer scholars did not want to, could not, or refused to write on these subjects but that institutional gatekeeping made it too risky to produce this scholarship. Black scholars, then, cleansed their work in order to survive within the institution. Johnson observes generational shifts at play—while many in the earlier generation still shy away from explicit queer sex in academic writing and judge those who produce this work, many in the current generation not only produce it but do not realize that what they've come to expect in Black queer writing "could not even [be] imagin[ed] ten years ago."[133] Johnson notes that "the current children's work, to a degree, is not bound by the same institutional, disciplinary, and publishing politics," a gift from their academic parents and grandparents for doing the risky work of expanding what constitutes scholarship in terms not dictated by respectability.[134]

Johnson employs kinship and childhood metaphors to describe this relationship between the previous generation and current generation working on Black sexuality. While the field of "black queer studies has come of age," it is, according to Johnson, still practiced by children.[135] He says, "The House of Black Queer Studies was built by mothers and fathers (and those who embody both) who were/are grand and fierce, but it is the children who are constantly remodeling the house, keeping it updated, and making it the envy of the neighbors, all the while slaying and snatching trophies as their parents watch on with a careful side eye—no tea, no shade!"[136] In this metaphor, Black queer studies is an institution in and of itself, and the structure the field has produced is constantly "remodel[ed]" by the children. Practitioners of an earlier generation watch with pride but also "a careful side eye," anxious to protect that which they've invested in and risked so much to build.

This dynamic recapitulates the tension that exists in these schools among adults running them and children occupying them. The founders of institutions like Manassas took on huge financial and social risk to build these institutions. They knew that their hard work and labor could be for nothing at any time—the moment that a state official or white benefactor was displeased with the progress or training in the school, perhaps manifested through unclean conditions, financial resources could be withdrawn that would make it impossible to run schools already struggling to make ends meet. The careful management of sexuality in these schools was of course restrictive, and it continues today to harmful ends, as imagined in *Choir Boy*. In an effort to protect the future, sexuality was carefully managed; this careful protection could slowly shift the conditions for more expansive takes on sexuality, as Johnson admits happens within the fields of Black queer studies, or it could replicate the institution and strengthen it to violent ends, as *Choir Boy* demonstrates. In both cases, adults want to protect the institutions and the children who occupy them in order to guarantee the future of both (even if that intention manifests, at best, as a replication of the present or, at worst, as steps backward). But children and institutions are going to shape each other, and adults cannot always control that interplay. The impulse to manage children remains, nonetheless, but if the impulse can be converted into a step aside and a "careful side eye," maybe the kids—and the institutions they alter—will be all right.

5

Sexual Orphanings

Colonizing Native Erotics

In Cree author and boarding school survivor Tomson Highway's 1998 novel *Kiss of the Fur Queen*, he tells the fictional story of Cree brothers Champion and Ooneemeetoo, who are christened Jeremiah and Gabriel shortly after birth and forced to use these names when they attend a boarding school for Native children run by Catholic priests in the 1960s. In order to achieve ostensible assimilation, Jeremiah and Gabriel are not allowed to speak their Cree language, and the school's priests strictly enforce this rule, making "Cree a crime."[1] When Gabriel is caught singing a Cree song, one priest "lashed and lashed" Gabriel's body.[2]

This upholding of the English language over Cree, enforced violently on the surface of the Native child's body, works to distance the boys from the community and culture they have left behind. During a visit home on a school break after years at the school, the boys are with their father; he tells a joke in Cree, and it "plummeted, for on matters sensual, sexual, and therefore fun, a chasm as unbridgeable as hell separates Cree from English, the brothers were sadly learning."[3] Mandated loss of language entails a loss of Cree understandings of sexuality as well as the "sensual" and "fun"—the pleasurable—embedded in it. The children feel the effects of this loss as disconnection and alienation from their father, whose role has been replaced by the institution and its agents.

I understand this loss, enabled by the school's violently enforced kinship restructuring, as an orphaning. I argue that the process through which many Native children were taken from reservations and required to attend boarding schools in the nineteenth and twentieth centuries in the United States and Canada is usefully understood as a state-produced orphaning, an orphaning away from Native customs and culture and ultimately toward state-desired death. The education that children received in boarding schools can be seen as a process of further, mandatory orphaning, one that children learned to enact upon themselves. The intensity with which these boarding schools intervened into the sexuality of Native children was crucial to this process, and I argue that "sexual orphaning" was the goal of the boarding schools' alienation of Native children from their culture, a goal that oriented children away from futurity, reproductivity, and sexual capacity. I understand "sexual orphanings" as a mode of queer childhood that oriented children toward futures where their access to social, economic, and sexual possibilities was curtailed. This queer childhood was achieved paradoxically through heterosexualization, but a racialized heterosexualization oriented toward failure—children would never be straight (or white) in the settler state's eyes. I consider what "erotics" might remain for these orphans and look at ways in which the genocidal sexual orphanings of Native children might be recalibrated in Native fiction toward a survivance rather than disappearance.

Native children have been crucial to the settler state's attempts to alter Native communities' relationship to futurity. The state and its institutions and agents have structured gender, sexuality, and kinship for children so that settler understandings and practices are "straight"—and thus moral, proper, and state-sanctioned—and anything Native is consequently non-straight and thus queer.[4] This definition of queerness is drawn from Mark Rifkin's *When Did Indians Become Straight?*, in which he explores how "coordinated assault on native social formations . . . [can] be understood as an organized effort to make heterosexuality compulsory as a key part of breaking up indigenous landholdings."[5] Building on this settler preoccupation with sexual reorganization of Native communities, Joanne Barker has explored how "colonial-settlers were particularly obsessed with issues of gender and sexuality" since many Native modes of organizing, especially ones that included the political participation of women and gender and sexual formations incommensurate with settler identities, were perceived as "dangerous to proper Christian norms and civil society . . . [and] counter to God's designs for the order of things between the sexes. . . . It was believed that a complete transformation was needed in order to secure Native conversion and subjugation to God's will."[6] Native gender and sexual formations, kinship organization, and relationships to land were cast as immoral, and religiously determined valuation colluded with and enabled settler seizure of land. The settler state intervened into and attempted to violently restructure—or straighten—Native traditions, customs, and kinship to justify violent dispossession of Native land, conversion, and settler domination.

These straightening interventions were paradoxically a process of queering. Jodi Byrd has argued that "the queer in Indigenous studies . . . challenges the queer of queer studies by offering not an identity or a figure necessarily, but rather an analytic that helps us relocate subjectivity and its refusals back into the vectors of ongoing settler colonialism."[7] In approaching the tactics through which the settler state, its institutions, and its agents have attempted to straighten Native peoples, practices, relationalities, and modes of being as queer, I am working to bring queer and Indigenous studies together to understand how settler colonization has manufactured experiences for Native children that may *look* like identities (e.g., the proper settler, the domestic servant, the farmhand) but operate to further settler logics of elimination. These experiences that look like identity production are temporalities that curb Native futurity via gender and sexual regulation. The self-appointed parenting nation has narrated queerness in an effort to normalize, naturalize, and instantiate heteronormativity, which enables ongoing settler claims to land and constructions of property, inheritance, and the laws that govern them. Adult or child, all Native persons have been and continue to be queered by this narrative. Native children in particular have been crucial to the settler state's attempts to queer Native communities. Since the turn of the twentieth century, this queering has served to justify and enable state-sanctioned genocide under the guise of welfare and false promises of protection—the future functions as a trap, enabling violence.

The boarding school system of the late nineteenth and twentieth centuries in the United States and Canada was one mechanism through which many Native children were made to experience queer childhood. Susan Burch writes that "institutionalization" is a "distinctly non-Native process," capturing how the routines, order, and logics of the school imposed a settler mode of operating onto children that ran "counter to indigenous values, relationships, and ways of being."[8] Producing queer childhood was pivotal for eliminating Native populations through the promise of assimilation of their children. Children were removed from their reservations and required to attend the boarding schools, where they were violently forced to abandon their names, languages, and cultural practices. At school, they were educated to understand their Native communities and culture as backward, deviant, and something to abandon, an education that occurred alongside all-but-institutionalized sexual abuse.

I understand this abandonment as an orphaning and see it as compulsory for those Native children who passed through the boarding school. The boarding schools produced Native children as orphans in order to enforce metaphorical orphanings of Indianness. By Indianness, I mean all those features whose loss would facilitate cultural genocide—languages, custom, and practices and understandings of kinship, gender, and sexuality. I term the state-enforced abandonment of the latter a *sexual orphaning*, and its metaphorical loss had material effects: orphaning children from Native conceptualizations of gender and sexuality was a calculated attempt to alienate children from Native acculturated bodies, and this alienation oriented children toward non-reproductivity and circumscribed sexual capacities. I conceptualize sexual orphaning as a historical process that produced bodily practices, sensations, and affects lived out in the bodies of targeted children. Drawing on Rifkin's scholarship in *Erotics of Sovereignty*, I understand these practices and sensations as "erotics—sensations of pleasure, desire, memory, wounding, and interrelation with others, the land, and ancestors."[9] Queering Native children necessitated an education in erotics: how to apprehend and disavow them.

The schools violently educated children to understand and experience erotics as shameful, but these shamed erotics created avenues for decolonization. In her reading of M. Jacqui Alexander's concept of "radical self-possession," Ann Cvetkovich explains how decolonization can and must include "the senses and feelings."[10] Building on this claim, I argue that the Native child's body, a strategic target of colonization carried out by the boarding school and its agents, has a capacity for decolonization at the level of the individual body by reclaiming those senses and pleasures that education forced the child to disavow.

This claim does not metaphorize decolonization but rather takes seriously the expansive targets of colonization—land, bodies, minds, affects, habits—and considers different loci for responding to its forces.

In her reading of Linda Hogan's *Solar Storms*, Mishuana Goeman invites critics to "think of the various scales of space, starting with the body."[11] Goeman reminds readers that the individual body is never just about the individual but also connected to the "social body of the Native community and the national bodies" of settler states.[12] Since "bodies remember colonization and its processes," then "examinations of gendered bodies as a meeting space intensifies the interconnectedness of the various scales and breaks down the distances constructed by colonial knowledge and production."[13] The regendering, resexualizing, and shaming of Native children's bodies in schools occurred not just at the level of the body through abuse, habits, and discipline but also at the level of erotics. At schools, "colonialism [was] a *felt*, affective relationship" that created "emotional habitus" and pivoted on "manipulative management of [students'] emotions."[14] The education of children in erotics is what Kyla Schuller describes as "sensorial discipline," or the "imperative placed on . . . those aspiring to civilization and citizenship to learn to master their sensory impulses and thus direct the development of themselves and their descendants."[15] Education mandated sexual orphanings—children were told in exchange for these orphanings, experienced through "master[y over] sensory impulses," progress and survival for their communities and future offspring would be secured.

Sexual orphanings were a key feature of Native queer childhood in boarding schools. The attempt to orphan children from their sexualities was twofold. First, schools imposed heteronormative understandings of gender and sexuality on children, and this imposition necessitated that children renounce Native understandings of gender and sexuality, viewing them now as backward and sinful. Second, school agents violated children's bodies through sexual abuse that was "indeed institutionalized as to almost form a core part of the curriculum."[16] Chris Finley argues that "for many tribes . . . shame around sex started in the boarding schools, and sexual shame has been passed down for generations."[17] Dian Million reiterates this point when she writes about the "elaborately produced *shame*" in schools; schools have taught "Native children that their Indian bodies are by nature sexually depraved and that their entry into white society depends on their eternal vigilance against their own shamed and savage sexuality."[18] Sexual orphanings did not make all children non-reproductive—there are generations who still bear the legacy of those who survived the school, who are also testament to the ongoing presence of Native peoples and sexualities in the face of attempts at erasure. However, Finley and Million suggest a pervasive shame whose origin is in the schools, one that haunts many Native communities and has affected how Native peoples view and experience sexuality: it is filtered through a history of abuse.

Abuse and education in the schools helped the settler state center its understandings of sexuality. This sexuality, which Scott Morgensen calls "settler sexuality," permits a narrow heteronormativity for white bodies while sanctioning sexual violence against and abuse of nonwhite bodies.[19] Settler sexuality casts as queer more capacious understandings of sexuality that consider dispositions, affect, pleasure, and sensations, or what Rifkin terms *erotics*. Sexual orphanings make it difficult to inhabit erotics because of alienation from the Native acculturated body. Rifkin alludes to how more capacious understandings of sexuality are especially important for considering Native resistance because "sexuality points to a nexus of practices, desires, relations, and pleasures in which one could locate the presence of modes of indigeneity that exceed the 'oppressed, repressed, shamed, and *imposed* sense of reality' generated through institutionalized processes of settlement."[20] In other words, the settler state and its institutions—such as the boarding school—enforce an "*imposed* sense of reality" onto Native sexuality that narrate it as a source of shame and oppression. Rifkin invites readers to think about what to do with the presences of "desires" and "pleasures" that exist within and despite seemingly totalizing narratives of "oppress[ion]," "repress[ion]," and "shame."

I use this invitation to return to Native queer childhood as produced by and experienced in the boarding school. Sexual damage is a hallmark of the settler education of Native children. The violence, abuse, and neglect in schools that the settler state allowed to continue for close to a century is undeniable and inexcusable. I want to focus, however, on some unexpected effects of sexual damage. Accounts of Native queer childhood in the boarding school force us to contend with the presence of desire and pleasure amid violence and abuse, as well as the alternative times and spaces they might open up. How does pleasure come about in this setting? What do these moments of pleasure unsettle? How might they disrupt totalizing narratives of the school's production of oppression and shame? How much weight does pleasure actually carry in the context of ongoing genocide? Does pleasure enable access to alternative times and spaces, and if so, how? An examination of Native queer childhood asks us to consider the knotted problem of violence's relation to decolonization. Children's bodies and experiences both bear the legacy of and have the capacity to disrupt settler narratives of unmitigated colonization and disappearance; the schools and their agents colonized children's bodies, but this colonization did not go uncontested by children.

To consider these questions, I take up *Kiss of the Fur Queen*, by Cree author and playwright Tomson Highway, whose fictional text imagines possibilities for survival and Indigenous modes of being *despite* the historical phenomenon of sexual orphanings. Highway's novel functions as a counterarchive, recounting the sexual orphanings two brothers are forced to undergo, but also exploring how children might maintain a connection to their sexuality, even in the context of violent education and abuse.

The boarding school is a nineteenth- and twentieth-century historical institution whose effects are ongoing; looking at a contemporary text that represents the boarding school is important to the present because Native children, most visibly in the modern-day foster care system, continue to be targets of settler policy that seeks to erase Indigenous presence under the guise of welfare, putting children in precarious situations—a genealogy I explore further in a coda to this chapter through a brief investigation of Sherman Alexie's *Flight* (2007). From the perspective of the settler state, the only future for Native children is the white future they help preserve; Bethany Schneider contends that "Native children are the diet of white supremacy and colonization," enabling settler futures not intended for them.[21] The boarding schools educated children in a normativity to which they could never accede, guaranteeing the failure of the Native body: education attempted to result in children unable to grow up or move forward into a reproductive future. They were left, as Kathryn Bond Stockton puts it, to "grow sideways," and I grapple with the pleasures and possibilities accessible to children in this liminal time and space to which the schools oriented them.[22] I examine the history of the boarding schools, which helps us understand how sexual orphanings that position children for no future existed in a larger context that neglected the Native body through biopolitical practices. I then turn to

Kiss of the Fur Queen as a text to think through the issues of violence, pleasure, and decolonization in Native queer childhood, considering how sexual orphanings are enforced in the narrative and looking at alternative modes of embodiment that Highway imagines as possible responses to an education that leaves children orphaned from their bodies and sexualities.

Managing Life at the Boarding School

While I focus on literal children in this chapter, it is important to understand how the settler state has historically narrated Native peoples as figural children in order to justify colonization and deny Native communities sovereignty. In *Fathers and Children*, Michael Rogin examines the rhetoric and actions of U.S. president Andrew Jackson, engineer of the 1830 Indian Removal Act, to reveal how his carefully manufactured project of "'inevitable' Indian extinction" necessitated a conceptual kinship reordering.[23] Jackson and his contemporaries conceived of Natives as stuck in the time of "'childhood' of the human race," whereas white males were understood to be endowed with an "adult white maturity," which legitimized their role as the rule-wielding parent nation.[24] The settler state's perceived duty to discipline Native populations materialized in policies that sanctioned genocide and legalized the seizure of Native land. Through these acts, the father nation "grounded their growing up in a securely achieved manhood, and securely possessed [Native] land."[25] These policies were undergirded by and helped strengthen settler "logics that primarily cast Native people as inherently dependent wards and settlers as primarily benevolent humanitarians"—Native people were cast as ontological children who had to yield to the moral, upright superior father nation.[26]

Kinship rhetoric continued to be deployed to explain why Native communities needed to be under the settler state's parental care. In the introduction to "Sexuality, Nationality, Indigeneity," a special issue of *GLQ*, Schneider points us to a critical statement in Chief Justice John Marshall's decision in *Cherokee Nation v. Georgia* (1831), in which he suggested that Native nations' relationship to the United States "resembles that of a ward to a guardian."[27] Schneider's reading of this seminal definition of Native nations understands the dynamic of father nation /

colonized child as one where "Native people were requeered as children, eternally stunted, the sexualized wards of the state."[28] This maneuver was a "requeer[ing]" since the state initially "queered" Native culture and sexuality by casting it as deviant and backward; the "sexual[ization]" of Natives was a heterosexualization, as the state attempted to "force Indians into a heteronormative futurity defined by private property, inheritance, and the nuclear family."[29] This *requeering* names the temporal outcomes of failed racialized heterosexualization: to be locked in an "eternally stunted" relationship with the settler state. For the United States to gain access to the land, the government made Native people into "wards of the state," orphaned communities who must be taken care of by the parenting nation.[30]

A crucial step in creating orphaned communities was intervening in, destroying, and restructuring kinship structures to fit into colonial understandings of personhood and property relations. Rifkin has demonstrated how "imperial interventions into Native residency, family formation, collective decision-making, resource distribution, and land tenure" broke down Native traditions, customs, and kinship formation to achieve this violent restructuring.[31] And, to ensure that many of these interventions would succeed, the state targeted children, most visibly in the form of educational policies focused on assimilation.

The first off-reservation Native American boarding school that produced queer Native childhood in the United States was the Carlisle Industrial School. Founded by Colonel Richard Henry Pratt in 1879 and in operation until 1918, the school served as a model for other Native American boarding schools that proliferated into the latter half of the twentieth century in the United States and Canada. Pratt's vision for the school was inspired by his work in a prison for Native adults in Florida, capturing the carceral logics and mechanisms that underpinned this institution for children, where the lines demarcating school from prison were indistinguishable. These institutions that emerged out of child-removal policies functioned as biopolitical tools of the settler state because they helped to control Native kinship and futurity. Michel Foucault explains that "biopolitics deals with the population, with the population as a political problem, as a problem that is at once scientific and political, as a biological problem and as power's problem."[32] The "population" of Native peoples had to be managed, and management of children functioned as a ruse for furthering the mission to eliminate Native peoples from the colonial landscape. The settler state's intervention into kinship was an intervention into Native reproduction, and children helped the settler state exercise its "power to 'make' live and 'let' die."[33] As Margaret Jacobs explains, "Indigenous child removal constituted another crucial way to eliminate indigenous people, both in a cultural and a biological sense"—the children were stripped of their Indianness in the schools, forced to abandon their language, cultural practices, names, and separated for years if not a lifetime from their Indigenous communities, accounting for the cultural elimination that Jacobs describes.[34]

While biological elimination of Native communities had been occurring since the first settlers arrived in North America, the turn of the century marked a shift from biological elimination through war to cultural elimination through assimilation. However, the latter did not preclude the former. Patrick Wolfe asserts that "the imposition on a people of the procedures and techniques that are generally glossed as 'cultural genocide' is certainly going to have a direct impact on that people's capacity to stay alive."[35] In other words, trying to rid children of their Indianness culturally, especially when this ridding is inextricable from violence, trauma, and abuse, has a direct relationship with children's ability to survive, flourish, and inhabit the future as productive and reproductive beings—preconditions for population growth in a settler capitalist system. Sexual orphanings, a consequence of cultural genocidal tactics, enabled cultural genocide to effect biological elimination under the guise of welfare.

One immediate way schools impacted Native futurity was by neglecting students' health in schools, resulting in many deaths. A brief look at the conditions of the schools shows that they were sites where children's "capacity to stay alive" was compromised. From their inaugural moment in 1879, boarding schools operated at institutions that took in healthy children and made them ill. Lack of regulation and oversight made it so that schools were never an environment that fostered health, growth, and general well-being. Schools produced what Jasbir Puar terms "debilitated bodies."[36] This created debility, exacerbated by disregard for the limits on children's capacity for manual labor, hastened the "slow death" of Native populations.[37] Debility meant fewer children had to be educated and the "Vanishing Indian" vanished faster, allowing the state to expend fewer resources on fewer Native Americans. In his 1976 report on the comprehensive state of Native American health, physician Everett Rhoades explains that at the end of the nineteenth century "[w]hen the federal Government assumed responsibility for the education of Indians, some degree of responsibility for their health was incidentally involved, and the first expenditures for their health was made from funds appropriated for education and 'civilization.'"[38] In other words, concern for Native American children's health was "incidental," and there were no funds specifically allocated toward overseeing health and regulating living conditions in Native American boarding schools. As a result, many children never saw a physician and were not examined for preexisting illnesses or symptoms prior to enrolling in the schools.

Sequestered in this restrictive environment that was supposedly committed to civilizing children, children were forced to live in squalid conditions. Many became ill when arriving at the schools because of environmental factors; children sent east experienced harsh climatic changes, not to mention the physiological stress of travel itself, but they did not receive medical attention once they arrived.[39] For example, David DeJong shares how a group of fifteen Shoshone boys were sent to Carlisle, and eleven died shortly after arrival. Children experienced overcrowding, often sleeping two or three to a bed in closed quarters that had poor ventilation.[40] Food available at schools resulted in inadequate nutrition, which was especially concerning because children were forced to engage in strenuous physical labor. These conditions, coupled with "strict military discipline," meant "some schools . . . became synonymous with death and disease."[41] DeJong outlines how illnesses, including tuberculosis, smallpox, and trachoma, were widespread in schools at levels statistically greater than among white people. Furthermore, when children became fatally ill, they were often sent back to their reservations; this practice allowed infected children to come into contact with their uninfected communities, enabling the transit and transmission of illness among Native peoples. Racist ideology fueled, in part, by social Darwinism considered Native American children, even if civilized, nonwhite and thus inferior and justified to be less invested in than their white counterparts.[42] The state's oversight of their own institutions worked to "'let' die" Native children. Boarding schools were holding stations, sites for producing an experience of queer childhood that would mitigate children's access to future social, economic, and political opportunities.

For those who did pass through and survive the boarding school, the schools sought to educate them in ways that would ensure no future for Native peoples. The often-cited motto of the schools, "kill the Indian, save the man," captures the schools' violent project of ridding children of their Indianness to "save" their humanity—for their Indianness was conceived as nonhuman.[43] This motto exemplifies Russ Castronovo's theory of necro citizenship, or the ways that the state necessitates a death, especially for members of marginalized groups, before an individual can be made into a political subject. This necessary "death that structures national identity" *is* the orphaning that children must undergo.[44] Orphaning Indianness was synonymous with "kill[ing] the Indian"—the projects were one and the same, inextricably linked because educating children to orphan their Indianness enabled the state to advance their project to eliminate Native peoples. If children abandoned their Indianness, they could not sustain Native lineages; Native reproductivity would stall, and Native Americans would start to disappear from the colonial landscape. The settler state's attempt to orphan the Native child functioned to ensure no future for Native peoples as well as Indigenous modes of being. Viewing the schools as institutions of "biophilanthropy," Schuller argues the logics of these institutions "reverse . . . death, seizing members of a primitive population marked for expiration and forcing them to live by rendering deleterious milieus out of the body layer by layer and violently imposing a new vitality on them."[45] Native children were forced to undergo a death in order to be kept alive—not for their own futurity and progress, but to enable the forward movement of the nation through providing labor and becoming "assets of the middle classes' capitalist accumulation, rather than threats to civilization."[46]

Pratt's rhetoric positioned Native children as the means through which a future would be secured for both children and their communities. In his treatise on the development of Carlisle, Pratt writes about how he convinced a group of Sioux parents to send their children away: "Your own welfare while you live and the welfare of your children after you, and all your interests in every way, demand that your children should have the same education that the white man has."[47] But this "same education" did not mean the same future as settlers; according to Pratt, Indian children could be "convert[ed] in all ways but color" and thus could never fully enter into white civilization.[48] Rifkin reiterates this point, explaining that eventual "interracial coupling" with whites was never foreseen for these children; the schools vehemently "preserv[ed] the reproductively constituted color line while arguing for a malleability in Indian character."[49] In other words, the Native body would never permit children to take part in a white future. Million also captures the built-in failure of this educational project when she notes that "Indian women's training could not be identical with one for white, middle-class 'femininity,' even if this is what was imagined as a model. White racial and gender stereotypes often led to an odd reversal for tribal women, who were rarely free to establish their own homes as 'havens' of domesticity."[50] Million identifies the gap here between the white settler model and impossibility of the educated Native child to replicate this model, as well as the ways that children were trained for futures they couldn't enact upon leaving the schools. Attempts to "reproduce middle-class sexual mores in Native children would always run against the 'known' available nature of Native sexuality"—schools were educating children in racialized sexual norms that their Nativeness prevented them from inhabiting or imitating.[51] In Million's words, "Indians had been considered assimilable but in actuality were barred by race."[52] Carmen Nolte-Odhiambo reads the ultimate unassimilability of Native children as a mode of "unbecoming: they do not fit within the desired parameters, and therefore present a potential challenge to a vision of the future characterized by the continuance of the status quo."[53] "Unbecoming" captures the social death and sexual orphanings that children were made to undergo in the schools.

Thus, Native children were educated to abandon Indianness culturally, but they would never be able to leave behind their Native bodies in the eyes of the state; politically, legally, socially, and biologically, they could never be white citizens or access the rights, privileges, and futures available to white citizens. But without their heritage or an understanding of Native customs, traditions, or languages, their Native bodies could not reproduce Indianness. "Kill the Indian, save the man" could succeed—except that "the man" saved was the white community that the state never intended for the children to join. In other words, "kill the Indian, save the man" was a peculiar kind of orphaning; the inability of orphaned children to carry on Indianness through the Native body was an attempt to preserve the future for white bodies at the expense of a generation of orphaned Native children, suspended in a liminal space between whiteness and Indianness, past and future. This liminality was temporal, spatial, cultural, and sexual, and it resonates with other settler-colonial attempts to restrict possibilities for Native sovereignty and survival.[54] Children's bodies were the vestiges of this orphaning; since the body remained, the schools needed to alienate children from these bodies to succeed in a complete orphaning of Indianness.

The state, then, attempted to complete this orphaning from the body through queering Native childhood, and crucially through the sexual orphanings that enabled this queer production. Children were paradoxically queered through being educated in white heterosexual norms. This queering was a double bind. On the one hand, the boarding schools' ostensible heterosexualization of Native children orphaned them from Indigenous modes of sexuality; on the other hand, that heterosexualization was racialized so as to arrive at normative failure, leaving Native children in a liminal space. The outcome of this queering was an orientation to a limited social, economic, and political future. Queerness names the liminal state in which many Native children who survived the boarding school experience found themselves.

Genre and Method

I now turn to Highway's *Kiss of the Fur Queen* to explore how sexual orphanings were enforced and consider what possibilities the text imagines despite these orphanings. Can they be disrupted? Undone? Reversed? Paying attention to the bodily sensations that the orphanings effect in *Kiss of the Fur Queen*, and how the children refuse or acknowledge these sensations and pleasures, shows us how the Native child's body might operate as a site for responding to colonization.

I explore *Kiss of the Fur Queen* in particular because, as a piece of Native literature, it can "supplement forgetting with new narratives of affirmation and presence."[55] Violent colonization continues into the present, but the rhetoric of the modern-day nation-state obscures the history and presence of violence, often masking it as care, thus producing what Lisa Lowe calls a "violence of . . . forgetting." Native literature forcefully asserts that *not everyone has forgotten*. Despite ongoing colonization, Native communities have survived and *continue to survive*, and literature is one site where Native peoples can affirm their survival, presence, and remembering. Lowe uses historian Stephanie Smallwood's statement that "I try to imagine what could have been" as a jumping-off point to consider how "the *past condition temporality* of the 'what could have been' symbolizes aptly the space of a different kind of thinking, a space of productive attention to the scene of loss."[56] I suggest that Native literature is a site where "what could have been" is imaginatively and productively enacted to resist the settler state's imperative to forget.[57]

Native literature that depicts sexuality participates in both a resistance to forgetting and a refusal of erasure. Daniel Heath Justice explains that "as indigenousness itself has long been a colonialist target, so too has our joy, our desire, our sense of ourselves as being able to both give and receive pleasure."[58] Justice asserts that seemingly quotidian bodily experiences and affects—"joy," "desire," "pleasure"—are not isolated from but intimately tied up with settler colonialism; paying attention to these sensations, especially in literature, then, is a way to track the violence of settler colonialism as well as responses to it at the level of affect, interiority, and self. Justice continues, explaining that since "Aboriginal peoples [are viewed] as historical artifacts, degraded vagrants or grieving ghosts," then "to take joy in our bodies—and those bodies in relation to others—is to strike out against five hundred plus years of disregard, disrespect, and dismissal."[59] Justice connects being viewed as remnant anachronisms with limited claims to humanity—"artifacts," "vagrants," "ghosts"—to being viewed as without bodies or without sexualities. Asserting sexuality is a way to assert presence, resist erasure, and combat the narrative that views Native peoples as disappeared or their sexualities as damaged. Justice sees writing about these experiences as critical: "Our sexuality isn't just part of our Nativeness—it's fuel for the healing of our nations."[60] Representing Native sexuality in literature, then, depicts sensations at the micro level that have potential to enable pathways toward "healing."

Highway's fictional text initially started as a memoir, based on his own time in a residential school in Canada. The role that his experience plays in the production of the text is crucial because Native knowledge and experience have historically been and currently are dismissed and devalued—Million argues that "literature of experience" can disrupt settler version of truth that enable ongoing colonization.[61] The story's final form as a novel allows it to imagine a "what could have been" that permits readers to approach some of the vexed issues surrounding Native queer childhood. Linking fiction to social change, Sam McKegney examines how Native fiction and Highway's text in particular enact political resistance in ways that differ from memoir or testimonial because it can "unsettle comfortable power relations by creatively reimagining Indigenous culture and identity in the contemporary moment."[62] Focus on the "contemporary moment" is crucial because of the ongoing legacy and ramifications of the boarding school, which is arguably most visible in the modern-day foster care system disproportionately made up of Native children; Native children continue to be targets of state intervention into Native kinship and futurity.[63]

Sexual and Temporal Orphanings in *Kiss of the Fur Queen*

Kiss of the Fur Queen is divided into six parts and follows the brothers Champion-Jeremiah and Ooneemeetoo-Gabriel throughout their childhoods, first in northern Manitoba and then in a Catholic-run boarding school, as well as their adulthoods in Winnipeg, where Jeremiah becomes an accomplished pianist and Gabriel a successful dancer who identifies as a gay man.[64] An omniscient narrator gives readers access to their diverging trajectories and also introduces readers to the Fur Queen, the trickster figure who watches over and confronts the boys at moments when the settler world is splintering them from their Native roots. Highway's choice to tell the story about two brothers, who are fated to different experiences and futures in the text, allows him to render two plots that differently present and imagine the effects of queer Native childhood. I focus mainly on the boys' time in the boarding school and where I see it bearing on their adulthood in order to think through some of these effects.

The first orphanings that the boys experience are geographical and kinship related. As young children, their local priest shares that according to the law and the Department of Indian Affairs, they must attend the faraway Birch Lake Indian Residential School, despite their father Abraham's "wish . . . that he had some say in the matter."[65] The state reorders kinship so that the authority figures within the school take on a parenting role. On his first day at the school, Champion tries to resist the "assault" of the school's authority by protesting the haircut and name change they require.[66] He stops when he remembers that his father "would have decreed that this [priest's] word bore the weight of biblical authority and therefore was to be listened to; [he was] feeling his father's eyes looking over his shoulder."[67] In this moment, fatherhood transfers from the Native father to the religious, institutional priest. While the Native father mediates the transfer, the priests are the ultimate father figures for the boys while they attend school, creating a new kinship structure that replaces and overrides the Native family.

The orphanings I consider in the remainder of this chapter are sexual orphanings, which enable temporal orphanings. The education acquired in the school inaugurated the children into a settler Christian linear temporal framework. A clock furtively appears in the first scene at the Birch Lake Residential School; six-year-old Champion waits to have his hair cut and "thought the holy brother might leave some hair, but as the seconds ticked on, this appeared unlikely."[68] The ritual of haircutting is one of the first violent acts the school takes in order to orphan Champion from his Indianness, carried out in a visible way on his body.[69] The introduction of time coincides with an act that leaves Champion thinking, "His hair was gone; he has no power."[70] This moment leaves Champion particularly vulnerable and thus more receptive, even if unwillingly receptive, to the institution's desires. The "seconds tick[ing]" during this scene structure the inevitability of the violence—Champion hopes that the act will not be completed, but as time moves forward "this appeared unlikely." Vine Deloria explains that the omnipresence and organizing power of time is a specifically modern Euro-American phenomenon. Particularly in the United States, "time . . . consume[s] space," emerging as the medium through which persons are made to understand all experiences.[71] Joseph Bauerkemper argues that "nonlinear[ity] . . . [is] crucial to . . . [I]ndigenous nationhood," critiquing the U.S. settler linear narrative that has supplanted "place-based" understandings of how the world works with time-based frameworks.[72] Vine Deloria warns that "if time becomes our primary consideration, we never seem to arrive at the reality of our existence in places but instead are always directed to experiential and abstract interpretations rather than to the experiences themselves."[73] In other words, time, especially as deployed in the boarding school, forecloses Native modes of being and reality. And yet, in the context of the settler state, it functions as an inescapable framework with which all "are inevitably involved," and in the case of boarding schools, involved through coercion.[74] So this initial scene of haircutting, marked by "seconds ticking," introduces Champion to a mode of being that time structures. This introduction is visibly marked through violence and loss on the Native body and folds him into a temporal framework intent on erasing his Indianness.

The school further imposes a settler temporality on Champion through a revision of his origin. After the priest cuts his hair, he says, "According to Father Bouchard's baptismal registry, you are named Jeremiah Okimasis."[75] Champion's birth name commemorated his father's legendary win at a dogsledding competition, a victory that family lore says enabled Champion's conception. This baptismal name, captured in the archive of the "registry," is meant to replace Champion. Diana Taylor explains that "archive" has its roots in "'arkhe' . . . mean[ing] a beginning, the first place, the government."[76] In this moment, the institution that has catalogued Native births imposes a new "beginning" onto Champion, erasing his Native identity for a settler Christian one.

The school's renaming attempts to extricate Champion from his Native genealogy. Initially, Champion resists, finally settling on "Champion-Jeremiah—he was willing to concede that much of a name change, for now."[77] This temporal disclaimer—"for now"—on Champion's concession reveals that he is already contending with the force of the institutionally imposed forward motion of time. Champion attempts to stall this motion, but his attempts are thwarted; the summer that Gabriel joins him at Birch Lake, the narrative shifts from calling him "Champion-Jeremiah" to only "Jeremiah."[78] Becoming Jeremiah serves to further orphan him from the Cree history, subjectivity, and kinship attached to Champion.

The boys' father, Abraham Okimasis, notices this loss of history and tracks his children's temporal displacement. While the musically gifted Champion plays the accordion as a young boy, Abraham thinks, "it [was] his greatest pride to have finally sired a child with a gift for the making of music, one to whom he could pass on his father's, his grandfather's, and his great-grandfather's legacy . . . this ancient treasure of the Okimasis clan could rest intact for at least another generation."[79] Abraham recognizes that Indianness will survive "at least another generation" through Champion. However, after Champion goes to school, Abraham's understanding of what will facilitate the boys' futures shifts. He tells Gabriel, "Father Lafleur [a priest at Birch Lake] is taking care of you just fine . . . with him guiding you, your future is guaranteed."[80] In this moment, that which guarantees Native survival and futurity transfers from the "ancient treasure of the Okimasis clan" to Father Lafleur. This transfer of responsibility for the future also serves to further orphan the boys from their Native kinship—Native futurity has been preserved through Native fathers (Abraham's "father's, his grandfather's, and his great grandfather's"), but here the institutional father replaces the Native father.

Abraham as the Native father, then, is unable to intervene in this reorientation of kinship and co-option of futurity. The longer the boys are at school, the more Abraham realizes that "visit by visit, word by word, these sons were splintering from their subarctic roots, their Cree beginnings. Yet he knew that destiny played with lives; the most a parent could do was help steer."[81] The Native father, once responsible for his child's survival, surrenders to "destiny," seeing himself in a more passive role where he can only be someone who "help[s]." While this admission might be a way to refuse to acknowledge the school's complete hold on his children—it is "destiny" and not the school "play[ing]" with and "steer[ing]" his children—it is still a recognition of his children's orphaning from their Cree past. "Destiny" is a temporal term and affective state of resignation produced by settler colonialism and child removal.

The school also temporally restructures the brothers' bodies through an education in settler heteronormativity. Champion is educated in the rhythms of what J. Jack Halberstam terms "repro-time," learning the proper practices that will enable heterosexual reproduction and (white) futurity.[82] Education *about* repro-time is not recruitment *into* repro-time, and this distinction becomes clear once the boys pass through the school. Nonetheless, the school works to ensure that the students who enroll are successfully internalizing this education in repro-time. The school carefully monitors children's bodies, and particularly its interactions with the opposite sex. The school separated girls from boys: "Girls had their own yard on the other side . . . away from the view of lusty lads."[83] Enforcing this separation of boys and girls works to teach children the appropriate object to desire *while also* implying that this desire is inappropriate and must be prevented through strict separation. In this way, the school constructs heterosexuality as the appropriate end for children while teaching them that desire is not permitted in this heterosexual paradigm. Rifkin understands this construction to be a crucial component in the "romance plot" that the school narrates.[84] In this plot, schools "regulate social interaction between the sexes . . . [and] orchestrate and manage the process of courting."[85] More than just "orchestrating and manag[ing]" this process, they *produce* it through their regulations. Deborah Miranda notes that "the strict separation of boys and girls during long stints at Indian boarding school . . . not only changed Native courtship and coming-of-age experiences, but also inscribed a European, Christianized dogma regarding the 'dirtiness' of Native bodies and sexuality in general."[86] Educating children in "courtship" and heterosexual practices necessitated teaching them how to look back on "Native bodies and sexuality" as "dirty" while also apprehending their present desires as "lusty" and inappropriate. Producing gendered categories and teaching appropriate romantic and sexual affect and behavior worked to queer Native children's bodies and produce shame and disavowal of sexuality. Children were taught what a heterosexual future looked like, but sexual orphanings would preclude them from gaining access to that future.

This production and structuring of appropriate desire at the boys school is not in the service of making sure that Native children will heterosexually reproduce—*straightening children is what queers them*, or orients them toward a future where sexual and reproductive capacities will be mitigated. After the boarding school, it is impossible for Jeremiah to return home, at least geographically—"he had absolutely nowhere to go."[87] He settles in Winnipeg, where "in this metropolis of half a million souls . . . he seemed to be the only Indian person."[88] Isolated and demarcated from the whiteness surrounding him, Jeremiah is left extricated from his Native community. While on a bus in this city, Jeremiah remembers how the school monitored "every bodily secretion"; conjoined with this memory of surveillance is the realization that in this city, unlike at the school, he was "free to talk to girls. Except there were no girls to talk to. At his [current high] school, there may have been a thousand, but they were all white."[89] Since Native reproductivity cannot cross racialized lines, the heterosexual desire in which Jeremiah has been educated cannot be enacted outside of the school. The girls he has been educated to desire "were all white" and thus are inaccessible to his Native body. This illusory, constructed "romance plot" halts Jeremiah's sexual and reproductive possibilities.

Despite being barred from repro-time, Jeremiah cannot unlearn this education that privileges the "biological clock . . . [and] bourgeois rules."[90] As an adult, he comes face-to-face with the Fur Queen, the larger-than-life embodiment of Cree culture who has "no gender" and structures the text.[91] The trickster asks him what the point of life is, to which Jeremiah responds, "You are born. You grow up, you go to school, you work—you work like hell—you get married, sometimes, you raise a family, sometimes, you grow old. And then you die."[92] This understanding of life follows the "biological" and "bourgeois" markers that are characteristic of repro-time, recognizing a clear beginning (birth) and end (death) punctuated by heteronormative life events (marriage and family). The mandate of marriage and family is twice spliced by a perhaps hesitant, perhaps qualifying "sometimes," which might illustrate Jeremiah's recognition that he himself will not participate in this hetero-time. This is juxtaposed with an emphasis on work, suggesting that this is the feature of heterotime that rings most true for him. The boarding school has cultivated within Jeremiah an understanding of what existence *should* look like according to a linear, settler heterosexual model, but he does not achieve these heteronormative milestones. He does, however, achieve capitalist participation through laboring.

Jeremiah attempts to reconnect with his Indianness by keeping up with his music lessons as a young adult. He takes the stage at a piano competition, and the narrator describes how the "flowing-haired Indian youth . . . was about to perform."[93] Previously, his haircut left Jeremiah with "no strength" and "no power."[94] When his hair was cut at school, "He was being skinned alive, in public; the centre of his nakedness shriveled to the size and texture of a raisin."[95] Losing his hair is linked with a "shrivel[ing]" of his sexuality, and so having hair might allow for him to reconnect with his sexual body. While he played the accordion as a child, the piano is the only instrument he is allowed to play in school. Music functions as a hybrid activity, fusing the talent that might preserve Native futurity with an instrument that the settler state introduces him to, thus holding potential for subversion.

This reading, however, is complicated by other moments in the text that suggest pursuing his musical talent after the boarding school might actually work to *further* orphan Jeremiah temporally and sexually. While at a party with Gabriel and Gabriel's lover, someone looks at Jeremiah and "the pianist's scrotum shrank to raisin size," connecting it textually to the moment that his hair was cut at school.[96] It is not haircutting, then, but perhaps being looked at and put on public display that "shrinks" and "shrivels" Jeremiah's sexuality. Being acknowledged in his Native skin divorces him from the erotics of his body. It is distinctly the "pianist's scrotum" that shrinks in this moment, linking his musical talent with his orphaned sexuality. Piano playing appears here to assist the settler state in keeping Jeremiah distanced from his body.

Music cannot entirely reverse the impact of Jeremiah's temporal or sexual orphanings. Piano playing ultimately affirms Jeremiah's impotence. Gabriel accuses Jeremiah of having orphaned his sexuality, exclaiming, "You'd rather diddle with a piano than diddle with yourself. You're dead Jeremiah. At least my body is still alive."[97] Later in a sexual encounter, "[Jeremiah] couldn't get erect. His sex was dead."[98] While playing the piano perhaps is a way for Jeremiah to remain connected to pieces of his Cree past and assert a Cree present, he is unable to reconnect with his sexuality. This disconnect suspends him between being alive and dead. The piano functions as the medium through which his inability to reconnect with his body is ascertained. Gabriel tells him "you are dead" and later "his sex was dead"—he and his sexuality experience the same "no future," stunted and unable to participate in the reproductive order.

Not participating in the reproductive order does not necessarily entail no future. However, any future or alternative temporality seems inaccessible to Jeremiah by the text's conclusion. Gabriel, on his deathbed in the final scene, asks Jeremiah, "If Native languages have no gender, then why should we?" to which Jeremiah responds, "Father Lafleur would send you straight to hell for saying that."[99] Jeremiah tries to support his brother, who he feels did not "take care of" growing up but is unable to think or interact with him in a way that has not been structured by the school.[100] This response that Gabriel would go "straight to hell" for contemplating a life with "no gender" reveals that Jeremiah cannot reconnect with a Native conceptualization of sexuality or time; he has been successfully folded into settler understandings of both, which means he has been successfully orphaned from time and sexuality by the text's conclusion. The image of Jeremiah with which we are left is an impotent one; he seems stuck in a liminal space, with minimal capacity to resist the forces that have sapped his vitality.

The settler state successfully queers Jeremiah through educating him in heterosexuality. He is educated in a reproductive futurism in which he cannot participate. Jeremiah is unable to move forward but unable to return home temporally, sexually, or in terms of kinship. He, then, is orphaned from sexuality—enabled by an orphaning from his Cree past and resulting in an orphaning from a potential reproductive future; his experience and education in the school have left him with a body from which he is disconnected. Native queer childhood bars Jeremiah from occupying the future as a sexual or reproductive being.

Pleasure and Violence in Gabriel's Orphanings

The sexual orphanings that Jeremiah experiences differ from Gabriel's, who is raped by a white priest, Father Lafleur, during his time at school. Jeremiah is left orphaned from his sexuality; however, the abuse Gabriel experiences produces sensations that alter the totalizing effects of this orphaning. Gabriel's sexuality both as a child and as an adult is inextricably linked with and perhaps even a product of his experience of sexual abuse—elements present in the scene the first time the priest rapes him are also present in his adult sexual encounters. While the sexual abuse of Father Lafleur asserts colonial control over the bodies of Native children, the scenes of violation present abuse alongside sensations of pleasure.[101]

I use Qwo-Li Driskill's concept of the sovereign erotic to think about how possession of one's body might paradoxically come through damage. Driskill writes, "We were stolen from our bodies / We were stolen from our homes" and defines the sovereign erotic as "an erotic wholeness healed and/or healing from the historical trauma that First Nations people continue to survive, rooted within the histories, traditions, and resistance struggles of our nations."[102] For Driskill, the sovereign erotic allows for an "erotic wholeness" even after being "stolen"—or orphaned—from the Native body. While Driskill envisions an "erotic wholeness," I am interested in how the body might heal in ways that do not necessarily result in wholeness but nonetheless open up pathways for decolonization at the level of bodies, affects, and sensations. Elizabeth Freeman notes that "erotics . . . traffic less in belief than in encounters, less in damaged wholes than in intersections of body parts."[103] *Kiss of the Fur Queen* gives us a way to consider if and how local features of the body that constitute the erotic—bodily sensations and pleasures—disturb the totalizing narrative and violence of settler colonialism.

Driskill understands the body as home, which resonates with M. Jacqui Alexander's understanding of coming to "home in the body" as a way to counter state violence. Driskill argues that the body "is the first homeland" and one of many homes from which Native children are orphaned.[104] This conceptualization of "home" is not strictly geographically determined or rooted to land; it is an expansive understanding of "home" that takes seriously the body's role and allows us to consider the relation between Alexander's "radical self-possession" and the dispossession of Native land. In other words, settler colonialism dispossesses Native Americans not just of their land but also of their bodies through a violent education that imposes settler sexuality and teaches children to apprehend erotics as shameful. Rifkin explains that the settler state requires that "to gain 'individuality' [a necessity for white understandings of property and land ownership] Indians must shift the horizon of their thinking and, more importantly, their feeling, connecting 'home' not to specific tribal territories but to the great expanse of the entire United States."[105] Children were educated to abandon attachment to their communities and understand "home" as a nation that would never welcome them. The reality of colonization makes a return to "home" in terms of kinship and geography impossible—some orphanings are irreversible. However, if the body can serve as a "home" through a reclamation of erotics that the schools disallow, decolonization might begin to occur at the level of individual bodies.

Gabriel's abuse and the pleasure it produces enable him to maintain a connection to the Native body despite abuse. His reaction to the abuse and how this first sexual violation recurs during his lifetime reveal that within traumatic, sexual violence there is space for him to disrupt the sexual orphanings that this abuse has worked to incur. Embracing the pleasure produced in these encounters allows him to *return home through the body*. This return is not a temporal one; he is not returning to some pristine Cree past untouched by colonial violence. Gabriel returns to a body that has been violated and colonized, but allowing himself to experience pleasure and sensation—the very bodily practices the school produces in order to shame—enables a connection to the sovereign erotic that is life-affirming.

Father Lafleur's violation of Gabriel's body builds on a longer history of institutional violation. When Gabriel is baptized, the priest says, "'*Abrenuntias satanae?*' The words, meaningless to Cree ears, pierced the infant's fragile bones and stayed here."[106] The assault on Gabriel's body begins with the ritual of baptism's violent penetration of Gabriel's physical body. These "meaningless" words will "stay there," demonstrating how the Church not only makes itself a part of Gabriel's body at this moment but will remain present with his body across time. This "piercing" violation lays the groundwork for his experience of later violations.

The first sexual violation in *Kiss of the Fur Queen* is bound with and even contingent upon Gabriel's pleasure. Gabriel performs in a school play and "beamed with pleasure" as he dances across the stage, where an audience that includes Father Lafleur watches him.[107] When Gabriel sleeps later that night, he dreams he is dancing and that his "little body was moving up and down . . . producing, in the crux of his being, a sensation so pleasurable," but upon waking, "the face of the principal [Father Lafleur] loomed inches from [Gabriel's] own."[108] This sequence of events reveals that it is the performative act of dancing—an act that produced "pleasure" within Gabriel—that triggers Father Lafleur to approach Gabriel's bed that evening. Gabriel's pleasure, then, comes prior to the priest's and is actually responsible for the priest's own pleasure. Native sexuality takes precedence—the young Gabriel has not been rid of his sexuality yet, nor is it something primitive and in the past; his sexuality is present and powerful and apprehended as a sensation "in the crux of his being."

When Gabriel wakes up and realizes what is happening to him, his experience of pleasure disrupts the power dynamics of the encounter. The description of the rape that occurs reveals that Gabriel, while a victim, is not a passive object onto whom the priest inflicts violence during the act:

> From some tinny radio somewhere off . . . [Gabriel] could hear Elvis Presley singing "Love Me Tender." . . . Gradually, Father Lafleur bent, closer

and closer, until the crucifix that dangled from his neck came to rest on Gabriel's face. The subtly throbbing motion of the priest's upper body made the naked Jesus Christ—this sliver of silver light, this fleshly Son of God so achingly beautiful—rub his body against the child's lips, over and over and over again. Gabriel had no strength left. The pleasure in his centre welled so deep that he was about to open his mouth and swallow whole the living flesh—in his half-dream state, this man nailed to the cross was a living, breathing man, tasting like Gabriel's most favourite food, warm honey.[109]

Gabriel sees himself as an object over whom "holy men" have a "right."[110] This passage depicts an unexpected consequence of that right: the "pleasure" in Gabriel's "centre [that] welled so deep." Highway's narration of this pleasure forces readers to pause and consider how to account for pleasure, and specifically sexual pleasure in a child, in a scene of vivid, unquestionable violence. Acknowledging the presence of this pleasure is crucial, even if uncomfortable. As Justice asserts, "To ignore sex and embodied pleasure in the cause of Indigenous liberation is to ignore one of our greatest resources. . . . Every orgasm can be an act of decolonization."[111] The presence of sexual pleasure in an act of sexual violation suggests the potential for the sovereign erotic and the "resource" of pleasure. Gabriel's pleasure disrupts the attempted colonization and orphaning of his body by creating space for and allowing the erotic.

Allowing for the erotic means that Gabriel is not orphaning it; the sexual orphaning on which the state depends fails in this moment. Audre Lorde argues that Euro-American conceptualizations of sexuality, particularly as they are tied with "suppression," interfere with an ability to see the erotic as a site and "source of power and information."[112] Connecting with rather than suppressing the erotic, acknowledging rather than refusing the erotic, enables Native peoples to retain and reclaim what colonizers have attempted to destroy and restructure. If erasing the erotic is part of the colonization and queering of Native communities, connecting to and allowing the erotic functions as an important step toward decolonization. It also allows the possibility to reclaim, maintain connection with, or heal ties with Native conceptualizations of sexuality, thus resisting the state's project of queering and rendering backward Native cultures, traditions, and epistemologies.

Importantly, the erotic is not limited to the domain of sexuality. Lorde explains how it involves the political, spiritual, emotional, and social spheres, and Driskill reiterates this point when they explain that the erotic is "not . . . a realm of personal consequence only. Our relationships with the erotic impact our larger communities, just as our communities impact our sense of the erotic. A Sovereign Erotic relates our bodies to our nations, traditions, and histories."[113] Thus, Gabriel's erotic encounter with the priest, even though "confusi[ng]" for him, helps him maintain a crucial connection to his "nation, traditions, and histories."[114] His pleasure interrupts a complete sexual orphaning.

Gabriel's pleasure further disrupts the act of the colonizing priest because it enables him to connect to erotic power rather than orphan it. The first time the school introduces pleasure is in the classroom, when Gabriel's older brother, Jeremiah, learns about heaven and hell. Jeremiah is taught hell is a place where "there appeared to be no end to the imagination with which these brown people took their pleasure; and this, Father Lafleur explained earnestly to his captive audience, was permanent punishment."[115] This moment is an important one in the boys' education because it frames Native pleasure as inevitably linked with and even synonymous with "punishment." The school folds the Native body into a narrative with specific temporal outcomes (i.e., "permanent" hell), and these temporal outcomes are a *consequence* of Native pleasure. The depiction of hell reveals this pleasure to be responsible for both bringing someone to hell as well as the "punishment" itself once there. Since pleasure leads to hell and pleasure is hell, the boys are educated to want to orphan this pleasure.

While there is potentiality embedded in Gabriel's experience of pleasure, the boarding school structures how Gabriel makes sense of this pleasure. While at Mass, Gabriel and his brother recite, "'Through my fault, through my fault, through my most grievous fault' . . . [and] both had concluded that they were being asked to apologize for something beyond their control. . . . They had also independently concluded that it was best to accept blame; it *was* their most grievous fault."[116] Alongside the sexual violence he experiences, the school educates Gabriel to acquire shame, recognizing himself as responsible for "something beyond [his] control." Gabriel internalizes this structure of feeling cultivated in the rituals of the mass, convinced that an unnamed "something" is his "most grievous fault." That this moment comes so soon after the first incident of sexual abuse suggests that it might be shame from the abuse and the experience of pleasure resulting in this "accept[ance of] blame."

Comments that Gabriel makes later about his experience in the boarding school confirm this shame he feels as a result of the abusive encounters. When recognizing a homosexual desire he has for an older male, "a terrible guilt pummeled his heart. *Mea culpa, mea culpa, mea maxima culpa* [my fault, my fault, my most grievous fault]. Suddenly, a terrible need came over him, to run into his mother's arms and hide, crawl back into her womb and start over."[117] Recognition of his erotic desire results in "guilt" and the repetition of the Latin phrase that previously connected him to feelings of self-blame and responsibility. His sexual desire triggers shame. The shame is so strong it makes Gabriel want to impossibly return to his mother's womb, revealing a desire to erase his experience in his Native body by returning to a time prior.

This shame further orphans Gabriel from kinship. When they return from school on a break, Gabriel talks with Champion in English about "what Father Lafleur do[es] to the boys at school."[118] Their mother asks them to explain what they are talking about, and Gabriel is "silen[t] . . . and then [Champion] said, his voice flat, '*Maw keegway.*' Nothing."[119] Gabriel's sexual abuse can be articulated only in the language of the colonizer, and it cannot be communicated to his family. Finley notes that "one of the methods Native communities have used to survive is adapting silence around sexuality";[120] "silence around sexuality," in this instance, helps Gabriel to "survive" while simultaneously weakening his ties to his Native community.

The silence around his sexuality continues to assist in orphaning Gabriel from his Indianness as he gets older. When he leaves the school, he joins Jeremiah in Winnipeg, and he has frequent homosexual encounters. When he returns to his family during a vacation, he talks to his father, to whom "he lied . . . his voice incapable of masking shame or guilt. Supposing this beautiful man could see . . . the hundreds of other men with whom his last-born had shared . . . [if he] could see his baby boy pumping and being pumped by a certain ardent young Jesuit with grey-blue eyes."[121] Gabriel is unable to name what he has "shared" with these men, making the imagining and acknowledgment of his sexuality impossible; silence remains. While he is older and has been with "hundreds of other men," he returns to his first sexual encounter by wondering what his father would think if he knew about the sex he had with "a certain ardent young Jesuit." Gabriel acknowledges "being pumped by" the priest, but also names his own "pumping" in the encounter; while he might feel "shame or guilt" over the experience, he recognizes himself as an active participant in the encounter as well as the possibility that he also received pleasure while in the passive position. This recognition is significant because, while it is infused with "shame" and "guilt," it also implicitly acknowledges the pleasure of the encounter. In *Touching Feeling*, Eve Sedgwick explains that pleasure is a requirement for shame: "Without positive affect, there can be no shame; only a scene that offers you enjoyment . . . can make you blush."[122] So while shame might be a product of the boarding school experience, it serves an important function because it includes pleasure. In *Beautiful Bottom, Beautiful Shame*, Stockton posits that shame can simultaneously hold "beautiful, generative, [and] sorrowful" power.[123] The inextricable link between shame and pleasure is one of the "generative" outcomes of shame. Shame, then, is one of the affects that comes out of sexual violation because it can come only after an acknowledgment of pleasure—and it is through this affect that Gabriel navigates damage.

Once he leaves the school, Gabriel experiences sexual pleasure as an adult, and these experiences parallel his initial sexual encounter with Father Lafleur. When Gabriel joins Jeremiah in Winnipeg, he almost immediately has sex with a man who was "transported by [his] cool beauty. . . . Ulysses' sirens had begun to sing 'Love Me Tender' and the Cree Adonis could taste, upon the buds that lined his tongue, warm honey."[124] The return of the song "Love Me Tender" and the honey—features present in the first scene of violation with Father Lafleur—in this new sexual encounter suggest that his traumatic experience shapes his adult sexuality. Elements of this first encounter continue to crop up in his sexual experiences outside of the boarding school, especially "the naked Jesus Christ" crucifix the priest is wearing the first time he rapes Gabriel.[125] This repetition of the first sexual violation enables the colonizing power to have control over his body long after he leaves the school, which works to keep Gabriel disconnected from his body.

Ann Cvetkovich offers a way to begin to see the recurrence of trauma as a site of potentiality. She asserts that there can be "unpredictable potential [in] traumatic experience."[126] She seeks a conceptualization of trauma that is "not pathologize[d]" but "that forge[s] creative responses."[127] Seeing trauma outside of this pathologizing framework is crucial in a Native context; Million has investigated how governmental approaches to historical and contemporary state-sanctioned harm against Native communities make it so that "the colonized subject became a trauma victim," where trauma and its attending pain and suffering are viewed as "a pathology" responded to with "state-determined biopolitical programs for emotional and psychological self-care."[128] The "creative" responses may, then, link sexual trauma to the "creative" power of the erotic—both are capable of opening up new spaces. Cvetkovich is particularly interested in the productive power of flashbacks. Flashbacks, characterized by the fact that they force a subject to repeat a traumatic event, may contain "subversive possibilities of repetition with a difference."[129] In other words, if an experience can be repeated but part of the experience can be changed or altered, it may "provide the basis for healing rituals and performances . . . [which] exemplifies Eve Sedgwick's notion of a queer 'shame-creativity,' which reclaims that which has been debased and repudiated."[130] "Embracing rather than refusing" trauma can actually be a way to disrupt the overdetermining temporal rhythms of trauma.[131] It can counter sexual orphanings through this "shame-creativity." The very repetition of trauma and the fact that it brings the past into the present might help counter the temporal orphanings that the school enforces; it disrupts the normal unfolding of the forward timeline, creating a space in which to "grow sideways."

This temporality of repetition enables Gabriel to further disrupt his state-produced temporal orphaning. In another sexual encounter, "Gabriel found himself in a wood-panelled living room. Somehow, time had passed through him . . . everywhere he looked, naked limb met naked limb met naked limb, an unceasing domino effect of human flesh, smell, fluid."[132] During the encounter, "the silver cross oozed in and out, in and out . . . on his lips," another repetitive element that was present during his encounter with Father Lafleur.[133] In this orgy, "time had passed through" Gabriel—his body is not consumed by time but rather functions as a medium through which time can "pass." This "pass[ing]" suggests that time is not determining his body's outcome; his body's relationship with time is altered within the sexual encounter. His traumatic encounter in the boarding school keeps Gabriel connected to his erotic self, rather than distanced from it. The repetition of the experience across his lifetime does not stunt the development of his sexual self or suspend him in a liminal space.

We can see the limits and possibilities of these "queer healing practices" in Gabriel's adult life.[134] Gabriel grows up to identify as a gay man, a description of same-sex desire that is an effect of his induction into a modern settler sexuality. In an argument during which his brother, Jeremiah, realizes that Gabriel is gay, Jeremiah says, "How can you let someone do what that disgusting old priest did to you? How can you seek out . . . people like that?" Gabriel responds, "And you? . . . You'd rather diddle with a piano than diddle with yourself. You're dead. . . . At least my body is still alive."[135] Being alive allows Gabriel to experience sexual pleasure and erotic power. That he qualifies this survival of his body with "at least" might dwarf the impact of this survival; however, colonization and education have orphaned Gabriel from much of his Indianness, and he sees how in his brother, "kill the Indian" has succeeded in killing the Native body and its sexual capacities. Gabriel's body is an individual site that has remained alive and connected to pleasure and erotics in the face of ongoing violent assault. In this moment, we see definitively that the traumatic violence of the boarding school does not succeed in orphaning Gabriel from his sexuality—rather, it keeps him connected to it and alive.

The final scene shows us how this connection to his body, sexuality, and erotics enables Gabriel's survival in an alternative time and space through the trickster narrative. *Kiss of the Fur Queen* is, crucially, an AIDS narrative. in his early adult life Gabriel is diagnosed with AIDS, which indicates that his life will be cut short and that he will not participate in the reproductive order: he is the target of multiple genocides.[136] While Gabriel is on his deathbed, "the Fur Queen swept into the room. . . . Rising from his body, Gabriel Okimasis and the Fur Queen floated off into the swirling mist."[137] Gabriel "ris[es] from his body," leaving behind the Indian body from which the settler state has so vehemently tried to alienate him. The scene suggests that while his body is left behind, his subjectivity continues—he "floated off," an open-ended conclusion that does not suggest finality. The settler state has attempted to educate Gabriel to orphan his own sexuality. Highway imagines Gabriel's refusal to orphan his sexuality, and this imagining enables a final scene where Gabriel can orphan his body but still survive. Highway explains that the "continued presence of this extraordinary figure" of the trickster prevents "the core of Indian culture [from] be[ing] gone forever."[138] The final image of Gabriel and the trickster is one of survival and continuance not bound to linear time or material space. It is still able to emerge despite fractures caused by sexual orphanings. Gabriel is denied the settler future, but Highway imagines an alternate way to endure. *Kiss of the Fur Queen* offers some possibilities for what "growing sideways" might look like—it is a site of pleasure and repetition, full of potentiality and continuance even if not future oriented.

Exchanges between queer and Indigenous studies have been marked by productive tensions around issues such as kinship, institutions, pleasure, reproduction, and temporality. Both fields critique the state's management of bodies and sexualities for the purpose of excluding queer and Native communities from state-sanctioned futures, exclusions that have been justified by rendering both Native and queer peoples in similar temporal terms: backward and childlike. However, key and revealing differences have emerged, for instance, in divergent views of kinship. While queer studies tends toward a utopic view of alternative kinship structures, Indigenous studies reminds practitioners that intervening into and supplanting kinship with new structures has been a violent tactic used by the settler state to access and steal Native land over the last two centuries. Queer studies attends to pleasure, rejects normativity, and embraces non-reproductivity, but Indigenous studies asks us how these issues must be taken up differently in the face of ongoing cultural and biological genocide. Native peoples have not disappeared, but the attempts to disappear them make reproductivity salient and not something that can easily be dismissed or theorized as a conservative value. In other words, queer studies' embrace of pleasure and non-reproductivity can happen when there is a guarantee that bodies and populations will be there and will reproduce and survive; queer studies has limits in Indigenous contexts where survival and futurity are at stake.

In this chapter, I have turned to the children of Native American boarding schools as especially charged figures through whom to consider these historical and theoretical tensions at the intersection of queer and Indigenous studies. This argument has taken a seemingly non-queer approach to reproduction by casting it as a litmus test for viewing how the settler state prevents Native peoples from accessing the future, thus aligning reproduction and the future. However, Native children are not synonymous with or guaranteed a future in the context of settler colonialism; in fact, I argue that promises of futurity to Native children in the form of education obscure violences intended to prevent that very future. Second, since the settler state saw literal Native bodies as an obstacle to the seizure of land, legal and otherwise, preventing the literal reproduction of Native populations was crucial to settler expansion; taking seriously Native reproduction and its relationship to the production of Native queer childhood allows us to track how the settler state attempted to prevent the expansion of Native populations through sexual education of their children. My argument reveals the double bind of Native children's education: children were educated to understand and experience their Indianness as queer, and thus orphaned from it, and then they were educated in white heterosexual norms, norms in which they would always fail because of their race. Paradoxically, then, ostensible heterosexuality queers these children. Queer, here, is not liberatory but genocidal. The settler state's refusal of the future to Natives is not liberatory but genocidal. And the promise of a future—through education—is a false one that enables the queer outcome of the schools in the form of limited social, economic, political, and sexual futures.

Coda: Sexual and Temporal Orphanings in Foster Care

The ramifications of the boarding school still impact Native communities today, and we can see the boarding school as an ancestor to the modern-day foster care system, which is disproportionately composed of Native children who are wards of the state. The 2013 Supreme Court decision in *Adoptive Couple v. Baby Girl* to disregard features of the Indian Child Welfare Act (ICWA) of 1978, a law meant to protect Native parents' rights when it comes to custody of their children, is just one way that Native children remain unprotected by the settler state. In *Somebody's Children: The Politics of Transracial and Transnational Adoption*, Laura Briggs explores how at the time of its passing the "ICWA was founded on a tribal definition of peoples' rights—hence defined by the nature of their political and legal, not 'racial,' status."[139] Despite Native communities' attempts

to make the ICWA about sovereignty, not race, the settler conceptualization of Indianness as a race has often impeded the implementation and
preservation of the act. Briggs describes this process of "trying to turn
tribal peoples into a 'race' as a matter of law is to try to fit the square
peg of Native governance questions into the round hole of a black-white
racial paradigm."[140] The settler state has needed to cling to its conceptualization of Native peoples as a race in order to limit Native governance.
These racializing processes that obscure ongoing colonization continue
to gain new traction and energy—at the time of this writing in summer
2022, the ICWA will once again be challenged in *Brackeen v. Haaland*,
specifically over whether it "discriminate[s] on the basis of race."[141]

The settler state's continual targeting of Native children and occlusion
of colonization through racialization disrupts Native kinship, aiding the
state's attempt to restrict Native futurity. In order to examine what futures might be for Native children today as well as how those futures are
a legacy of the boarding school, I turn to Sherman Alexie's *Flight* (2007),
a text that explores the fate of a "half-breed" Native child, Zits, in the
foster care system.[142] Zits recognizes his connection with the boarding
school and inserts himself into a genealogy that recognizes he is a product of the boarding school system. Zits travels across time in the text,
and during one episode that has taken him to a Native community in the
nineteenth century, Zits looks around and laments,

> All these old-time Indians are doomed . . . the children are going to be
> kidnapped and sent off to boarding schools. Their hair will be cut and
> they will be beaten for speaking their tribal languages. . . . All of them are
> going to start drinking booze. And their children will drink booze. And
> their grandchildren and great-grandchildren will drink booze. And one
> of those great-grandchildren will grow up to be my real father. . . . That's
> what is going to happen to all these old-time Indians. That's what's going
> to happen to me.[143]

Zits hails himself as a direct descendant of children who were "kid-
napped and sent off to boarding school." That it is "what's going to
happen" to Zits suggests an inevitability to this fate he recognizes for
himself; his use of the future tense for the old-time Indians works to
doubly seal the fate of the past (since he is traveling back in time, "what

is going to happen" has already happened, so in fact he narrates that it is "going to happen" *again*), which simultaneously seals his own since the two are linked. He realizes that this past impedes any possibility of a "what could have been"—futurity seems limited for him in this moment. Qwo-Li Driskill observes that "boarding schools continue to have severe repercussions on our communities," and the foster care system continues to be one of the "severe repercussions" of this violent colonial project.[144] John Sheridan Milloy explains that colonial violence "was not simply visited on the individual child in school; it spilled back into communities, so that even after the schools were closed it echoed in the lives of subsequent generations of children."[145] Zits is one of those "subsequent generations of children" subject to the temporal and sexual orphanings imposed by the state in an effort to eliminate the Native body, that which remains after sexual orphanings.

Like children in the boarding school, the text's narrator Zits is also a state-produced orphan. However, the foster care system conceals his orphaning, instead rotating him in and out of white kinship structures. Furthermore, temporal orphanings need be enforced only in one direction; unlike the children of the boarding school, Zits does not have a remembered experience of a Native past. Thus, the state must focus on preventing Native orphans in foster care from the possibility of a Native future. Despite the lack of a Native past, the threat of the Native body to the future remains an issue for the state to resolve. Sexual orphanings in foster care pivot on preventing reproduction of the Native body.

Flight immediately introduces the problem of the Native body. Zits knows that he had a white mother and Native father, but that is the extent of his knowledge regarding his origins. Zits has "inherited his [father's] ruined complexion and black hair and big Indian nose," making his Indianness unknown but physically present.[146] Despite the biological presence of his Indianness, Zits explains, "There's this law called the Indian Child Welfare Act that's supposed to protect half-breed orphans like me. . . . My Indian daddy gave me his looks, but he was never legally established as my father. Since I'm not a legal Indian, the government can put me wherever they want."[147] The inability of the government to uphold the ICWA in the case of Zits by placing him with a Native family points to how the ICWA is unevenly enforced. Briggs explains that "many children who might be readily identified as 'racially' Indian are not covered by ICWA."[148] Not classifying "half-breed" children like Zits as "'racially' Indian" works in the favor of the state because it becomes a way to restrict Native kinship and futurity. Briggs states that "many states kept no statistics on the percentage of their foster care population that was Indian . . . [and] many Native kids passed into foster, institutional, or even adoptive care outside the legal system and hence would not have turned up in the statistical picture."[149] While Zits identifies as Native, is seen and treated as Native by others, and sees his Indianness as a crucial role to his identity in the text, he is documented as white; the state erases his Indianness legally. This erasure is the first step toward eliminating the Native child's potential for Native futurity.

We get an early glimpse of the disappearance of Native reproductivity when Zits reflections on his own conception. He says, "I remember my mother and father slow-dancing to that Blood, Sweat & Tears song . . . I remember how they conceived me that night. Okay, I don't exactly remember it. I can't see my mother and father naked in bed."[150] While Zits often "remembers" what he is "not supposed to," he is unable to imagine this scene, making the imagining of Indian reproduction and sexual pleasure unable to be realized.[151] While Zits's physical appearance acts as proof of Native reproductivity, this exclusion of his father's reproductive power as well as its omission from his memory assist in the disappearance of Native sexuality, which has implications for Native reproduction and thus futurity.

In the text, Zits travels through time and inhabits a different body during each time period he visits. One of these bodies that Zits inhabits is the Native father whom he has never met; occupying this body is the catalyst for disavowing the Native body. When Zits suddenly realizes that he "[is his] father," he "force[s] hi[s father's mind] to remember" the birth of Zits.[152] Recalling this memory brings Zits as his father to the realization that "somewhere on this floor, my mother is giving birth to me. But my father cannot be a participant. He cannot be a witness. He cannot be a father."[153] Zits removes his father from both the scene of his birth and the performance of his birth. Taylor states that the "French etymological root [of 'perform' is] . . . 'to complete.'"[154] Native reproductive capabilities are rendered impotent in this moment: the Native father's ability to carry on a Native future will remain "incomplete." The possibilities for the Native body to exist in the future are extinguished.

Time travel functions to eliminate Zits's Native origins by removing his father from the scene of his birth. When he returns to the present, this elimination enables him to experience a white rebirth. This white rebirth begins with finding a white father. Zits turns himself in for a crime to a police officer, Dave. While Zits inhabited his father's body, he walked around repeating, "I want some respect."[155] In an interaction with Dave, he says, "Officer Dave . . . I want you to know that I respect you."[156] In giving "respect" to Dave, Zits grants the desire of the Indian father to the white police officer, reappropriating fatherhood from the Native to the white man. Zits painfully participates in the extinction of Native fatherhood and reproduction and the sustaining of white fatherhood. As the child, he is the future; as a "half-breed" child, he has the burden of determining whether this future is his white "half" or his Indian "half"—the extrication of the child from kinship and extinguishing of past ties increase the stakes of the child's decisions and movements. The settler production and valuation of the individual are critically at play. The Native father has already birthed Zits, and Zits helps to retroactively erase Native fatherhood. In doing so, Zits erases his own Indianness—he has "inherited" his Indianness from his father, but he extricates himself from his inheritance when he transfers paternal power from the Native father to the white authoritative male.

While relatives of Dave adopt Zits, this act solidifies the impossibility of Native futurity. Officer Dave tells Zits that he will be adopted, and Dave introduces the information to Zits by saying, "You're going to die . . . you are going to die."[157] While Officer Dave's use of "to die" might imply a death from happiness, it still frames Zits's adoption as one that will result in a death—this is the modern-day version of "kill the Indian." A white man commands this death, and Zits accepts the death imposed on him: "So I'm going to die."[158] Officer Dave narrates the imminent death of Zits's Native self, but Zits has to accept this mandate.

Zits's white rebirth completes the prophecy that "he will die." Officer Dave's brother and sister-in-law are the couple that will adopt Zits, and Dave tells Zits that they "always wanted a baby," regressing Zits to a pre-Native infancy.[159] They revert Zits to a temporal space where revision is possible. This reversion is partly necessary because of a desire that Officer Dave has to "go back in time."[160] In his early days as a police officer, Dave reported to a home where he found two white babies who had been drowned in a bathtub. This death of white offspring has haunted Dave over the years. Zits worries that Officer Dave will always "look at [him] and see him as those two babies," who were white and whom he could not "keep . . . safe."[161] Officer Dave has been unable to escape this traumatic recurrence in his life; however, by incorporating Zits into his extended family, he can transform Zits into a white child whom he *can* "keep safe." This incorporation halts the repetition of his traumatic past, thus enabling him to move forward into the future—the memory of white death can be replaced by the existence of a surviving white child. While Dave's brother is officially adopting Zits, Dave "is going to take care of [Zits], too . . . [Zits] needs as many fathers as possible."[162] Zits comes to occupy a space in this new family that necessitates him to be white, and becoming a white child enables white male virility.

The final scene of the text further sets the stage for his white (re) creation. The morning of his rebirth, Blood, Sweat & Tears plays on his radio, linking this morning with his original conception during which the song also played. This return to his conception creates space for his birth to be revised. Mary, his adoptive mother, takes on this revision when she gives him acne cream, stating that "a few months from now, you'll be brand new."[163] Zits will be made "[a]new" in this new family through a removal of his Native physicality. The final remnants of his father, his "inherited" zits, will disappear. The white family can revise his body, and this revision preserves white futurity by making Native present and thus futurity "vanish." Zits's "half-breed" status is undone; in being made new, there is potential for him to be made wholly white. This elimination of his "half" Native self is necessary if he is to enter the future with this family. The Native body cannot move forward in time.

Mary begins the process of Indian removal, and Zits completes this removal by renaming himself. When Mary gives him the acne cream, he recognizes the "beginning[s]" on which he is embarking, and says, "Michael . . . my real name is Michael. Please, call me Michael."[164] Vine Deloria argues that "time has an usual limitation. It must begin and end at real points, or it must be conceived as cyclical in nature."[165] Zits's story opens with, "Call me Zits . . . that's not my *real* name, of course. My *real* name isn't important";[166] he concludes the narrative by stating, "My *real* name is Michael."[167] He asks to be called Michael after he is "begin- ning to think . . . beginning to think . . . beginning to think," marking his conclusion as a "beginning" that ends on this "real name," and thus "real point."[168] This name supplants the nickname that literalized his Native physicality. This move, then, establishes the conclusion of *Flight* as a beginning of settler linear time. A new time with a real beginning is established, and this establishment disavows Native time for a white-settler conception of time, which extinguishes Native futurity.

Thus, *Flight* resolves the issue of the Native body through violently making it disappear. The physical markers of Zits's Indianness are shed; he will be "brand new" in white skin. The death of the Native father, the proliferation of the white father, and the removal of Native physicality ensure that there is no room for Native resistance in this system. The foster care system deals with the vestiges of sexual orphanings—the Native body—through a violent assimilation. Lisa Lowe explains, "What we know as 'race' or 'gender' are the *traces* of . . . modern humanist forgetting. They reside within, and are constitutive of, the modern narrative of freedom but are neither fully determined by nor exhausted by its ends. They are the remainders of the formalism of affirmation and forgetting."[169] Indianness as a racialized category is a "trace" of the "forgetting" of colonization. Texts like *Flight* force readers to remember how this racialization process has been produced and reconfigured in order to meet the state's desires. Zits has no Indianness to remember as a result of state-sanctioned child removal. Despite Zits's ability to literally travel across time and space, he cannot alter "what could have been." *Flight* calls for an understanding of the genocidal production of Indianness as a race to eliminate Native queer childhood as a temporal form and absorb it into white futurity. Colonization gets "forgotten" through viewing Indianness as solely a racial category but must be remembered in order to shift from "what could have been" to "what can be."

Epilogue

What's My Damage? On Attachments to Queer Theory

Why Is This a Queer Project? Answer 1

When I began this project my chapters were organized by institution type—that is, reform schools, schools for children with disabilities, African American industrial schools, and Native American boarding schools. Part of this impulse was to mimic the historical establishment of these schools into types—schools were distinct in the populations they served, and I did not want to collapse these divisions. Furthermore, I wanted to do justice to the experiences of these children and not subsume them all under the category of "marginalized" or "other." Although many of these schools emerged in the same historical moment and were often established and funded by persons with similar progressive agendas, they each have their own relationships to histories of racism, eugenics, and colonization, as well as different resonances in the contemporary moment.

The bigger rationale for this taxonomy, though, was so that I could precisely examine the contours of "queer" in each institution. I did not want (or anticipate) my arguments to be analogous or for the queering processes to look parallel in each school. I wanted to think about how "queer" intersected with each chapter differently depending on the histories and fields needed to understand an institution type—so, for example, I was interested in how queer and Indigenous studies (as well as queer Indigenous studies) interacted in chapter 5, while chapter 3 examines how queer theory bears on this disability history and literature. Queer studies has long been in tension with Black studies, disability studies, and Indigenous studies in part because of its tendency to erase, dismiss, and subsume with its impulse to queer all the things.

Queer theory imagines itself to be a field of resistance, but when other fields push back, it brooks no resistance. Queer theory charges forth, sometimes deferring to the limitless capacities of "queer" to obscure its dominating tendencies.

The field of queer studies emerged out of minoritarian fields, and it has been in an oppositional relationship with these fields since its institutionalization in the early 1990s. While "queer" resists demarcation and boundaries, other minoritarian fields have long been asking whether queer needs some limits. Calling for such limits need not impede productive engagement across fields; rather, it is simply to insist on the significance of history and context.

Would this insistence un-queer the field? In 1993, Judith Butler defined the "queer" of queer theory as that which has to "remain . . . in the present, never fully owned, but always and only redeployed, twisted, queered from a prior usage and in the direction of urgent and expanding political purposes."[1] These other fields are asking—and have been asking—if queer's commitment to staying "in the present" has obscured histories, overdetermined the contours and future of the field, and participated in the "hierarchizing mission of higher education."[2] Is queer as limitless as the field posits when it continues to reproduce hierarchies and unevenly confer value on knowledge production? Is disciplinary kinship with other fields always destined for generational impasses, rifts, erasures, and gatekeeping? What happens when queer's "present" has now been decades long? How might new generations of scholars "redeploy and twist" queer when the material possibilities of pursuing this work are increasingly diminished with the adjunctification of faculty labor, austerity measures that defund programs supporting queer work, and political campaigns to defund and delegitimize queer and queer-adjacent work across educational institutions? How does tapping queer's potential relate to, exacerbate, and/or respond to restrictive material conditions for exploring and pursuing knowledge?

As this project progressed, I realized that my neat taxonomy of institution type was anything but. There was significant crossover in these institutions. For example, children in reform schools could be transferred to industrial schools if they modeled improvement. Children in reform schools could be transferred to state hospitals and sterilized if they failed to improve. While the institutions looked different on paper, the experiences, depictions, and practices within could, at times, be indistinct from one site to the next. Schools separated children by race, gender, and ability; but racialized, criminalized, and disabled children have shared experiences of bodily management, labor training, and quotidian sexual violence across institution type, and racialized, criminalized, and disabled queer childhoods have produced what appear as gendered and sexual identities formed through and defined by loss, deferral, disavowal, and restriction. Queering processes resonate across populations of children, and my delineation of the queering process specific to each school (displacing home, internalized sterilization, contaminating sexualities, and sexual orphanings) could be interchangeable. Is this an inevitable outcome of filtering these histories through a queer lens? Or does a queer lens allow one to bridge fields and histories that the state and its institutions have attempted to keep separate?

On one hand, my attempts to be intersectional actually reified identities, and the organization of this project may have obscured (or at least made harder to disentangle) other ways to draw connections across these institutions and bridge queered disabled, criminalized, and racialized children. On the other hand, this project is true to queer theory's origins, whether one traces it through feminist of color critique or gay male activism or the sociology of deviance—queer as deeply linked to damage. Heather Love writes that "acknowledging damage—and incorporating it—was crucial to the turn to queer politics and queer studies in the 1980s."[3] The damage that these institutions attempted to incur was deeply queer—it was tied to children's experiences and understandings of their sexualities, invested in punishing homosexuality, and key in shaping children's potential, mitigated futures. Is sexual damage enough justification for viewing these histories alongside one another? Material damage—of genocide, institutionalization, subjugation—cannot be undone. Can queer theory provide tools and roadmaps for exploring damage without qualifying it as resistance, pleasure, or productive? Do these histories and presents dwarf the power of any potential, or does the scale of erotics still hold? This project is invested in illuminating actual and epistemological damage done by the state without reinscribing damage through imposing queer theory. This may be an impossible project.

Why Is This a Queer Project? Answer 2

The ghosts of gay children haunt queer theory; queer theory is haunted by the ghosts of queer theorists. Imagined personal attachments to dead queer figures have been an animating force in queer theory. Which queer figures are available for attachments? Are these attachments fantasy, material, both, something else? How do these attachments function particularly in the field of queer theory, which claims to be anti-teleological, anti-oedipal, and anti-elitist, while also seeking institutional security, advancement, and recognition? Can imagined personal attachments enable solidarities, community, and theorizing? Or do they calcify limited genealogies that narrow the scope of queer theory's possibilities? Are romanticization and fetishization at play in these attachments, critical and otherwise, and are those bad things? What is queer work without attachments, good and bad, healthy and toxic, institutionally recognized and perverse, material and delusional, generative and destructive?

Forging intimacies with the dead has been a critical and generative enterprise for queer theory since its founding moment—exemplified by Sedgwick herself. In the midst of the AIDS crisis in 1993, Sedgwick opened one of the founding texts of queer theory, *Tendencies*, with the claim that the deaths of queer youth were the "motive" for "everyone who does gay and lesbian studies."[4] Sedgwick also imagined herself as part of a generation of scholars who were themselves metaphorized queer children— queers stuck in a state of perpetual arrested development shunned by social, professional, and political worlds. Nonetheless, Sedgwick saw herself and her colleagues as accessing a future unavailable to dead queer youth—doing queer work was a way for Sedgwick and company to "keep faith with vividly remembered promises made to ourselves in childhood," a move that elided the past child self and a generation of dead queer youth in an effort to establish the field and justify its advancement.[5]

Sedgwick continues to shape queer theory, and she has been an available figure for critical attachment and cathexis from a new generation of queer scholars who have only known an academy after Eve. Eve Sedgwick died April 12, 2009. I took my first undergraduate class that taught queer theory a few months after her death, in fall 2009. Rather, this fall 2009 course was my first conscious encounter with queer theory—in a discussion that semester on Jo March's tomboy identity in *Little Women*,

I raised my hand with that combination of confidence and naïveté only a sincere sophomore could have when I said, "This reminds me of something I read in my Renaissance Literature class. I don't know if you've heard of this person, Judith Butler, but she has this idea about gender performance that seems connected." My professor didn't sneer at or condescend to me. Modeling generosity and seeing me in my context—enthusiastic, desperate for teacherly attention, closeted, and without attachment, proper or otherwise, to this academic figure—she invited me to share about the Judith person to the class.

Later that semester the same professor invited me to apply for a summer fellowship where I could pursue a funded humanities research project. With her help and building on themes that interested me in her course, I proposed a project on studying orphans in children's literature who I wanted to read as queer. It was during this summer I first encountered Eve Sedgwick. Her essay "How to Bring Your Kids Up Gay" was transformative and showed me that there was a whole world of theorizing available for thinking about childhood sexuality and specifically childhood queerness. I felt like I was getting away with something illicit—using the college's money, which felt exorbitant to me then (and still would now), to read and understand characters in canonical and beloved children's books as queer and to further read the violences undergirding their queerness. All the characters, I would argue, are wrested of their queerness by the texts' ends through harmful homophobic mentorship from queer adults in their lives that left the cherubic conclusion of each text coexisting with a queer haunting, dead child lesbians abounding. Years before reading *Tendencies* and Sedgwick's motive for doing gay and lesbian studies (but seventeen years after Sedgwick asserted it), I was also haunted by dead gay children.

My professor told me this could be a career, and it was at that point I started to learn a little bit about what academia is and what professors do (besides emotional labor for emerging homosexuals). When she told me what PhD programs were and that I might be able to get into one with funding, my jaw dropped. I didn't know there were funded ways to obtain a postgraduate degree, and I didn't realize research could be a career. I was told in very explicit terms to have no attachments to geography or stability, economic or otherwise, during graduate school or the time after if this is what I decided to do. Most of my fundamental attachments at this point were structured by asymptotic impossibilities, so this didn't seem to be a problem. I was a baby dyke peacefully resigned to her isolation and unfulfilled connections. (Queer theory would later teach me that this is the condition of the spinster.) I wasn't interested in what I *wouldn't have* by pursuing queer theory as a career. I could only hear all that would be possible and that I could maybe eke out a living if I wasn't attached to attachment.

Around this time, my professor connected me with her other literature student in this summer fellowship cohort, who already had a rich relationship to queer theory and was eager to introduce me to more. Our friendship blossomed as the next academic year started. In my Methods to Literary Studies class that fall, I was excited to see Sedgwick on the syllabus, only to feel bereft when I learned that she had recently died. Coming into the field meant beginning to forge attachments with the living, breathing humans behind the articles I read—the author is dead, I was learning, but I was learning this interpretive mode at the same time I was understanding that these authors who were writing the scholarship I was voraciously devouring are (or were, or still linger) very much here. Joan Lubin recounts a similar discovery in an essay for *Post45* reflecting on *Gender Trouble* at thirty—upon discovering Lauren Berlant's blog SuperValent around the same time I found out Eve had died, Lubin recalls, "It had not occurred to me that texts had authors, that academics were people, that blogs had content. I mistook it for a diary, not knowing that the ordinary was available for analysis."[6]

In our class meeting on *Epistemology of the Closet*, my professor mentioned offhand that there was a bench dedicated to Eve in Madison Square Park in New York. The next week I visited the bench when I commuted to New York for my Tuesday therapy appointment, an obligation I fulfilled out of both necessity and attachment. That night, I was telling my friend about the bench (as one does), and she told me about an event honoring Eve earlier that year, the text of which was on Lauren Berlant's blog: "You have to read this beautiful one about cheese by Berlant." She emailed it to me:

IV. Cheese
 Once we [Lauren Berlant and Eve Sedgwick] discovered that we'd be landing in a small airport at the same time to pick up connecting flights.

So we met at the food court for lunch. It was after her first round of chemo. As I entered she was already laying in heartily to a double bacon cheeseburger and fries. I tend toward the ascetic, but I am always scavenging for relief from my "predictable choreography" by imagining what it might do to assume the form of other people's guesses at living. But still: at that time I was sure that if *I'd* had cancer, I would defend against future shame and vulnerability by adopting an astringent regime of eating the right diet and doing the right things and becoming pure for the future in reparation for the past. I said, I guess *you're* not doing that, and she said no, she thought her health would flourish more if she had fidelity to her pleasures. I loved her for this, and I am still learning it.[7]

We were profoundly moved by this passage, and particularly the line about Eve having "fidelity to her pleasures." At this point in time, I was engaged in a multiyear struggle with the facts and material reality of having a body, having a gendered body, having a sexual body, and the Venn diagram of all those. This field of queer theory—and this sociality enabled by queer theory—was offering me relief, giving me language and discourse and modes of not just thinking but being, that felt like it created some space, some breathing room for the very tight, very rigid structures of existence I permitted for myself. My affective and social life to that point had been very much structured by shame, self-destruction, punishment, and disavowal of even having a body—a desire for "purity" and "astringency" that manifested in and as a very intense, anxious young adult. Looking back, I see how these are all the features of queer theory (and pretty much most queer theorists). But what's striking to me in retrospect is that while these features were perhaps preconditions for my entry into the field, that was not what attracted me to the field and its figures, like Eve; instead, it was flourishing, pleasure, heartiness, and community. I saw a future. I even started to have desire for one. It was a romanticized one, yes, but one where I saw that maybe there was space—not just for my mind but maybe, too, for my body.

Inspired by Berlant's reflection, some members of our little summer fellowship cohort started ordering takeout once a week. We would get veggie burgers from a local spot and began calling these evenings Eve Sedgwick Burger Night. The motto of these evenings had become F2OP, "fidelity to our pleasures," transforming Berlant's description of Eve's—

"her pleasures"—into a collective statement, a description, an imperative, and an aspiration.

In 2013, I completed my first year of graduate school and wanted to commemorate the moment—which wasn't about a year of the profession under my belt but rather about beginning to inhabit a new rhythm. I finally understood that the cruelly optimistic pace I had been operating at wasn't sustainable for a future in the profession, and I radically recalibrated, finding space for pleasure, community, and queer sociality—which were still coexistent with pain, shame, and hardship, particularly in my body, but the ratios had started to shift incrementally yet dramatically. I chose to commemorate this work with a tattoo (right at the height of the surface reading debates!) that reads "fidelity to our pleasures." Getting this tattoo was about a fantastical attachment to Eve routed through Berlant, but it was also commemorating the community I was being continually regifted in a very queerly reproductive fashion. I came of age in the field being trained by persons shaped by the loss of their colleague, whose careers were, in part, enabled by the paths Sedgwick forged. The figure of Eve enabled so many lateral relationships and what would become lateral relationships as my mentors transformed into colleagues and friends and I connected with scholars across time and space; forming attachments *with* Eve enabled present-day attachments *through* Eve. I was involved in many of "Eve's triangles," but also quadrangles and octagons and other dimensions entirely.[8]

I would not be here if not for the idealized attachments that defined my coming of age and "professionalization." At the moment I encountered it, queer theory gave me language, genealogy, and the possibility of a future. The field gave me not just the theorizing but the tools for survival. From my position now, I am certainly disillusioned by how the field can at times seem to see itself as strictly a "disruptive cog within the system rather than a producer of 'palace discourses.'"[9] But something I remind myself when teaching is that my students are encountering these concepts, often for the first time, at a critical moment in their growth and applying it to their lives: someone learning that given family doesn't have to be the predominant or privileged mode of belonging, or a student who has never felt safe in their body being given a language for understanding how that individual pathologized feeling could be an effect of structure. These are moments that *do* open up lifeworlds.

That doesn't erase or undo other damaging effects of the field or the institutions in which they're encountered. But the micro-moments of connection, understanding, and engagement—from professors, texts, classmates, colleagues—have had incalculable impacts on the way my life has unfolded and the work I've been able to do, and I continue to see those play out every day.

I feel somewhat hesitant recounting my narrative of this privileged entry (albeit likely fairly normative of those who experienced queer theory at institutions of "Rich Queer Studies") into the field and the extent of my attachments to Sedgwick.[10] I feel I am exposing a cringe-worthy but honest trajectory of how I've arrived at a queer project, institutionally and affectively. Idealization got me here, but it is not the only animating force behind my work. In her contribution to the *GLQ* twenty-fifth anniversary issue, Chase Gregory reflects on some of these, at times, paradoxical and complicated affective spaces inhabited by what she calls the "third generation" of queer theorists:

> I like reading "Queer Bonds" because it affirms things that I feel but am embarrassed to admit: namely, the power of the bonds that structure this field. . . . Here are some of the things these academic and pedagogical bonds can feel like/can be: mentorship, friendship, rivalry, embarrassment, flirtation, celebrity stalking, the family romance, regular romance, acting, spectating, capitalist exploitation, coaching, having a nemesis, having an uncle, awkwardness, debt, networking, pen pal correspondence, hatred, love, uncertainty, failure, anger, exchange, ambivalence. I am only six years out of college, and that means that right now I still negotiate what it means when my academic bonds, now a decade old, shift from mentorship into collegiality.[11]

What I love about this list—a very Sedgwickian method—is that, in listing, there isn't a hierarchization of any of these bonds over the other. One might want to impute value saying some of these are better than others, but this is a descriptive list that captures the many frequent, sometimes ephemeral, sometimes overlapping modes one might inhabit as one navigates the multiple and ever shifting and inevitable socialities and attachments—not good, not bad, but inevitable—that emerge in and beyond professional and institutional spaces.

Love described a similar shifting in a reflection on Sedgwick. Love refers to Sedgwick's essay on paranoid and reparative reading and notes "the oddness of the direct address in [Sedgwick's] essay's subtitle: 'You're so paranoid, you probably think this essay is about you.' It's true, I do. So what next?"[12] While there is the plural possibility of the "you"—Sedgwick "could be speaking to anyone"—Love takes "the title personally." Reading herself in the title, in part, enables a somewhat uncomfortable intimacy; it's an "exposure" that is "damning" and "embarrassing."[13] It also reveals Sedgwick's deployment of paranoid method.

Love's reading also enables a new type of relation—with Sedgwick herself. Sedgwick's address is one of teacher to student, but Love is "the teacher now."[14] Love recounts the realization that "my pedagogical crushes have finally migrated inside the text."[15] Here, Love's position as teacher has made those teachers with whom she wanted to form intimacy exist in a different form; the intimacy of the student-teacher relationship transitions to an intimacy between teacher and text: the essay that is "about you" and the newly realized "teacher and teacher." Ultimately, Love reads Sedgwick as calling "to deidealize what must be the most idealized relationship, for many of us in queer studies: the relation between student and teacher."[16] Recognizing being shamed through a paranoid method of exposure is, ultimately, the deidealization that Love states is ultimately that which can bond. Love says that "recognizing that it is not only reparation but damage at work in Sedgwick's late essays will let us begin the hard work of deidealization. And that's love too."[17]

I've been trying to reflect on what exactly my attachment to Sedgwick—and, by extension, queer theory—is and if it's an idealization. Kadji Amin has observed how "a Queer Studies without idealization would not be Queer Studies at all," while urging practitioners to adopt deidealization as a mode that opens up sites, objects, methods, and figures that aren't necessarily aligned with liberation, affirmation, futurity, and political value.[18] My idealization of the figure of Eve was an attachment from a position I became very accustomed to and comfortable with as an early closeted queer: fantasy, imagination, and longing for that which cannot be. It was also enabled by a mixture of privilege, capital, luck, and being in the right place at the right time. My relationship with Sedgwick the scholar is, in some ways, deidealized. I engage with, critique, and build on her work regularly in my own research, trying to create economic and social futures for myself in an ever-increasing landscape of precarity, austerity, and the neoliberalization of higher education. I don't know what the line, if any, is between Eve the figure and Sedgwick the scholar, and if I'm truly oscillating between idealizing and deidealizing modes. I want to say I am post-idealization, but the tattoo remains, the body remains, and the work to be done remains. There are queer times to be inhabited, forged through damage, coexisting with damage, and perhaps at times incurring more damage.

ACKNOWLEDGMENTS

The critical energy against institutions in this project stems from a belief that institutions are not top-down, overdetermining forces but have the capacity to be shaped and reshaped—and perhaps even queered—by those who constitute and inhabit them, whether by choice or coercion (or some ambivalent space outside of that framework). I am indebted to the many institutions, communities within institutions, and people who compose those communities who have sustained and supported me across the many phases of this project with their generosity, friendship, and patience. I will do everything I can to pay it forward.

Many thanks to everyone at NYU Press who has helped to strengthen, shepherd, and shore up this project, especially Ann Pellegrini, Joshua Takano Chambers-Letson, Tavia Nyong'o, Eric Zinner, and Furqan Sayeed. I am grateful to the external readers, whose provocations helped me to critically address and develop key issues of the project.

The research in this project was generously supported by fellowships and grants from the University of Pittsburgh as well as the University of Pennsylvania's Fontaine Society, School of Arts and Sciences, and Gender, Sexuality, and Women's Studies Program. Many thanks to the librarians and archivists at the Library of Virginia and Manassas Museum for their help and patience. I am grateful to those who worked to preserve, digitize, and make accessible online holdings from the Carlisle Industrial School and Perkins School for the Blind.

I had the opportunity to share different iterations of this work with Penn English's Gender and Sexuality Studies Reading Group; Penn's Gender, Sexuality, and Women's Studies Graduate Colloquium; a dissertation writing group convened by David Kazanjian including Clare Mullaney, Laura Soderberg, Najnin Islam, Jazmín Delgado, Ana Schwartz, Evelyn Soto, and Alex Eisenthal; the School of Humanities at Penn State Harrisburg; a colloquium at the University of Pittsburgh's Humanities Center with responses by Jules Gill-Peterson and Mark Paterson; and panels at conferences for ASAP, ACLA, ASA, MLA, NWSA, and C19. I am grateful for the rich feedback and incisive insights I received from all of these audiences. I shared a chapter draft with my seminar led by Ivy Schweitzer at the 2016 Futures of American Studies Institute—many thanks to the wonderful Jack Gieseking, Hannah Bailey, Joshua Bartlett, Grant Palmer, Robin Smith, Chen Chen, Daniel Grace, Eun-hae Kim, and the late Jeanine Ruhsam.

At the University of Pennsylvania I was part of a brilliant community of scholars who buoyed and buttressed me at every turn. Heather Love pushed me to stretch the bounds of my critical thinking and has provided an incomparable model for how to be a generous and kind scholar. David Kazanjian taught me to "say yes to the text" and to always bring precision to my analyses and prose. Nancy Bentley has been a supportive and insightful resource for this research. Melissa Sanchez's belief in and engagement with this work helped me pursue and clarify many of the project's animating questions. Sharrona Pearl's wisdom and friendship continue to inspire me (as does her amazing family). I am also thankful to Michael Gamer, Paul Saint-Amour, Julia Bloch, Ian Petrie, Lance Wahlert, Jim English, Melanie Adley, Demie Kurz, Nancy Hirschmann, Anne Esacove, Luz Marin, and Amy Jordan for their support during my time at Penn.

A postdoctoral fellowship at the University of Pittsburgh's Humanities Center gave me a fantastic community in which to engage this research. Thank you to Jonathan Arac—his confidence in my work has meant the world to me, and I am grateful for his model of kindness, leadership, and critical engagement. I was lucky to be affiliated with Pitt's Gender, Sexuality, and Women's Studies and Children's Literature Programs; many thanks to Courtney Weikle-Mills, Todd Reeser, Nancy Glazener, Rachel Kranson, and Scott Kiesling for their support during my fellowship. Before Pitt, Vanderbilt's Women's and Gender Studies Program was a terrific home in which to research and teach, with especial thanks to Katie Crawford and Elizabeth Covington.

I completed this project at Penn State Harrisburg, where the School of Humanities and Program in American Studies have provided camaraderie, resources, and a fantastic atmosphere to work. I would like to especially thank my school director, Jeff Beck, and my three chairs, Anne Verplanck, John Haddad, and Anthony Buccitelli, for their leadership, guidance, and mentorship. Many thanks, too, to Ellen Stockstill, Jeff Tolbert, Charlie Kupfer, Jen Hirt, Catherine Rios, David Witwer, Emily MacLeod, Mariah Kupfner, Laura Feibush, Hannah Lair, Stephanie Winklejohn Black, and Jeremy Boorum.

I was first hailed as a literary and queer scholar by members of the Bryn Mawr College English Department, and I am forever indebted to them for helping me gain access to a future I didn't think was available to me. Bethany Schneider and Kate Thomas are superb mentors and marvelous friends who have taught me more than they will ever know (beyond canasta). I am also grateful to Jennifer Harford Vargas, Jamie Taylor, Sharon Ullman, Gail Hemmeter, Jen Callaghan, Jane Hedley, Anne Bruder, Raima Evan, and the late Karen Tidmarsh.

Beth Freeman, Sharon Marcus, Anna Mae Duane, Sarah Chinn, Robin Bernstein, Rebekah Sheldon, Kathryn Bond Stockton, Jules Gill-Peterson, Mark Rifkin, Scott Herring, Lindsey Reckson, Matt Brim, Lucia Hodgson, and Allison Giffen have been generous and generative editors, respondents, and/or reviewers of my work, and I have learned so much from their examples. I am grateful for opportunities to have presented alongside and/or exchanged work with Jacob Breslow, Thomas Dichter, Brie Owen, Ilana Larkin, Amy Fish, E. Feinman, Halle Singh, and Phil Nel.

I am grateful for the friendship of Omari Weekes, Patrick McKelvey, SaraEllen Strongman, Julia Cox, Rachel Corbman, and Ashley Cohen. My life (and text threads) would be dull and unmerry without them.

I am lucky my paths crossed with Liz Reich. Her utterly dazzling brain pushed this project to new heights. I would not have gotten to this point without her enthusiasm, crankiness, and queer kinship.

I finished this project while settling into a rich life in Harrisburg. Many thanks to everyone at Harrisburg Area Roller Derby (HARD), who push me (literally and figuratively) to take up more space and motivated me to get this project done so I could skate more! Love to Yay or Neighbors and the community at Chaka CrossFit. Many thanks to Barry Loveland and the LGBT Center of Central PA's History Project.

There are too many people to thank across institutions, times, and spaces, and the following list is incomplete. In no particular order and perhaps in the Sedgwickian method of nonce taxonomies, many thanks to Susan Balée, Don James McLaughlin, Benjamin Brown, Will Clark, Kersti Francis, Sierra Lomuto, Aundeah Kearney, Laura Soderberg, Margaret Galvan, Jack Gieseking, Mairead Sullivan, Anthony Petro, David Tenorio, Serena Rivera, Aaron Goldsman, Aaron Winslow, Clare Mullaney, Kami Bates, Melanie Adley, Jason Fitzgerald, Ittai Orr, Kate Severance, Brittney Thornburley, Ray Bailey, Alessandra Lembo, Lily Scott, Rachel Roepke, Nicole Gervasio, Davy Knittle, Ben Stanley, Jess Shollenberger, Joan Lubin, Dianne Mitchell, Didem Uca, Julia Dauer, Alicia Meyer, Matty Hemming, Riley McGuire, Shona Adler, Mayelin Perez, Najnin Islam, Travis Chi Wing Lau, Sara Sligar, Sal Nicolazzo, Elias Rodriques, Eleni Palis, Keyana Parks, Evelyn Soto, Ana Schwartz, Kevin Gotkin, Sunny Yang, Marina, Bilbija, Alice McGrath, Tim Griffiths, Erin Loughran, Leona Casella, Michaela Ablon, Theresa Dougherty, Molly Wolfe, Claire Pizzurro, Laura Quigley, Manuel Lopez, Christina Lovaglio, Pete Lovaglio, Donna Miele, Nick Miele, Rocky, Molly, and Lily.

Many thanks to my parents, ZMan and Maggie, for the enormous sacrifices they have made for my education. I appreciate my siblings, John and Annie, and my brother-in-law, JJ, for helping to instill and maintain my arguably healthy competitive drive. My Aunt Pat always supported my love of reading, from which this project ultimately stems. The Convent of the Sacred Heart community nurtured the gifts that have enabled me to do this work. I am thrilled to include my nephew and niece in these acknowledgments—Michael Roch and Catherine Patricia have invited me to question a few (but certainly not all) of my ideas about the Child.

Queer Childhoods includes versions of the following previously published work:

1) "Queering Black Girlhood in the Virginia Industrial School," *Signs: Journal of Women in Culture and Society* 45, no. 2 (Winter 2020): 373–94—a revised and expanded version of this article serves as the first chapter.
2) "Sexual Orphanings," *GLQ: A Journal of Lesbian and Gay Studies* 22, no. 4 (2016): 605–28—a revised and expanded version of this article serves as my fifth chapter, and some of the article's arguments appear in the introduction.
3) "Eve Sedgwick's Queer Children," *GLQ: A Journal of Lesbian and Gay Studies* 25, no. 1 (Winter 2019): 29–32—the opening paragraph appears in the introduction.

NOTES

INTRODUCTION

1 Edelman, *No Future*, 29.
2 Foucault, *History of Sexuality*.
3 Rubin, "Thinking Sex."
4 See hooks' *Ain't I a Woman*, Moraga's *Loving in the War Years*, Lorde's *Sister Outsider*, Anzaldúa's *Borderlands*, and Collins's "Meaning of Motherhood in Black Culture and Black Mother-Daughter Relationships."
5 Freeman, *Time Binds*, 83.
6 Sedgwick, *Tendencies*, 1.
7 For example, see Berlant's *Queen of America Goes to Washington City*; Bruhm and Hurley's *Curiouser*; Kent's *Making Girls into Women*; Abate's *Tomboys*; Stockton's *Queer Child*; Gilbert's *Sexuality in School*; the special "Child" issue of *WSQ*, edited by Chinn and Duane; the special "Child Now" issue of *GLQ*, edited by Gill-Peterson, Sheldon, and Stockton; Fischel's *Sex and Harm in the Age of Consent*; Gill-Peterson's *Histories of the Transgender Child*; Harkins's *Virtual Pedophilia*; Fielder's *Relative Races*; Breslow's *Ambivalent Childhoods*; Owen's *Queer History of Adolescence*; and Bradway and Freeman's *Queer Kinship*.
8 Cobb, "Childlike," 120.
9 Ibid., 119.
10 Ibid., 120.
11 Fawaz, "Stripped to the Bone," 363.
12 Stockton, *Queer Child*, 2.
13 Amar, "The Street, the Sponge, and the Ultra," 571.
14 In this way, queer theory's engagement with the child has mimicked larger cultural approaches to the child. James Kincaid argues that "the construction of the modern 'child' is very largely an evacuation" (*Erotic Innocence*, 16); children must be "evacuated" of sexuality in the cultural narratives to which adults subscribe so that children can become "a vacancy at the center of [a] story . . . controlled by our [adults'] fantasies" (4). Similarly, queer theory has "evacuated" its children, projecting onto and positioning them to serve the field's needs. Rebekah Sheldon more recently observed this dynamic, looking at ways that the child is made into a "resource" in a culture increasingly facing technological and ecological destruction—"the child as resource is freighted with expectations and anxieties about the future" (*Child to Come*, 3), pointing us to the ways that the child's link

to futurity is not just (or even at all) about hope but about other affective states that both reflect and increase the stakes of the child's signification.

15 Edelman, *No Future*, 2.

16 Muñoz, *Cruising Utopia*, 95.

17 Viego, *Dead Subjects*, 177.

18 Hurley, "Childhood and Its Discontents," 10.

19 Breslow, *Ambivalent Childhoods*, 4.

20 Ibid., 3.

21 Edelman, *No Future*, 29.

22 Chinn, "I Was a Lesbian Child," 160 and 161.

23 My project is certainly not the first to be using literary and historical cases to challenge Edelman's work but rather is part of a recent wave of queer scholarship that is critiquing the child with cases of children. For some examples, see Woubshet's "Epistles to the Dead" in *The Calendar of Loss* for his meditation on how Black children in African American literature challenge Edelman's opposition of child to queer and queer to futurity; Sheldon's analysis of the child beginning in the 1960s that focuses on how "the child's figuration of interlocking biological processes stands in the place of the complex systems at work in ecological materiality" (*Child to Come*, 5); and Soderberg's investigation of nineteenth-century childhoods that reveal how "the importance of childhood to the construction of the population did not extend protection to all children" (*Vicious Infants*, 12).

24 Halberstam, *In a Queer Time and Place*, 5.

25 Wexler, *Tender Violence*, 103.

26 Ibid., 107.

27 Carter, *Heart of Whiteness*, 2.

28 I am grateful to Melissa Sanchez and members of the 2015 Graduate Executive Committee in the University of Pennsylvania English Department (Emily Steinlight, Salamishah Tillet, and Nancy Bentley) for helping me to articulate this definition of queerness.

29 Some scholarship that constituted this turn includes Nealon's *Foundlings*; Edelman's *No Future*; Halberstam's *In a Queer Time and Place*; the special "Queer Temporalities" issue of *GLQ* edited by Freeman; Love's *Feeling Backward*; Muñoz's *Cruising Utopia*; Rohy's *Anachronism and Its Others*; Freeman's *Time Binds*; and Dinshaw's *How Soon Is Now?*

30 Berlant and Warner, "Sex in Public," 549.

31 Probyn, "Suspending Beginnings," 439.

32 Ibid., 440.

33 Chinn, "'I Was a Lesbian Child,'" 156 and 157.

34 Puar, *Terrorist Assemblages*, xix.

35 Keeling, *Queer Times, Black Futures*, 17.

36 Love, *Feeling Backward*, 6.

37 Ibid., 7.

38 While at first glance none of the children in my archives appear to immediately overlap with the trans archives that Jules Gill-Peterson elucidates in *Histories of the Transgender Child*, like the trans children in her study, those in *Queer Childhoods* were "subject to a regime of racially and gender normative governance by medical and other social institutions." Gill-Peterson notes that across the twentieth century, Black trans children were seen as "less deserving of care" (197) in comparison to their white counterparts in medical and clinical settings, making these children "subject . . . to potentially infinite detention in psychiatric facilities, as well as more literal forms of incarceration" (31). This reality "structurally barred" (197) Black trans children from entering and embodying trans futures. Gill-Peterson's discernment of these unlived futures across the twentieth century for Black trans youth suggests that reform schools and other carceral spaces explored in *Queer Childhoods* may have enrolled trans children (as well as gay, lesbian, and otherwise queer children) who were disciplined into apparent gender and sexual normativity.

39 Wiegman and Wilson, "Introduction," 4.

40 Ibid.

41 Gill-Peterson, Sheldon, and Stockton, "What Is the Now, Even of Then?," 497.

42 Keeling, *Queer Times, Black Futures*, ix.

43 Chambers-Letson, Nyong'o, and Pellegrini, "Foreword," xi.

44 Amin, *Disturbing Attachments*, 4.

45 Chambers-Letson, Nyong'o, and Pellegrini, "Foreword," x.

46 Ibid., xiv–xv.

47 Amin, *Disturbing Attachments*, 6.

48 Puar, *Terrorist Assemblages*, 22.

49 Ibid., 24.

50 Ibid., 24.

51 Katherine Franke explores this link between queer liberalism and racial subjugation in *Wedlocked*, examining how the gay "right to marry help[s] us better understand the stubborn, even indelible nature of racial stigma" (21). In other words, the promises of state recognition and protection by the state can be false ones—inhabiting white sexual norms cannot liberate you if you are not white. The history of marriage as a way to increase state surveillance and policing of African Americans after emancipation reveals how marriage is a right that "can both burden you and set you free" depending on your ability to inhabit white heterosexuality.

52 Love, *Feeling Backward*, 4.

53 Kunzel, "Situating Sex," 254.

54 Keeling observes how "salient critiques of the extent to which 'queer' has been domesticated and fixed along lines of sexuality, gender, class, ethnicity, and race in various national contexts remain unimportant because they address how the politics that grow out of the disturbances through which 'queer' has become perceptible might be responsible to those who presently might claim and/or be claimed by that category" (*Queer Times, Black Futures*, 17).

55 Amin, *Disturbing Attachments*, 8.

56 Ibid., 7–8.

57 Soderberg, *Vicious Infants*, 15.

58 Ibid., 15.

59 Hartman, "Venus in Two Acts," 11.

60 Puar, *Terrorist Assemblages*, 2.

61 Duane, "Introduction," 10.

62 Kazanjian, *Colonizing Trick*, 5.

63 Benjamin Kahan has examined the ways that women workers could be barred from employment in the nineteenth and early twentieth centuries—some professions "essentially required [women] to be single," so schools' emphasis on economic training privileged children's futures as workers, not as sexual or reproductive (*Celibacies*, 15).

64 Freeman, *Time Binds*, 19.

65 Ibid., 18.

66 Ibid., 18.

67 Eng, *Feeling of Kinship*, 8.

68 Schuller, *Biopolitics of Feeling*, 159.

69 Stockton, *Queer Child*, 8.

70 Bernstein has done work on how innocence is preserved for white children, while racialized, and particularly Black, children are viewed as incapable of that innocence and thus "exclu[ded] . . . from the category of childhood" (*Racial Innocence*, 16). Thus, the contours of racialized queer childhood differ depending on the child's race and other vectors of identity, an issue I grapple with throughout this book.

71 Stockton, *Queer Child*, 30.

72 Bruhm and Hurley, *Curiouser*, xiii.

73 Foucault, *Discipline and Punish*, 26 and 25.

74 Ibid., 131, 131, and 137.

75 Kahan, *Celibacies*, 3 and 4.

76 Schuller, *Biopolitics of Feeling*, 21.

77 Ibid., 136.

78 Ibid., 147.

79 Ibid., 11.

80 Ibid., 165.

81 Wexler, *Tender Violence*, 10.

82 Foucault, *History of Sexuality*, 11.

83 Briggs, *Taking Children*, 7 and 8.

84 Ibid., 12–13.

85 Fleetwood, *Marking Time*, 39.

86 Freeman, *Time Binds*, 3.

87 Ibid., xv.

88 Ibid., 3.

89 Keeling, *Queer Times, Black Futures*, 18.
90 Amin, *Disturbing Attachments*, 14.
91 Ahmed, *Queer Phenomenology*, 91.
92 Menon, *Indifference to Difference*, 123.
93 Bradway and Freeman, *Queer Kinship*, 2.
94 Ibid., 5.
95 Gill-Peterson, Sheldon, and Stockton, "What Is the Now, Even of Then?," 496.
96 Platt, *Child Savers*, 3.
97 Fass, "Foreword," vii.
98 McLachlan, *American Boarding Schools*, 254.
99 Ibid., 254.
100 Schools would, in theory, lead to expansive employment opportunities, while factories could lead only to menial labor. This vision, however, failed to recognize that the image of the machine was always at the heart of U.S. education. In Chief Justice Marshall's 1819 *Dartmouth v. Woodward* decision that authorized the existence of private educational institutions, he claimed that the institution was a corporation where "many persons . . . may act as a single individual . . . a perpetual succession of individuals are capable of acting for the promotion of the particular object like one immortal being" (*Trustees of Dartmouth College v. Woodward* 1819). Bethany Schneider points to this statement to argue that "the small liberal arts college is . . . the American corporation's eldest and dearest sibling" and that institutions, educational and otherwise, obsessed with preserving and repeating themselves "immortal[ly]" have had trouble figuring out how to incorporate "non-white, non-Christian, and non-male bodies" ("Pleasures and Frictions," 2). In other words, progressive imaginings of institutions as sites that could begin to welcome disenfranchised children were in tension with the "old boys' club" nature of their origin. And, as I will demonstrate, when institutions attempted to incorporate nonwhite, criminal, and disabled children, they functioned as holding cells that all but guaranteed limited economic opportunities for these students. Specialized boarding schools were not the only educational institutions that promised children an expansive economic future only to reveal that future as false. Many educational historians subscribe to the idea of schools, especially during the Progressive Era, as sites for reproduction of class under the guise of democracy and equal access. Willis's *Learning to Labor* explores the ways working-class students were trained to access a future predetermined by their socioeconomic status. Institutional force set them up to rebel, and this rebellion guaranteed their failure at social mobility or class accession.
101 Wexler, *Tender Violence*, 103.
102 Ibid., 52.
103 This was often the case not only for state-run institutions but also for institutions founded and/or run by private organizations, including those affiliated with religious institutions. Many schools either had an official religious affiliation or were, on paper, secular but nonetheless included a religious component in their

curriculum. For example, some state-run industrial schools for delinquent boys prided themselves on teaching these boys to memorize biblical verses. Thus, often more than one institution—that is, the church and state—colluded in their management of these populations in boarding schools.

104 Bellingham, "Institution and Family," S37.

105 Ibid., S42.

106 Cooper, *Autobiography of Citizenship*, 2.

107 Ibid., 3.

108 D'Emilio, "Capitalism and Gay Identity," 132.

109 Historian of deviance Bruce Bellingham names this "assumption of custody by the child savers to promote the child's moral control" ("Institution and Family," S48) as "philanthropic abduction" (S42).

110 Halberstam, *Queer Art of Failure*, 72.

111 When institutionalized, these children were essentially adopted by the state, and their marginal status meant that the adopter/adoptee relation was similar to the dynamics Jerng observes in *Claiming Others*, where adoptees have "neither a sense of continuity nor entry into a specific history that is one's own" (x) and embody the "crises in the reproduction and naturalization of norms of personhood at the conjunction of familial, national, and racial logics" (x–xi).

112 Gill-Peterson, Sheldon, and Stockton, "What Is the Now, Even of Then?," 496.

113 Wexler, *Tender Violence*, 149.

114 Ibid., 107.

115 Wexler explains that many were being trained for no future because "black farmers all over the South los[t] their land in a rapid downward spiral of tenancy, debt, and depression. Thousands more, migrating north, would find a market for their labor and skills not as independent small businessmen at all but as an increasingly degraded industrial workforce" (*Tender Violence*, 149). Progressive institutions enabled failure and subjugation of Black youth trained in industrial education.

116 Stoler, *Race and the Education of Desire*, vii.

117 Ibid., 7.

118 Soderberg, *Vicious Infants*, 4.

119 Ibid., 5.

120 Ibid., 12.

121 Ariès, *Centuries of Childhood*, 107.

122 Foucault, *History of Sexuality*, 26.

123 Ibid., 26.

124 Ibid., 27.

125 Ibid., 28.

126 Ibid., 104.

127 McLachlan, *American Boarding Schools*, 13.

128 Educational historian James McLachlan notes that nineteenth-century boarding schools were "modeled on idealized 'families' in which the child's 'natural depravity' could be suppressed and his 'naturally good' impulses carefully nurtured"

(*American Boarding Schools*, 13–14). In the first half of the nineteenth century, many of these schools had students attend class during the day on campus and live with families in the local community (47).

129 Edwards, "Private School in American Life," 280.
130 McLachlan, *American Boarding Schools*, 13.
131 Rayback, *History of American Labor*, 70.
132 McLachlan, *American Boarding Schools*, 122.
133 Althusser, "Ideology and Ideological State Apparatuses," 144–45.
134 Ibid., 155.
135 The history of the doctrine of *in loco parentis* dates back to 1765 in England and was used to describe the role of schools in the United States in 1826. For more on the history of the doctrine, see Hogan and Schwartz's "In Loco Parentis in the United States."
136 Althusser, "Ideology and Ideological State Apparatuses," 155.
137 Goffman, *Asylums*, xiii.
138 Ibid., 4–5.
139 Foucault, *History of Sexuality*, 101; Povinelli, *Empire of Love*, 7.
140 Alexander, *Pedagogies of Crossing*, 297 and 329.
141 Ibid., 329.
142 Bellingham, "Institution and Family," S35.
143 Foucault, *History of Sexuality*, 45.
144 Ibid., 96.
145 James, *Resilience and Melancholy*, 4.
146 Bellingham, "Institution and Family," S39.
147 British psychiatrist Lionel Penrose coined this term in 1939 to describe the inverse relationship between the numbers of persons occupying prisons and psychiatric hospitals in industrialized societies; that is, if prison populations are lower, hospital populations are higher, and vice versa ("Mental Disease and Crime"). It has since become more widely used in the medical and social work fields to explain how deinstitutionalization in the latter half of the twentieth century is more accurately understood as transinstitutionalization—attendees left one institution only to be admitted to another. Burch asserts that "histories of institutionalized people often are histories of people experiencing *transinstitutionalization*—the process of moving individuals from one variety of institution to another—as part of sustained containment, surveillance, and slow erasure" (*Committed*, 16).

1. FALSE PROMISES OF HETEROSEXUALIZATION
1 Ferguson, *Aberrations in Black*, 84.
2 Hartman, *Wayward Lives, Beautiful Experiments*, 28.
3 Berlant and Warner, "Sex in Public," 553.
4 Ferguson, "Of Our Normative Strivings," 92.
5 Ibid., 92.
6 Ibid., 96.

7 Agyepong, "Aberrant Sexualities," 272.

8 Gross and Hicks, "Introduction," 359.

9 Manion, "Gendered Ideologies of Violence, Authority, and Racial Difference," 13.

10 Estelle Freedman argues that training in domesticity for all incarcerated women helped to "regularize inmates' lives and to train them for proper womanly roles" and was imagined to be a "means of restoring femininity to the fallen" (*Their Sisters' Keepers*, 55 and 56). This training did not liberate but limited them: "Although they claimed their goal for each inmate, and each prison, was female self-sufficiency, they trained inmates for dependency in domestic employment and in other ways treated them as juveniles" (17). I'm interested in how this training differentially impacted Black juveniles who encountered it as part of an educational program in reform school.

11 The Virginia Industrial School was later known as the Peaks Industrial School and then the Janie Porter Barrett School. It was open to Black and white girls in 1968, became coeducational in 1972, and then became a rehabilitation program for boys in 1977 known as the Pinecrest Program (later known as the Barrett Learning Center, which closed in 2006). Despite changes in name, management, and student population over the years, later iterations of the institution saw continuity with the 1915 mission. The school continued to celebrate Founders' Day, which commemorated Janie Porter Barrett, into the 1990s.

12 Kunzel, *Fallen Women*, 55.

13 Haley, "'Like I Was a Man,'" 55.

14 Fielder, *Relative Races*, 3.

15 Ibid., 3.

16 Webster, *Beyond the Boundaries of Childhood*, 38.

17 Hartman, *Wayward Lives, Beautiful Experiments*, 264.

18 Kunzel, *Fallen Women*, 2.

19 Lira, *Laboratory of Deficiency*, xiv.

20 Agyepong, "Aberrant Sexualities," 271.

21 Gross and Hicks, "Introduction," 363.

22 *The Booster*, 3.

23 For more on the history of Black children's admission into nineteenth-century institutions and the work to establish institutions specifically for them, see Webster's *Beyond the Boundaries of Childhood*, esp. chap. 2.

24 Ward, *Black Child-Savers*, 8.

25 For more on this aspect of reformatory history, see Wolcott's "Juvenile Justice before Juvenile Court"; Folks's *Care of Destitute, Neglected, and Delinquent Children*; and Brenzel's *Daughters of the State*.

26 Agyepong, "Aberrant Sexualities," 271.

27 For example, in *Daughters of the State*, Barbara Brenzel notes that for a white girl, her "sinfulness [was not attributed] to her nature, but rather to her environment . . . a rehabilitative environment could remedy the wrongs of [her] childhood and reform her to her previous state of grace" (3). White children had a

"previous state of grace" to return to, whereas racialized criminality rendered Black children always already deviant. Hicks elaborates on this idea: "Immigrant and native-born white working-class women certainly were targeted by reformers and the police for questionable moral behavior, but generally authority figures believed these women could be reformed. Rehabilitative efforts were less of a guarantee for women who were characterized as innately promiscuous because of longstanding negative stigmas associated with their African ancestry and legacy of American enslavement" ("'Bright and Good-Looking Colored Girl,'" 419).

28 Ward, *Black Child-Savers*, 11.

29 While some of these institutions permitted Black children to attend throughout the nineteenth century, their presence often functioned to heighten racially differential narratives of criminality in children. In her work on the Illinois Training School for Girls at Geneva, Agyepong observes that the school set Black girls up for "a different kind of segregation: an imaginative, discursive, and practical segregation from white girls that structured administrative decisions within the institution and resulted in the construction of a race-specific image of black female delinquency" ("Aberrant Sexualities," 283).

30 For more on the role of Black clubwomen in the establishment of reform schools, see Shaw's "Black Club Women and the Creation of the National Association of Colored Women," Ward's *Black Child-Savers*, and Young and Reviere's "Black Club Women and the Establishment of Juvenile Justice Institutions for Colored Children."

31 Barrett, *Sixth Annual Report*, title page.

32 "Virginia Industrial School for Colored Girls," 404.

33 Ibid., 404.

34 Ward, *Black Child-Savers*, 9.

35 Barrett, *Twentieth Annual Report*, 7.

36 Barrett, *Sixth Annual Report*, 31; Barrett, *Second Annual Report*, 31; Barrett, *Eighth Annual Report*, 23.

37 Barrett, *Eighth Annual Report*, 10.

38 Brenzel notes that this state intervention into, displacement, and replacement of the origin family was a strategy for dealing with poor, immigrant, and Black families throughout the late nineteenth and early twentieth centuries: "For those children deprived of adequate family life and reluctant or unable to take advantage of state education, the state intervened as supraparent. The teacher was mandated to act *in loco parentis*—in the place of the parent—daily in the schoolrooms; the state more completely displaced the natural family for those children in need of surrogate families. With this rationale, social reformers justified the creation of institutions for needy children, particularly reform schools" (*Daughters of the State*, 25).

39 Barrett, *Fourth Annual Report*, 7.

40 Bristow, *Making Men Moral*, 7.

41 Barrett, *Pictorial Record*.

42 See Davis's "A Virginia Asset."

43 Erin Bush has conducted a detailed digital mapping project that tracks the relationship between military camps and the sentencing of girls to both the Virginia Industrial School and Bon Air, an industrial school for white juvenile delinquent girls. Her findings suggest that the anxiety over interactions between girls and men in training camps was based on criminalizing narratives that didn't correlate with reality since the schools "did not accept proportionally more girls from war camp cities" in comparison with more rural counties during this time ("Attracted by the Khaki").

44 The age of consent in Virginia was sixteen during World War I, but the widespread criminalization of Black youth on the basis of sexual acts suggests that it was reinforced differentially across race and class. According to the school's ledgers, between January 1915 and December 1919, the age of the student body ranged from nine to seventeen, with the average age of an admitted student being fourteen (see Ledgers, Barrett Juvenile Correctional Center, Hanover, Virginia, 1915–2001, Accession 41782, State Government Records Collection, Library of Virginia, Richmond, VA).

45 Barrett, *Second Annual Report*, 7.

46 Barrett, *Twenty-Third Annual Report*, 6.

47 Ibid., 7.

48 Ibid., 7.

49 Ibid., 7.

50 Barrett, *Sixth Annual Report*, 21–22.

51 Ibid., 14.

52 Ibid., 33.

53 Barrett, *Fourteenth Annual Report*, 11.

54 Ibid., 17.

55 Barrett, *Twentieth Annual Report*, 9.

56 Another barrier to full entry to citizenship came in the form of lack of state support for the school. Girls were described as future citizens who would be useful to the state in order to convince the government to invest more resources in the school. Nonetheless, many of the school's material needs were not met. Barrett lamented in the *Seventh Annual Report*, "When it is fully realized that the girls are worth saving and that in order to make acceptable citizens of them they must be given every opportunity to develop I am hoping this need will be met" (11). Despite the labor girls provided for those in their community both while students at and then when parolees from the institution, their value could not be recognized. Barrett made this statement in 1921, and the 1941 inspections reveal little changed during that time. The latter concluded, "It may well be reemphasized that, inadequate and dangerous as most of the buildings are . . . the school's future usefulness to the state depends primarily on the provision of the type of personnel needed in a program of training and treatment for problem girls" ("Virginia Industrial School for Colored Girls," 415). With better staff and working conditions,

"it will be possible to achieve a well-rounded and effective program that will show good returns to the state in girls prepared to take their places in the community" (415). This subtle shift from centering the girls' usefulness to focusing on the school's usefulness suggests that the girls' ability to integrate into society as full citizens had been rendered impossible. The school had to focus on its own ability to be "useful" by consolidating the criminalized sexuality of Black girls in one site, protecting everyone besides the girls.

57 Barrett, *Fourth Annual Report*, 18.
58 Ibid., 18.
59 Barrett, *Sixth Annual Report*, 27.
60 Ibid., 28.
61 The ledgers reveal that several students were transferred to other educational institutions, including the Manassas Industrial School and the Daytona Educational and Industrial Training School, the former of which is explored in chapter 4. These schools share important features with the Virginia Industrial School, most notably that they were founded by Black women, Jennie Dean and Mary McLeod Bethune, respectively, and in their early years were supported by Black women's social clubs. They differed in that they were not reform schools for the delinquent but boarding schools for Black youth meant to educate and train them in a trade. The transfer of students among these institutions is one reason for thinking of reform schools in relation to other Progressive Era institutions established for specific populations.
62 Barrett, *Fourth Annual Report*, 19.
63 Consider, for example, statements and phrases like the following: "Several of the newly admitted girls have had contagious diseases which have given me the greatest concern because we have no place to segregate them. With the exception of the cases mentioned and a few of grippe and colds, the health of the girls has been very good" (Barrett, *Second Annual Report*, 12); "the good health record of the Institution" (Barrett, *Seventh Annual Report*, 11); "the general health has been very good this year" despite the fact that "we lost one girl by death . . . [who was] so seriously infected with venereal disease" (Barrett, *Eighth Annual Report*, 14); and "the general health has been good" (Barrett, *Twentieth Annual Report*, 6).
64 The 1941 inspection noted the lack of material conditions to sequester infected girls (369–70). The report quoted Barrett: "Conditions are such that the girls are exposed to many infections because there is no separate division for each group. To guard and protect the health of these girls, a building that serves as a hospital and reception division only is essential" (quoted in "Virginia Industrial School for Colored Girls," 383). This report, based on inspections conducted in the late 1930s and early 1940s, echoed what Barrett was asking for in the 1923 annual report, when she disclosed news of a girl who passed away from venereal disease, driving home the need "to have a place to segregate contagious cases. . . . We are as careful as possible, but with our inadequate facilities the whole population is in danger. A cottage, with a dispensary attached for the treatment of venereal

and other contagious diseases, would make it possible to give care and treatment without risk to others. Girls have been sent to us with small pox, chicken pox, diphtheria, and measles, and they are likely to come with any contagious disease. Sometimes the disease develops after they come" (Barrett, *Eighth Annual Report*, 14). The demonstrated need for facilities to help protect the health of the girls in the school remained unmet almost twenty years later, supporting the notion that the state's distribution of resources was in tension with and in this instance outweighed micro-level efforts to treat these girls. State neglect enabled the spread of contagious illnesses and the sharing of contaminated facilities.

65   Other reform schools did include mention of homosexuality in institutional materials for the public, so its absence in the Virginia Industrial School annual reports is curious and supports the idea of an assertion of and insistence on a narrative of sexual reform.

66   "Virginia Industrial School for Colored Girls," 387–88.

67   Ibid., 414.

68   See Kunzel's *Criminal Intimacy* and Hicks's "'Bright and Good-Looking Colored Girl.'"

69   Barrett, *Fourth Annual Report*, 6.

70   Ovington, *Portraits in Color*, 188.

71   Barrett, *Sixth Annual Report*, 13.

72   Barrett, *Eighth Annual Report*, 19–20.

73   Ibid., 19.

74   Examples of the expression of these sentiments include the following: "it is not the best thing to send a girl back to her home when she is first paroled" (Barrett, *Second Annual Report*, 13); "Experience teaches that the most favourable parole conditions are found by placing a girl in a good home other than her own at first. The parents who let a girl get beyond their control can seldom keep her headed right a year or two later . . . if she goes home, she begins to drop back after the first week or two, to the place where she left off"; and "at home she is too near the undesirable associates she left" (Barrett, *Fifth Annual Report*, 14).

75   Barrett, *Fifth Annual Report*, 13.

76   Ibid., 14.

77   Barrett, *Eighth Annual Report*, 17 and 19.

78   Barrett, *Twelfth Annual Report*, 8.

79   Haley, "'Like I Was a Man,'" 54.

80   Ibid., 54.

81   Ibid., 55.

82   Kunzel, *Fallen Women*, 52.

83   Ibid., 53.

84   Hartman, *Wayward Lives, Beautiful Experiments*, 266.

85   Lira, *Laboratory of Deficiency*, 5.

86   Gould, "Carrie Buck's Daughter," 335.

87   Ibid., 334.

88 Gould ultimately concludes that Buck and her kin were not feebleminded: "Her case never was about mental deficiency; it was always a matter of sexual morality" ("Carrie Buck's Daughter," 336). Gould makes this point not to say that Buck's sterilization would have been justified if she did have some kind of deficiency but rather to show how "the charge of imbecility was a cover-up" to exert control over threatening persons and populations under the guise of scientifically justified benevolence (337).

89 Willrich, "Two Percent Solution," 64 and 66.

90 For more on the links among feeblemindedness, sterilization, and juvenile delinquency, see Chamberlain's "Challenging Custodialism," Bailey's "'Saturated with Vice,'" Kunzel's *Fallen Women*, Lira's *Laboratory of Deviance*, Stubblefield's "'Beyond the Pale,'" and Zipf's *Bad Girls at Samarcand*.

91 Barrett, *Second Annual Report*, 7.

92 Barrett, *Fifth Annual Report*, 14.

93 Barrett, *Sixth Annual Report*, 32–33.

94 Barrett, *Eighth Annual Report*, 15.

95 There are several instances in the reports where the institution is described in disability terms. The *Sixth Annual Report*'s preface, written by the governor, noted that withholding money from the school would "cripple an institution like yours" (8). In the *Seventh Annual Report*, Barrett noted that the lack of trained staff "is a terrible handicap" (11). In the *Eighth Annual Report*, the institution was described as "seriously handicapped" by the presence of feebleminded girls (15). And in the *Fourteenth Annual Report*, Barrett wrote that "feeble-minded and borderline cases are a handicap" (5). The metaphorical use of disability shifts from descriptions of resources pertaining to the school to a metaphorical use that invokes literal disability—the institution was "handicapped" by girls perceived to be mentally deficient. Paradoxically, the very presence of feebleminded girls in the school was, according to Barrett, because of a lack of resources for mental testing and failure of the state to correctly place girls—but the blame for the conditions of the school shifted from this lack of resources to the bodies and minds of these girls.

96 Barrett, *Twenty-First Annual Report*, 3.

97 "Virginia Industrial School for Colored Girls," 384.

98 Barrett, *Twentieth Annual Report*, 6.

99 Ibid., 6.

100 "Virginia Industrial School for Colored Girls," 371.

101 Ibid., 400.

102 The series has generated a range of responses. Writing for the *New Yorker*, critic Doreen St. Félix notes how the series largely neglected to situate Madison in a "greater conversation about the efficacy of rehabilitative programs for juvenile women, or with the structural realities that lead to the incarceration of girls in the first place." She describes *Girls Incarcerated* as the "gendered photonegative of the troubled teen spectacle" popularized by the twenty-first-century media offspring

of the 1978 documentary *Scared Straight!*, such as A&E's docuseries *Beyond Scared Straight* (2011–15). While the Netflix show humanizes its participants, it fails them by accepting their criminality and not interrogating the conditions that have made residential institutionalization a method on which the state continues to rely when it comes to girls, especially girls of color.

103 Morris, *Pushout*, 10.

104 Ibid., 12.

105 Ibid., 12.

106 Ibid., 141.

107 Ibid., 146.

108 Crenshaw, Ocen, and Nanda, "Black Girls Matter," 5 and 8.

2. REFORMING SEXUALITY, DISPLACING HOME

1 Kunzel, *Criminal Intimacy*, 10.

2 Elman, *Chronic Youth*, 9.

3 Weinstein, *Pathological Family*, 98.

4 Freeman, "Reconsidering Kenneth B. Clark," 277.

5 The first time the protagonist is referred to as Claude and not Sonny is when he is attending reform school; since Sonny connotes his position in normative kinship (literally, as "son"), loss of this name in the institution reveals how the institution is displacing him from kinship.

6 Brown, *Manchild*, ii.

7 Goldman and Crano, "Black Boy and Manchild in the Promised Land," 169.

8 Jarrett, "Review," 207.

9 Ross, "Some Glances at the Black Fag," 208.

10 "Claude Brown 1937–2002," 105, and "Notable Books of 1965," 284.

11 Nelson, *African American Autobiographers*, 32.

12 Worth, "Claude Brown," 8.

13 Khan, "Dark Arts and Diaspora," 53.

14 Mathes, "A Negro Pepys," 456.

15 Baker, "Environment as Enemy in a Black Autobiography," 53.

16 Daley, "Cardozo Project," 17.

17 Rowell, "Interview with Henry Louis Gates, Jr.," 450.

18 Brown, "Harlem, My Harlem," 378 and 382.

19 Ibid., 378.

20 Ibid., 378.

21 See Worth's "Claude Brown" and Yagoda's *Memoir*.

22 Rotella, *October Cities*, 270.

23 Baker, "Environment as Enemy in a Black Autobiography," 53.

24 Rotella, *October Cities*, 211.

25 Baker, "Environment as Enemy in a Black Autobiography," 53.

26 For examples, see Glazer and Creedon's *Children and Poverty*, Sykes and Drabek's *Law and the Lawless*, Lundquist's *Education*, and Korn's *Juvenile Delinquency*.

27 *Manchild*'s realist, neutral tone was framed in value-laden ways in school contexts as well. For example, teacher Elizabeth Gates Whaley shared in 1974 how she was admonished for assigning the text in a Black Literature course when it "discuss[es] masturbation in graphic ghetto terminology"—it was deemed a "Dirty Book" (Whaley, "What Happens When You Put the Manchild in the Promised Land?," 62 and 64).

28 Carson, "Albert Murray," 890.

29 Murray, *Omni-Americans*, 98.

30 Ibid., 101.

31 Sánchez, *"Shakin' Up" Race and Gender*, 14.

32 Ibid., 15.

33 For more on how the Moynihan Report informed treatment models for juvenile delinquents, see Weinstein's *Pathological Family*.

34 Moynihan, *Negro Family*, 29–30.

35 Ibid., 38.

36 Rotella, *October Cities*, 270.

37 Ibid., 271.

38 Brown, qtd. in "Dialogue in Washington," 40.

39 Nelson, *African American Autobiographers*, 54.

40 Love, "Close but Not Deep," 386.

41 Ibid., 386.

42 Brown, *Manchild*, 107.

43 Ibid., 107.

44 Ibid., 107.

45 Rowell, "Interview with Henry Louis Gates, Jr.," 449.

46 hooks, *Black Looks*, 115.

47 The title also immediately calls to mind two other twentieth-century literary works concerned with sexuality, futurity, and education: James Baldwin's "The Man Child," published in his 1965 short story collection *Going to Meet the Man*, and Mary Antin's *The Promised Land* (1912). The former tells the story of an unnamed white father in an intense homosocial and likely homosexual relationship with his divorced, childless friend Jamie (see DeGout's "Masculinity and (Im)-maturity"). Jamie's failed attempts to participate in the heteronormative order make the father's son, Eric, read the thirty-four-year-old as borderline elderly, while the father and mother read Jamie as young and not his age: Jamie is a child to the man, but a man to the child. After the mother's second miscarriage, Jamie kills Eric, which cuts off futurity for the child but perhaps opens up a new future where the men's relationship can continue. Extricating the child from the plot enables the manchild to grow up or perhaps to remain a child. In the latter, Mary Antin illustrates how white immigrant children are inducted into straight, white American life through education. Schools function as spaces where state agents take on parental roles, replacing the immigrant parents and their "old ways" (24)—in this way, a queer form of kinship is created and attachments produced in

order to have a heteronormative effect. By the text's conclusion, Antin considers herself to have reached "The Promised Land"—the nation-state offered and fulfilled its promise. Antin's story asks us to consider the role of race and gender in Brown's narrative: whose promises are fulfilled, whose are deferred, and whose are denied?

48 Giroux, "From *Manchild* to *Baby Boy*," 528.

49 The *Oxford English Dictionary* notes usages ranging from *The Book of Margery Kempe* to Genesis to William Shakespeare's *Macbeth*. These usages typify the circulation of "manchild" to describe a baby until the end of the nineteenth century. Then, it appears "manchild" begins to describe a child who is somehow out of time, often because of race, in texts like Edgar Rice Burroughs's *Tarzan of the Apes* (1912) and Jan Carew's *Last Barbarian* (1961) ("man-child, n.").

50 "Promised land, n."

51 Muñoz, *Cruising Utopia*, 1.

52 Ahmed, *Queer Phenomenology*, 30.

53 Ibid., 27.

54 Ibid., 29.

55 Ibid., 30.

56 Brown, *Manchild*, ix.

57 Ibid., x.

58 Ibid., x.

59 Ahmed, *Queer Phenomenology*, 50.

60 Ibid., 59.

61 Brown, *Manchild*, 1.

62 Ibid., 12.

63 Ibid., 22.

64 Ibid., 55.

65 Ibid., 55.

66 Ibid., 139.

67 Ibid., 8.

68 Halberstam, *In a Queer Time and Place*, 2.

69 Brown, *Manchild*, 2.

70 Ibid., 2.

71 Ibid., 3.

72 See Bruhm and Hurley's introduction in *Curiouser*, Edelman's *No Future*, and Kincaid's *Erotic Innocence*.

73 Brown, *Manchild*, 47.

74 Claude doesn't always view himself as a child. He recalls, "Everybody was stealing from everybody else. . . . Although none of my sidekicks was over twelve years of age, we didn't think of ourselves as kids. The other kids my age were thought of as kids by me. I felt that since I knew more about life than they did, I had the right to regard them as kids" (13). Age is not a determinant for whether one is a child or an adult; it's certain kinds of life knowledge. That Claude asserts his identity as a

child in moments around sexuality suggests that childhood and adulthood aren't stable categories in the text, but fluid and able to be determined by oneself in addition to being determined by state institutions. The state doesn't have the last word when it comes to deciding whether someone is a child or an adult.

75 Brown, *Manchild*, 26.

76 Ibid., 104 and 105.

77 Ibid., 151.

78 The text presents girls' sexuality only through Claude's narrative lens, and it's hard to discern whether their experiences are as neutral or at times positive as Claude describes. One complicated scene is when Claude arrives home from his first stint in reform school at thirteen and participates in the gang rape of a white girl he was "even scared to dream of" (99). He doesn't depict this scene as one of violence or violation but instead says that "I just didn't enjoy it as much as I thought I would, but anyway, the dream came true . . . a lot of people had their first white girl that night, just about everybody in the building" (100). The only way the experience is legible as different from his other encounters is the lack of pleasure ("I just didn't enjoy it as much"); the erasure and avoidance of naming the brutality ask readers to be cautious in readings of girls' sexualities, Black and white, in the text.

79 Nyong'o, "Punk'd Theory," 26.

80 Brown, *Manchild*, 11.

81 Ibid., 8.

82 Ibid., 51.

83 Doyle, *Psychiatry and Racial Liberalism in Harlem*, 2.

84 Ibid.

85 For more on the psychiatric approaches and initiatives instituted in Harlem in this era, see Doyle's *Psychiatry and Racial Liberalism in Harlem*.

86 Claude describes Roosevelt as someone who "seemed to be a little crazy or something" who "wasn't around too much, just once in a while at Wiltwyck" (Brown, *Manchild*, 79). Brown dedicated the novel to her.

87 Trodson, "'Quiet' Man," para. 8.

88 Wright was a proponent of increasing mental health resources in Harlem, and his involvement with the Wiltwyck School informed his posthumously published novella, *Rite of Passage* (1994). In the text's afterword, Arnold Rampersad writes, "The Wiltwyck School is directly in the background of the story *Right of Passage*," and Wright "discussed his work in progress 'Rite of Passage' . . . with a black social psychiatric caseworker at Wiltwyck, who visited Wright at his home and facilitated Wright's visit to the school" (133, and 135). While he became a donor of the school, over time he became disillusioned and had "reservations about philanthropy" and the ability of the school to carry out its transformative mission (136).

89 Doyle, *Psychiatry and Racial Liberalism in Harlem*, 7.

90 Brown confirmed he attended at the time of filming in a 1965 interview, "Claude Brown Talks with Studs Terkel" (00:19:27). In a 2008 interview, former school

director Nate Levine "remembers [the film] . . . only had one purpose, to spread the word of the Wiltwyck School for Boys" (Trodson, "'Quiet' Man," para. 5). The film initially began as a project to raise funds for the school (para. 15).

91 Wallace, "Race, Gender, and Psychoanalysis," 268.

92 *Quiet One*, 00:55–01:14.

93 Ibid., 02:10–02:20.

94 Wallace, "Race, Gender, and Psychoanalysis," 267.

95 *Quiet One*, 02:35–02:40.

96 Ibid., 06:51–07:02.

97 Ibid., 46:05.

98 Ibid., 46:30–47:55.

99 Ibid., 58:04.

100 Ibid., 01:00:35–01:00:57.

101 Wallace, "Race, Gender, and Psychoanalysis," 268.

102 Weinstein, *Pathological Family*, 102.

103 Brown, *Manchild*, 123.

104 Ibid., 124.

105 Doyle, *Psychiatry and Racial Liberalism in Harlem*, 94.

106 Brown, *Manchild*, 130.

107 Foucault, "Of Other Spaces," 4–5.

108 Ibid., 5.

109 Brown, *Manchild*, 7.

110 Ibid., 7.

111 Ibid., 52–54.

112 Nyong'o, "Punk'd Theory," 22.

113 Ibid., 26.

114 Ibid., 28.

115 This fear isn't isolated to this event but recurs as Claude continues to occupy institutional settings. When Claude comes home from his two and a half years in reform school, he feels depressed and "girls would come around, but I didn't want to be bothered with them. Mama used to worry about me. I guess she was scared—she figured I had been with nothing but boys for a long time, maybe too long" (109). Claude's mother's fear reemerges and is exacerbated by the passage of time. The institution may not have produced homosexuality in Claude, but his depression makes him unable to stir heterosexual interest, which scares his mother.

116 Brown, *Manchild*, 131.

117 Ibid., 131.

118 Edelman, *No Future*, 19.

119 Freeman, "Introduction," 162.

120 Brown, *Manchild*, 131.

121 Willrich, "Two Percent Solution," 64.

122 Brown, *Manchild*, 132 and 131.

123 Ross, "Some Glances at the Black Fag," 218.

124 Brown, *Manchild*, 184.

125 Ibid., 185.

126 Ibid., 186.

127 In another moment between institutions, Claude is playing cards with friends and "after a while, Earl wanted to show up how to play a card game called Strip Me. Nobody was interested in it, mainly because we knew that Earl liked guys" (114). There is no commentary, judgment, or violence in this scene. He reveals Earl's sexuality as an unremarkable and accepted fact.

128 Ibid., 132.

129 Ross, "Some Glances at the Black Fag," 213.

130 This is also not to say that Claude isn't preoccupied with his own masculinity. He later describes the phenomenon by which his peers started calling one another "baby": "At Warwick in 1951 [was] . . . the first time I heard it, [and] I knew right away I had to start using it. It was like saying, 'Man, look at me. I've got masculinity to spare.' . . . [it] meant that you had to be sure of yourself, sure of your masculinity" (153). He notes, "Only colored cats could give it the meaning that we all knew it had without ever mentioning it—the meaning of black masculinity" (153). Claude is fascinated with the way that the phrase "baby" is used by Black boys and men to assert their masculinity; using what might seem like an infantilizing term is a way to actually prove *excessive* masculinity ("masculinity to spare"). In order to prove one's strength and manhood, one might divest oneself and one's peers of it in name. While Claude is preoccupied with demarcating himself from homosexuality for fear of it encroaching on his manhood, here merging oneself with an identity with which one might want to be distinguished is actually a way to strengthen that demarcation.

131 Brown, *Manchild*, 67.

132 Ibid., 68.

133 Ibid., 86.

134 Haley, "'Like I Was a Man,'" 61.

135 Brown, *Manchild*, 87.

136 Ibid., 87.

137 Ibid., 88.

138 Ibid., 80.

139 Ibid., 84.

140 Ibid., 14.

141 Ibid., 54.

142 Ibid., 354.

143 Ross, "Some Glances at the Black Fag," 211.

144 Althusser, "Ideology and Ideological State Apparatuses," 174. Especial thanks to David Kazanjian for reminding me of this critical component of Althusser's formulation.

145 Brown, *Manchild*, 128 and 130.

146 Ibid., 109.

147 Ibid., 129.

148 Ibid., 136.

149 Consider, for example, "things kept changing, and I'd always been able to change with them and keep up with the neighborhood [but now can't]" (89); "Harlem had changed a lot. Everybody had changed. I had changed too, but in a different way. I was moving away from things. There was no place for me. I felt lonelier in Harlem than I'd felt when I first went to Wiltwyck. I couldn't go back to Wiltwyck—I had been trying to get away from there for years to get back to this. Now it seemed as though 'this' wasn't there anymore. It was really confusing for a while" (93); "We had to do the same old things, or we had to find our own new things to do. . . . We were all kind of lost. Nobody knew what to do" (94); "I was losing out on all fronts in Harlem. I was losing my bearings there, and I was losing whatever hold I'd had on my own stamping ground, my home town, my family, and my friends. I was just losing my place" (205); "sometimes I wanted to run back to Harlem, but I couldn't find anything up there any more . . . I didn't feel a part of it" (208–9); "We were too old to hang out any more, and the Harlem we'd known had gone. In three years, it had all gone" (226).

150 Brown, *Manchild*, 109.

151 Ibid., 141.

152 Ibid., 141.

153 Ibid., 156.

154 Ibid., 149.

155 Ibid., 183.

156 Ibid., 160.

157 The latter half of the novel is concerned largely with what Claude calls the "plague" that hit Harlem in the form of heroin addiction: "drugs were killing just about everybody off in one way or another" (170). He is concerned that "the only thing that seemed to matter now to my generation in Harlem, was drugs. Everybody looked at it as if it were inevitable" (249). This misplaced generation, many of whom passed through reform schools or other welfare institutions, becomes largely impacted by drugs, and their dependency is viewed as "inevitable"—this is one of the futures that the institution envisioned for the boys. Earlier in the text, Claude even alludes to how the institution might be responsible for drug addiction. Heroin, referred to as "horse" in the text, hits Harlem while Claude is at Wiltwyck. Claude says that "the only way I felt I could come out of Wiltwyck and be up to date . . . was to get in on the hippest thing, and the hippest thing was horse" (89). The institution's displacement of boys creates a desire in them to reintegrate back into their communities, and experimenting with heroin is a way to accelerate becoming connected once more with his peers. Claude has a bad reaction to heroin, and it "turned out to be a real drag" (98) for him, which is the only way he can explain his resistance to the "plague."

158 Brown, *Manchild*, 139.

159 Ibid., 140.

160 Ward, *Black Child-Savers*, 182.

161 Brown, *Manchild*, 165.

162 Ibid., 166–67.

163 Ibid., 212.

164 Ibid., 160.

165 Ibid., 183.

166 Ibid., 185.

167 Ibid., 399.

168 Ibid., 400.

169 Ibid., 394.

170 Ibid., 394.

3. COMPULSORY STERILIZATION

1 Schuller, *Biopolitics of Feeling*, 18.

2 Heather Tilley has examined how in the nineteenth century the societally held image of blind persons had to be transformed from one of dependency, destitution, and social ill to one of self-sufficiency and health. Tilley argues this led to an increased preoccupation with how blind persons appeared in public, as evidenced by an increase in blind portraiture and especially of blind persons reading ("Portraying Blindness," paras. 1 and 2). Appearing in public as an intellectual and moral contributor to society also required adherence to gender and sexual norms, as I explore in this chapter.

3 Hayden, *Erma at Perkins*, 57.

4 Ibid., 20.

5 See Kline's *Building a Better Race*, Ordover's *American Eugenics*, and Schoen's *Choice and Coercion*.

6 Kim, "Asexuality in Disability Narratives," 482.

7 Przybylo, *Asexual Erotics*, 92.

8 Kleege, *Blind Rage*, 45.

9 Kafer, *Feminist, Queer, Crip*, 29.

10 Ibid., 31 and 28.

11 For more on the history of the establishment of schools for the blind, see Koestler's *Unseen Minority*, esp. chap. 23, "The Birthright of Every Child."

12 Trustees, *Fifth Annual Report*, 8.

13 Howe, *Seventeenth Annual Report*, 30.

14 Howe, *Sixteenth Annual Report*, 49–50.

15 Ibid., 50.

16 Ibid., 50.

17 Mollow, "Is Sex Disability?," 288.

18 Howe, *Sixteenth Annual Report*, 51.

19 Howe, *Forty-Second Annual Report*, 111.

20 Howe, *Seventeenth Annual Report*, 21.

21 Koestler, *Unseen Minority*, 455.

22 Ibid., 22.

23 Howe, *Thirty-Fifth Annual Report*, 38–39.

24 Howe, *Seventeenth Annual Report*, 28–29.

25 Walter Benn Michaels argues that homosexual families are non-reproductive families that can be incorporated into the larger American family in the early twentieth century because they can serve "as the model for purified American-ism" since they aren't reproducing threats to American identity via homosexuality (*Our America*, 49). Similarly, homosexual disabled persons can be incorporated into a national schema by the fact of their non-reproductivity in the logic of this moment.

26 Howe, *Forty-Second Annual Report*, 111–12.

27 Ibid., 114.

28 Howe, *Eighty-First Annual Report*, 30.

29 Burch and Patterson, "Not Just Any Body," 124.

30 Ibid., 124.

31 Markotić and McRuer, "Leading with Your Head," 166.

32 Ibid., 167.

33 Hayden, *Erma at Perkins*, 143.

34 Ibid., 142.

35 For example, Hayden spoke on "Advanced Braille" at the Adult Blind Teachers Open Conference, gave talks at Perkins, and published articles like "What to Do for the Mentally Retarded Pupil" in the *Teachers Forum for Instructors of Blind Children* (1941). Hayden also published textbooks such as *The Braille Code: A Guide to Grade Three* (1958). She stayed in contact with Perkins, submitting notes to their annual reports over the years, updating them on her employment.

36 Hayden, *Erma at Perkins*, 2.

37 *The Lantern*, 7.

38 Clipping in *Perkins Institution Scrapbook*, 71.

39 "Bookshelf," 12.

40 Hayden, *Erma at Perkins*, 83; Howe, *Eighty-Second Annual Report*, 53.

41 Hayden, *Erma at Perkins*, 93.

42 Ibid., 38.

43 Ibid., 134.

44 Ibid., 148.

45 "Peabody Bimonthly Booknotes," 187.

46 Chinn, "Gender, Sex, and Disability from Helen Keller to Tiny Tim," 242.

47 "Bookshelf," 12.

48 Ibid., 12.

49 Ruth recalls one classmate caught stealing who was eventually sent home because of the "recurrence of the weakness" (30); schoolgirl crushes that become love affairs "weaken characters that are already weak" (123); when a teacher disciplines Erma for being unable to control herself and humiliates her in the process, "never again would Erma parade her poor weaknesses" (130); and when a new student

doesn't understand why two people who became blind by accident can't be in a relationship, he is told "a weakness has to begin somewhere" (186).

50 Hayden, *Erma at Perkins*, 7.
51 Ibid., 8.
52 Ibid., 9.
53 Ibid., 9.
54 Ibid., 10.
55 Ibid., 10.
56 Ibid., 11.
57 Ibid., 11.
58 Ibid., 12.
59 Ibid., 12.
60 Trustees, *Annual Report*, 8.
61 See Thompson's "Time, Work-Discipline, and Industrial Capitalism" and Smith's *Mastered by the Clock*.
62 Foucault, *Discipline and Punish*, 128–29.
63 Ruth is preoccupied with distinguishing herself and her classmates from persons in other institutions. She recounts how "two little sisters arrived. . . . Their arrival is remembered because they had on bright turkey-red dresses . . . it may be that the red dresses were a give-away that these little girls may have spent the summer vacation in a State institution. . . . This may not be true, but it is mentioned here because it is one of the vivid memories of those first days at school, and also because many people think that Perkins is an asylum for the blind; but it is not. It is a school, and both pupils and teachers are required to go elsewhere during vacations" (22). Ruth is adamant to recount this potentially fabricated story—it is punctuated at every turn with how "it may be" or "may not be true"—in order to make a point about Perkins being a school for students, and not an institution for patients, wards, or the destitute. The school also enforces this distinction, teaching girls to contribute to charity and training them in trades so they could be provided work "instead of charity" upon graduation (140). As the girls get older, the school is able to distinguish who is capable of joining the workforce after graduation and who will always be dependent on institutions: "gradually, we are being separated into the rich or the poor, the able or unable, the successful or defeated," and where one is sorted will determine if one is a self-supporting alumna or one of "the 'needy blind'" (141, 150). Students' desire for normalcy through joining the labor force requires them to demonize their fellow classmates who will "never get beyond the needs of institutional care" (64). In order to save some students from stigma associated with disability, others have to be left behind, and students themselves are made to pronounce these condemnations.
64 Hayden, *Erma at Perkins*, 92.
65 Ibid., 14.
66 Ibid., 46.
67 Ibid., 61.

68 Ibid., 21.
69 Dawson, "Miniaturizing of Girlhood," 70.
70 Foucault, *History of Sexuality*, 28.
71 Hayden, *Erma at Perkins*, 23.
72 Ibid., 38.
73 Ibid., 94–95.
74 Ibid., 113.
75 Ibid., 83.
76 Ibid., 82.
77 Ibid., 58.
78 Ibid., 176.
79 Ibid., 134–35.
80 Foucault, *History of Sexuality*, 101.
81 Hayden, *Erma at Perkins*, 64.
82 Ibid., 67.
83 Ibid., 138.
84 Ibid., 15.
85 Ibid., 15.
86 For example, Topsy's hair is cut to give her a "more Christian-like" appearance in *Uncle Tom's Cabin* (Stowe, 205); the unnamed narrator in Zitkala-Ša's *American Indian Stories* tries to hide from the teachers at the Carlisle Industrial School when they cut her hair, and when they find her, the loss is traumatic; and Dr. Flint cuts Linda's hair in *Incidents in the Life of a Slave Girl* to assert his power over her.
87 See "despoil" in the *Oxford English Dictionary*.
88 Hayden, *Erma at Perkins*, 31.
89 Ibid., 31–32.
90 Ibid., 44.
91 Ibid., 44.
92 Ibid., 118.
93 Ibid., 118–19.
94 For more on situational homosexuality and how it has been central and not peripheral to modern understandings of normative sexuality, see Kunzel's "Situating Sex."
95 While "cottage life" refers to the literal cottage system that the school employs to mimic house and family, it is also a pun on gay cruising culture, emphasizing the sexual deviance of these "misfits."
96 Hayden, *Erma at Perkins*, 119.
97 Ibid., 118.
98 In the *Forty-Third Annual Report*, Howe writes that in coed institutions teachers must monitor children's behaviors, but the effects can be unexpected: "Teachers and attendants dislike to be spies and informers. The pupils must all be watched, or none; which is annoying to those who are well disposed; and may even suggest disobedience, otherwise not likely to have been thought of. . . . They must

establish and maintain rules and regulations in the household, to prevent what they consider undue intimacies, perhaps even innocent, if not desirable acquaintance, between the sexes. The blind almost universally revolt, in spirit, against these regulations, and consider them as arbitrary and unnecessary. Often, they show resolution and ingenuity in breaking or evading such rules, though obedient to all others; and they generally succeed in doing so" (115). Scrutinizing children's behaviors means reading "innocent" connections as "undue intimacies"; hypermonitoring can also "suggest disobedience" to students. *Erma at Perkins* reveals how these effects can also occur in single-sex institutions.

99 Hayden, *Erma at Perkins*, 119–20.
100 Ibid., 174.
101 Ibid., 98.
102 Ibid., 147. Race makes sparing but telling appearances in the text. While Ruth says, "In honor of Perkins training, be it known that there was never the slightest prejudice against creed or color in the school," the few times race does come up suggest that race and education around race at Perkins exist for the advancement of white blind students (146). One Black student, Joe Rodrigo, makes two appearances in the text—the first is when Erma has a successful violin performance at the Boston Theater, and her success is possible because "she could not remember the bowing . . . [but stood] behind a little colored boy named Joe Rodrigo who always did his bowing correctly" (59). Joe then doesn't appear again until the end of the novel when we learn that Erma wrote a song to "play at Joe Rodrigo's funeral" (194). Readers learn he unceremoniously died in a swimming accident at the school. His sole job in the text is to advance Erma's artistic production. When international students attend the school, they "add much to our understanding of other races and cultures and have also given us a cosmopolitan feeling" (177)—these international students are object lessons to make white students feel more "cosmopolitan."
103 Hayden, *Erma at Perkins*, 161.
104 Ibid., 121.
105 Kent, *Making Girls into Women*, 2.
106 Ibid., 2.
107 Ibid., 5.
108 Hayden, *Erma at Perkins*, 121.
109 Ibid., 123.
110 Foucault, *History of Sexuality*, 29.
111 Hayden, *Erma at Perkins*, 122.
112 Ibid., 123.
113 Ibid., 124.
114 Ibid., 124.
115 Ibid., 125.
116 Ibid., 126.
117 Ibid., 126.

118 Ibid., 127.
119 Ibid., 145.
120 Ibid., 146.
121 Ibid., 165.
122 Ibid., 167.
123 Ibid., 170.
124 Ibid., 185.
125 Ibid., 185–86.
126 Ibid., 186.
127 Carter, *Heart of Whiteness*, 2.
128 Hayden, *Erma at Perkins*, 187.
129 Ibid., 195.
130 Ibid., 196.
131 Lehrer, "Golem Girl Gets Lucky," 242.

4. CLEANSING AND CONTAMINATING SEXUALITY

1 The choice of this clip is more loaded in light of Cambridge's contested sexuality. Cambridge, a comedian, was married to a woman, but there is speculation
  that he was a closeted homosexual. He incited anger in the LGBTQ community
  for incorporating homophobic slurs into his routines. An October 28, 1971, letter
  to the editor of *Jet* magazine criticized a recent performance by Cambridge: "I
  saw nothing humorous in Godfrey Cambridge's joke about homosexuals, and I
  am sure 3,000,000 other Black homosexuals agree with me. . . . We consider a
  'straight' (heterosexual person) using the word 'fag' or 'faggot' derogatory. . . . We
  Black homosexuals will be silent no longer. Whether you straights wish to admit it
  or not, we are the most oppressed group in America. The whites reject us because
  we are Black and the Blacks reject us because we are a threat to their 'new-found'
  manhood. . . . I don't think the Black revolution can afford to alienation 3,000,000
  potential revolutionaries" (Holmes, "Don't Knock Homosexuals," 4). The author
  of the letter critiques Godfrey on the assumption that he is heterosexual and so
  acting as a gatekeeper of "'new-found' manhood" in the Black community—Black
  homosexuality "threat[ens]" the respectability that gender and sexual propriety
  has newly afforded some members of the Black community, who exist in a nation
  that "infantilizes" all Black sexuality. In light of Baldwin's critique, this response
  to Cambridge suggests that Black homosexuality in this historical moment is
  legible, even to other Black homosexuals, only when accompanied by an open
  declaration—for them, cultural labor is also absent of sexuality but implies a tacit
  heterosexuality.
2 Peck, *I Am Not Your Negro*, 00:50:00–00:50:45.
3 Ibid., 00:50:45–00:50:58.
4 Woubshet, "Imperfect Power of *I Am Not Your Negro*," para. 10.
5 Story, "On the Cusp of Deviance," 264.
6 Woubshet, "Imperfect Power of *I Am Not Your Negro*," para. 11.

7 Repudiating Black male homosexuality in the cultural sphere was also happening during the civil rights movement. For example, Bayard Rustin's "sexuality brought him trouble again and again" (D'Emilio, *In a New Century*, 93–94); Rustin was a leader whose political and activist work was impacted by discrimination from within and beyond his community. Leaders like Adam Clayton Powell and NAACP director Roy Wilkins didn't want "Rustin's influence in the civil rights movement, and they used his sexuality to isolate him" (94).

8 This is not to erase Black readership of Baldwin's oeuvre, nor to center white readers as consumers of his work—rather, I point this out to show how members of a dominant group can exert control over how work circulates, especially if it contains (perceived) threats to the dominant order.

9 For example, see Herron's "Baldwin Documentary 'I Am Not Your Negro' Is Mostly for White People."

10 Story, "On the Cusp of Deviance," 366.

11 While this investigation is largely centering Black male sexuality, scholars like Patricia Hill Collins in *Black Feminist Thought* and Dorothy Roberts in "Paradox of Silence and Display" have also noted this dynamic in the perception of Black female sexuality in dominant culture, where images of the sexless mammy and oversexed jezebel act to "control" Black female sexuality in the public and private spheres.

12 Lott, *Love and Theft*.

13 Yousman describes this dynamic as "blackophilia and blackophobia," where those who celebrate Black artistry are also threatened by it and so work to control it ("Blackophilia and Blackophobia," 370). Through generating these particular terms, Yousman displaces pathology from Black sexuality onto white consumers/managers.

14 Raney, "Encroaching Dark," 4.

15 hooks, *Black Looks*, 370.

16 Ibid., 370.

17 Ibid., 380.

18 Story, "On the Cusp of Deviance," 371.

19 The relationship between imposed cleanliness and hygiene and control and management of populations is explored in McClintock's *Imperial Leather* and Douglas's *Purity and Danger*. My investigation is interested in how this plays out specifically in the context of boarding schools for Black children.

20 The Atlanta Compromise was an agreement based on an 1895 speech Booker T. Washington gave at the Atlanta Exposition that southern whites would allow African Americans the right to education and due process. In exchange for financial support of educational institutions, African Americans wouldn't fight for more rights or contest racial violence and instead would focus on self-support.

21 Cooper, *Autobiography of Citizenship*, 3.

22 Ibid., 3, 8.

23 Ibid., 3.

24 Ibid., 8.
25 Ferguson, "Of Our Normative Strivings," 92.
26 Ibid., 92.
27 Ibid., 96.
28 Somerville, *Queering the Color Line*, 3.
29 Ferguson, "Of Our Normative Strivings," 90.
30 Reddy, *Freedom with Violence*, 39.
31 In the *Encyclopedia of African American Education*, Kofi Lomotey attributes this decline to the 1915 death of Booker T. Washington, reduction in donations during World War I, and increased concern that this educational model was limiting African Americans to industrial work, work for which their white counterparts were better trained because their industrial schools were better resourced (131).
32 Ferguson, "Of Our Normative Strivings," 92.
33 Ibid., 98.
34 Hartman, *Scenes of Subjection*, 140.
35 Manassas Industrial School, *1915–1916 Annual Report*, 17.
36 Lewis, *Undaunted Faith*, 90.
37 McCraney won the Oscar for Best Adapted Screenplay for *Moonlight* (2015), based on his play *In Moonlight Black Boys Look Blue* (2003). The play, like *Choir Boy*, explores coming of age as a gay child in a community that sees queer sexuality as at odds with mandates for Black masculinity.
38 At their peak, there were about a hundred boarding schools for African Americans in the United States ("Status of African Americans at the Nation's Most Prestigious Boarding Schools," 26).
39 Lewis, *Undaunted Faith*, 42.
40 For example, Berthold explains how in the Progressive Era "cleanliness was associated explicitly with civility, high class, and whiteness," and "slippage[s took] place between the exclusion of 'dirt' and the exclusion of 'dirty people'" from domestic, social, and cultural spheres ("Tidy Whiteness," 2). Raney argues that "a set of despised characteristics was first presumed to attach stereotypically to blacks, then associated with disease, then—once germ theory provided the model— regarded as transmissible," and "the visual analogy between dirt and black skin eased the middle step of this syllogism" ("Encroaching Dark," 5). In *Imperial Hygiene*, Bashford notes how this metaphorical link literalized: "The eugenics *mentalité* created contagions out of many human qualities. . . . This was driven by longstanding cultural usage of hygiene metaphors, or of folk theories of contamination. But it was not just that. . . . Epilepsy, feeble-mindedness, homosexuality, criminality, prostitution, alcoholism were all rendered into pathologies considered transferable between generations through reproduction. They were 'caught' by one generation from another. This literal not just metaphorical pathologisation of certain attributes into transmissible phenomena is yet another reason for the convergence of public health and eugenics, under 'hygiene'" (183–84). Fears of

how deviance could morally contaminate the population led to fears that deviance could be transmitted through reproduction.

41 Berlant, *Queen of America Goes to Washington City*, 60.

42 Ibid., 59 and 60.

43 Manassas Industrial School, *Manassas School Journal.*

44 Hartman, *Scenes of Subjection*, 156.

45 See Washington's *Working with Your Hands* and Du Bois's *Morals and Manners among Negro Americans*, both published in 1904. Both express preoccupation with cultivating hygiene routines and concerns with sexual immorality among African Americans.

46 Hartman, *Scenes of Subjection*, 129.

47 Wright, *Black Girlhood*, 147.

48 Ibid., 148.

49 Ibid., 157.

50 Andrews, "Introduction," xx.

51 Washington, *Up from Slavery*, 34.

52 Ibid., 102 and 103.

53 Ibid., 110.

54 But this insistence on cleanliness could not always be enacted in the institution; for example, "The students have been taught to bathe as regularly as they take their meals. This lesson we began teaching before we had anything in the shape of a bath-house" (Washington, *Up from Slavery*, 103). Students were at times trained in hygiene regimens that they could not fulfill, a paradox I'll elaborate on further in this section.

55 Thompson, "Letter to William Loeb," 2.

56 Ibid., 7.

57 While the school was officially taken over by the state in 1938, the leaders had been petitioning for the state to take control of the institution for at least a decade prior due to its financial struggles. Dean's leadership was often undermined by local patrons who saw her as uneducated and ignorant in manners of institutional management (Lewis, *Undaunted Faith*, 57).

58 Roosevelt, qtd. in Hagedorn, *Works of Theodore Roosevelt*, 676.

59 Ibid., 677.

60 Ibid., 677.

61 This investigation is part of a longer tradition of thought that has considered the relationship between compulsory heterosexuality and capitalism (for example, see Hayes's "Marxist Bedroom") and specifically scholars thinking about the mandate of (white) sexual propriety for racialized laborers (for example, see Kyungwon Hong and Ferguson's *Strange Affinities*).

62 Manassas Industrial School, *1908 Financial Report*, 6–7.

63 Manassas Industrial School, *1910 Financial Report*, 7.

64 "Manassas Industrial School," 277.

65 Manassas Industrial School, *1915–1916 Annual Report*, 14.

66 Ibid., 14.

67 Ibid., 17.

68 The same report suggests that the anxiety over sexual propriety, especially as it relates to cleanliness, might differ according to gender. The report notes that the girls' dormitory is "equipped with shower baths, tub baths, and modern toilet conveniences" (7); the boys' dormitory is also described, but there is no mention of the facilities. This absence suggests that there may have been more preoccupation with girls' cleanliness. In this moment, there was widespread concern over venereal disease, a public health crisis after World War I. Preoccupation over girls' cleanliness might reflect an anxiety over their role as transmitters of venereal disease to men, and infecting men risks the strength of the nation they have or may have to serve.

69 Manassas Industrial School, *1915–1916 Annual Report*, 42.

70 Ibid.

71 This trap was occurring in similar educational programs. "Keeping Fit," a health program developed by the Public Health Service and YMCA during World War I, spurred by anxieties over venereal disease and the (threatened) strength of the nation, had two versions of its program: one for white boys, one for Black boys. However, "although sexuality was usually defined in terms of race, evidence indicates that the Keeping Fit program for white boys was actually used to educate many African-Americans . . . [the education of] male adolescents was intended to provide for the salvation of the race, *specifically the white race*" (Lord, "Models of Masculinity," 130). The program trained Black boys in a program pitched at and intended for white boys—Black boys were receiving a sexual education that wasn't about improving or guaranteeing their own health, well-being, or futures.

72 Ritchie and Caldwell, *Primer of Hygiene*, 2–3.

73 Ibid., 73 and 76.

74 Ibid., 76.

75 Ibid., 191.

76 The ledgers record at least three students who were transferred from the Virginia Industrial School (VIS) to the Manassas Industrial School (MIS) in its early years. One student was admitted to VIS in June 1916 and was transferred to MIS less than a year later in March 1917; another student was admitted to VIS at the age of thirteen in March 1915 and was transferred to MIS five years later in January 1920; another was sent to MIS after two years in March 1920.

77 Manassas Industrial School, *1907 Financial Report*, 1.

78 Manassas Industrial School, *Manassas Bulletin*.

79 Opager Baughn, "Modern School Plant," 44.

80 Ibid., 44–45.

81 Ibid., 45.

82 Taylor, *Archive and the Repertoire*, 19 and 20.

83 Broadwaycom, "Tarell Alvin McCraney & Jeremy Pope on Bringing CHOIR BOY to Broadway," 01:48.

84 "Status of African Americans at the Nation's Most Prestigious Boarding Schools," 26.

85 For example, Cymone Davis, a city manager, is working to establish a Black boarding school in Tullahassee, Oklahoma, as a "beacon for Black excellence in the form of a private independent institutions for students ages 12 to 18" (Eaton, "Can an All-Black Boarding School Bring an Education Revolution?," para. 4).

86 See "Final Four."

87 See Tucker's *Blood Work*.

88 McCraney, *Choir Boy*, 16.

89 Ibid., 6.

90 For work on how this song codes moral duties, see Reuschling's "'Trust and Obey.'"

91 McCraney, *Choir Boy*, 9 and 10.

92 Ibid., 17–18.

93 In this way, the school achieves "the major effect of the panopticon, [which is] to induce in the inmate a state of conscious and permanent visibility that assures the automatic functioning of power" (Foucault, *Discipline and Punish*, 201).

94 McCraney, *Choir Boy*, 12.

95 Ibid., 12.

96 Ibid., 16.

97 Ibid., 16.

98 Ibid., 17.

99 Lott, *Love and Theft*, 24.

100 Taylor, *Archive and Repertoire*, 28.

101 McCraney, *Choir Boy*, 17.

102 Ibid., 20.

103 Ibid., 20.

104 Ibid., 25.

105 Ibid., 26.

106 Ibid., 49.

107 Ibid., 49.

108 Ibid., 50–51.

109 Ibid., 51.

110 Ibid., 51.

111 Ibid., 31.

112 Ibid., 31.

113 Ibid., 70.

114 Ibid., 59.

115 "File, v.," *OED Online*.

116 "Rub, v.," *OED Online*.

117 McCraney, *Choir Boy*, 79.

118 Ibid., 100–101.

119 Ibid., 101.

120 Ibid., 115.
121 Ibid., 105.
122 Ibid., 107.
123 Ibid., 107.
124 Ibid., 117.
125 Ibid., 118.
126 Ibid., 118.
127 Ibid., 120.
128 Ibid., 118.
129 Baldwin, *Giovanni's Room*, 186–87.
130 McBride, "Straight Black Studies," 82.
131 Muñoz, *Cruising Utopia*, 11.
132 Johnson, "Introduction," 8.
133 Ibid., 10.
134 Ibid., 4.
135 Ibid., 1.
136 Ibid., 23.

5. SEXUAL ORPHANINGS

1 Highway, *Kiss of the Fur Queen*, 113.
2 Ibid., 85.
3 Ibid., 190.
4 While practices and understandings varied from nation to nation, the settler state homogenized these practices, seeing them all as deviant. This pan-Native outlook extended to the schools, where children from many nations resided. Interactions between members of the same nation were strictly monitored so as to prevent attachment and allegiance to the communities from which they came; for example, children from the same tribe would be separated to make sure they were not speaking their language. In Dian Million's discussion of the "gender interventions inherent in colonial schooling," she notes that "colonial 'schooling' flattened a complex constellation of Indigenous familial, economic, and ceremonial roles into several one-dimensional stereotypes," capturing the ways that schools projected a unified narrative of Native deviance onto students (Million, *Therapeutic Nations*, 42).
5 Rifkin, *When Did Indians Become Straight?*, 5–6.
6 Barker, *Native Acts*, 85.
7 Byrd, "Loving Unbecoming," 226.
8 Burch, *Committed*, 3 and 9.
9 Rifkin, *Erotics of Sovereignty*, 39.
10 Cvetkovich, *Depression*, 25.
11 Goeman, "Ongoing Storms and Struggles," 101.
12 Ibid., 101.
13 Ibid., 111 and 117.

14 Million, *Therapeutic Nations*, 46, 49, and 79.
15 Schuller, *Biopolitics of Feeling*, 18.
16 Schneider, "Introduction," 18.
17 Finley, "Decolonizing the Queer Native Body," 32.
18 Million, *Therapeutic Nations*, 44.
19 Morgensen, "Settler Homonationalism," 106.
20 Rifkin, *Erotics of Sovereignty*, 28.
21 Schneider, "Modest Proposal," 87.
22 Stockton, *Queer Child*, 6.
23 Rogin, *Fathers and Children*, 11.
24 Ibid., 6 and 8.
25 Ibid., 125.
26 Burch, *Committed*, 5.
27 Marshall qtd. in Schneider, "Introduction," 17.
28 Schneider, "Introduction," 20.
29 Ibid., 20.
30 In this same issue, Andrea Smith emphasizes the "eternal" element of this project, noting that "the Native is rendered permanently infantile . . . an innocent savage. She cannot mature into adult citizenship, she can only be locked into a permanent state of infancy" (Smith, "Queer Theory and Native Studies," 51). If Natives are "permanently infantile," then both the present and "future of the white, settler citizen" are always guaranteed—and the future of Native communities is always tied up with and in the service of this white future (51). Natives must remain in this orphaned state in order for the "white, settler citizen" to maintain their destructive and dominating acts over Native land and peoples.
31 Rifkin, *When Did Indians Become Straight?*, 8.
32 Foucault, *"Society Must Be Defended,"* 241.
33 Ibid., 241.
34 Jacobs, *White Mother to a Dark Race*, 4.
35 Wolfe, "Settler Colonialism and the Elimination of the Native," 398–99.
36 Puar, "Cost of Getting Better," 153.
37 Berlant, *Cruel Optimism*, 95.
38 Rhoades, *Report on Indian Health*, 28.
39 DeJong, *If You Knew the Conditions*, 10.
40 Ibid., 10.
41 DeJong, "'Unless They Are Kept Alive,'" 261–62.
42 Ibid., 274–75.
43 Pratt and Utley, *Indian Industrial School*, 46.
44 Castronovo, *Necro Citizenship*, 6.
45 Schuller, *Biopolitics of Feeling*, 163.
46 Ibid., 162.
47 Pratt and Utley, *Indian Industrial School*, 20.
48 Ibid., 5.

49 Rifkin, *When Did Indians Become Straight?*, 150.

50 Million, *Therapeutic Nations*, 42.

51 Ibid., 42.

52 Ibid., 95.

53 Nolte-Odhiambo, "'I Be Home,'" 377.

54 Million notes that reservations were "designed to be temporary," training grounds for Native peoples to exercise "democratic techniques of 'freedom'"—the perpetual status of "domestic-dependent" nations has worked to ensure this "temporary" status is enduring, visible in the material space of the reservation system (Million, *Therapeutic Nations*, 149).

55 Lowe, *Intimacies of Four Continents*, 41.

56 Ibid., 40–41.

57 Rifkin also sees Native writing about sexuality as a way to productively engage with the "what could have been." Building on Craig Womack's critical formulation of imagining as vital for the production of Native epistemologies, Rifkin asks if "the erotic might serve as a source of imagination? . . . Creative engagement with the erotic can . . . register . . . the largely unacknowledged presence of the past as well as opening heretofore (officially) unrecognized potentials for living indigeneity in the present" (*Erotics of Sovereignty*, 27). In other words, imagining an erotics that exceeds those mandated by settler sexuality opens up "potentials" for Natives in the present. Thus, Highway's rendering of the sexual orphanings in the 1960s boarding school in a 1998 fictional text has ramifications for available Native modes of being in the present.

58 Justice, "Fear of a Changeling Moon," 103.

59 Ibid., 104.

60 Ibid., 106.

61 Million, "Felt Theory," 58.

62 McKegney, "From Trickster Discourses to Transgressive Politics," 81.

63 Deborah Miranda observes that "separation from parents and extended family resulted in adult survivors of boarding school who had no idea how to parent" ("Dildos," 138). Lisa Poupart explains how this proliferation of "unparented parents" has been further complicated by "the erosion of traditional extended-family systems . . . [which means] many are without the traditional networks of emotional and economic support" ("Familiar Face of Genocide," 93). The boarding schools' intervention into kinship coupled with lack of institutional support has not completely halted Native reproduction, but it has altered and limited what the Native family and community can look like today.

64 Highway is a survivor of the boarding school system in Canada—there are certainly significant differences between the U.S. settler state and the Canadian settler state, but the school systems developed and functioned similarly, with Sam McKegney noting that "like American boarding schools, Canadian residential schools acted as a weapon in a calculated attack on Indigenous cultures" ("From

Trickster Discourses to Transgressive Politics," 79). I use this text to think about a broader Native North American experience of boarding/residential school experience and its effects.

65 Highway, *Kiss of the Fur Queen*, 40.

66 Ibid., 53.

67 Ibid., 54.

68 Ibid., 51.

69 Zitkala-Ša is one of many Native authors who capture the severe consequences of the violent ritual of hair cutting that occurred when a child entered the boarding school. The unnamed narrator of *American Indian Stories* describes the moment when she heard the scissors, saying, "[I] heard them gnaw off one of my thick braids. Then I lost my spirit . . . now I was one of many little animals driven by a herder" (91). Cutting hair is a dehumanizing act.

70 Highway, *Kiss of the Fur Queen*, 74.

71 Deloria, *God Is Red*, 74.

72 Bauerkemper, "Narrative Nationhood," 28.

73 Deloria, *God Is Red*, 73.

74 Ibid., 73.

75 Highway, *Kiss of the Fur Queen*, 54.

76 Taylor, *Archive and the Repertoire*, 19.

77 Highway, *Kiss of the Fur Queen*, 58.

78 Ibid., 68.

79 Ibid., 27.

80 Ibid., 109.

81 Ibid., 193.

82 Halberstam, *In a Queer Time and Place*, 5.

83 Highway, *Kiss of the Fur Queen*, 63.

84 Rifkin, *When Did Indians Become Straight?*, 147.

85 Ibid., 152.

86 Miranda, "Dildos," 140.

87 Highway, *Kiss of the Fur Queen*, 103.

88 Ibid., 100.

89 Ibid., 102.

90 Halberstam, *In a Queer Time and Place*, 5.

91 Highway, *Kiss of the Fur Queen*, vii.

92 Ibid., 233.

93 Ibid., 212.

94 Ibid., 54 and 74.

95 Ibid., 53.

96 Ibid., 202.

97 Ibid., 207.

98 Ibid., 260.

99 Ibid., 298 and 299.

100 Ibid., 301.

101 Mark Rifkin has explored how the text "perform[s] an erotohistoriography of indigeneity and settler colonialism" and draws on Lynda Hart to examine how the "incorporation of [Gabriel's] abuse into his sexuality provides a means of challenging 'the dominant order's symbolic,' refusing the negation of Indigenous eroticism" ("Queering Indigenous Pasts," 140). My reading aligns in part with that of Rifkin, who suggests that this incorporation resists the erasure of Native sexuality. However, Rifkin focuses on how the text maintains and "reimagine[s] Indigenous continuity" and tradition, while I read the text as resulting in orphanings, which are forms of discontinuity, that nonetheless open up ways for considering Indigenous sexuality (140).

102 Driskill, "Stolen from Our Bodies," 50 and 51.

103 Freeman, *Time Binds*, 12–13.

104 Driskill, "Stolen from Our Bodies," 53.

105 Rifkin, *When Did Indians Become Straight?*, 151.

106 Highway, *Kiss of the Fur Queen*, 37.

107 Ibid., 76.

108 Ibid., 77.

109 Ibid., 78–79.

110 Ibid., 78.

111 Justice, "Fear of a Changeling Moon," 106.

112 Lorde, "Uses of the Erotic," 53.

113 Driskill, "Stolen from Our Bodies," 52.

114 Highway, *Kiss of the Fur Queen*, 78.

115 Ibid., 61.

116 Ibid., 81.

117 Ibid., 126.

118 Ibid., 91.

119 Ibid., 92.

120 Finley, "Decolonizing the Queer Native Body," 32.

121 Highway, *Kiss of the Fur Queen*, 190.

122 Sedgwick, *Touching Feeling*, 116.

123 Stockton, *Beautiful Bottom, Beautiful Shame*, 8.

124 Highway, *Kiss of the Fur Queen*, 121.

125 Ibid., 132, 169, 185, 204, and 263.

126 Cvetkovich, *Archive of Feelings*, 102.

127 Ibid., 102.

128 Million, *Therapeutic Nations*, 6.

129 Cvetkovich, *Archive of Feelings*, 74.

130 Ibid., 74.

131 Ibid., 74.

132 Highway, *Kiss of the Fur Queen*, 168–89.

133 Ibid., 169.

134 Cvetkovich, *Archive of Feelings*, 74.

135 Highway, *Kiss of the Fur Queen*, 207.

136 In *Epistemology of the Closet*, Sedgwick states that AIDS is "unlike genocide directed against Jews, Native Americans, Africans, or other groups" because "gay genocide, the once-and-for-all eradication of gay populations . . . is not possible short of the eradication of the whole human species" (130). While Sedgwick counterposes the genocides against Native Americans and gay persons because of her understanding of how Native and gay identities emerge, Highway proposes seeing Native and gay genocide as intertwined in *Kiss of the Fur Queen*. Both are genocides enacted on queered populations, and as a gay Native American, Gabriel occupies the position of the child queered by Native genocide who will be queered by AIDS. Many thanks to Scott Herring for helping me to understand the text in this manner.

137 Highway, *Kiss of the Fur Queen*, 306.

138 Ibid., vii.

139 Briggs, *Somebody's Children*, 59.

140 Ibid., 61–62.

141 *Brackeen v. Haaland*, para. 1.

142 Alexie, *Flight*, 8.

143 Ibid., 67.

144 Driskill, "Stolen from Our Bodies," 54.

145 Milloy, *National Crime*, 298.

146 Ibid., 4.

147 Ibid., 9.

148 Briggs, *Somebody's Children*, 63.

149 Ibid., 91.

150 Alexie, *Flight*, 3.

151 Ibid., 2.

152 Ibid., 150 and 152.

153 Ibid., 156.

154 Taylor, *Archive and the Repertoire*, 3.

155 Alexie, *Flight*, 141 and 142.

156 Ibid., 163.

157 Ibid., 168.

158 Ibid., 168.

159 Ibid., 174.

160 Ibid., 171.

161 Ibid., 176 and 171.

162 Ibid., 176.

163 Ibid., 180.

164 Ibid., 180 and 181.

165 Deloria, *God Is Red*, 71.

166 Alexie, *Flight*, 1, my emphasis.

167 Ibid., 181, my emphasis.

168 Ibid., 181.

169 Lowe, *Intimacies of Four Continents*, 207.

EPILOGUE

1 Butler, "Critically Queer," 19.

2 Brim, *Poor Queer Studies*, 9.

3 Love, "Feminist Criticism and Queer Theory," 313.

4 Sedgwick, *Tendencies*, 1.

5 Ibid., 3.

6 Lubin, "Haircut Theory," para. 2.

7 Berlant, "Pedagogies of 'Pedagogy of Buddhism,'" para. 11.

8 Wiegman, "Eve's Triangles," 51.

9 Brim, *Poor Queer Studies*, 9.

10 Ibid., 3.

11 Gregory, "Critics on Critics," 103.

12 Love, "Truth and Consequences," 236.

13 Ibid., 236.

14 Ibid., 237.

15 Ibid., 236.

16 Ibid., 240.

17 Ibid., 240.

18 Amin, *Disturbing Attachments*, 4.

BIBLIOGRAPHY

Abate, Michelle Ann. *Tomboys: A Literary and Cultural History*. Philadelphia: Temple University Press, 2008.

Agyepong, Tera. "Aberrant Sexualities and Racialised Masculinisation: Race, Gender and the Criminalisation of African American Girls at the Illinois Training School for Girls at Geneva, 1893–1945." *Gender & History* 25, no. 2 (2013): 270–93.

Ahmed, Sara. *Queer Phenomenology: Orientations, Objects, Others*. Durham, NC: Duke University Press, 2006.

Alexander, M. Jacqui. *Pedagogies of Crossing: Meditation on Feminism, Sexual Politics, Memory, and the Sacred*. Durham, NC: Duke University Press, 2005.

Alexie, Sherman. *Flight*. New York: Black Cat Press, 2007.

Althusser, Louis. "Ideology and Ideological State Apparatuses (Notes toward an Investigation)." In *Lenin and Philosophy and Other Essays*, translated by Ben Brewster, 127–86. New York: Monthly Review Press, 1971.

Amar, Paul. "The Street, the Sponge, and the Ultra: Queer Logics of Children's Rebellion and Political Infantilization." *GLQ: A Journal of Lesbian and Gay Studies* 22, no. 4 (2016): 569–604.

Amin, Kadji. *Disturbing Attachments: Genet, Modern Pederasty, and Queer History*. Durham, NC: Duke University Press, 2017.

Andrews, William L. "Introduction." In *Up from Slavery*, by Booker T. Washington, vii–xxii. 1902. Oxford: Oxford University Press, 1995.

Antin, Mary. *The Promised Land*. 1912. New York: Penguin, 2012.

Anzaldúa, Gloria. *Borderlands / La Frontera: The New Mestiza*. San Francisco: Aunt Lute Books, 1987.

Ariès, Philippe. *Centuries of Childhood: A Social History of Family Life*. New York: Random House, 1962.

Bailey, Hannah Anneliese. "'Saturated with Vice': Angelic White Children, Incorrigible Youth, and Reformable Subjects." *Left History* 23, no. 2 (Spring/Summer 2020): 36–59.

Baker, Houston. "The Environment as Enemy in a Black Autobiography: Manchild in the Promised Land." *Phylon* 32, no. 1 (1971): 53–59.

Baldwin, James. *Giovanni's Room*. New York: Dial Press, 1956.

———. "The Man Child." *Going to Meet the Man*. 1965. New York: Vintage, 1995.

———. "Sidney Poitier." *Look Magazine* 32, no. 15 (July 23, 1968).

Barker, Joanne. *Native Acts: Law, Recognition, and Cultural Authenticity*. Durham, NC: Duke University Press, 2011.

Barrett, Janie Porter. *The Second Annual Report of the Industrial Home School for Colored Girls*. Peake's Turnout, VA: Virginia State Federation of Colored Women's Clubs, 1917.

———. *The Fourth Annual Report of the Industrial Home School for Colored Girls*. Peake's Turnout, VA: Virginia State Federation of Colored Women's Clubs, 1919.

———. *The Fifth Annual Report of the Industrial Home School for Colored Girls*. Peake's Turnout, VA: Virginia State Federation of Colored Women's Clubs, 1920.

———. *The Sixth Annual Report of the Industrial School for Colored Girls*. Peake's Turnout, VA, 1921.

———. *The Seventh Annual Report of the Industrial School for Colored Girls*. Peake's Turnout, VA, 1922.

———. *The Eighth Annual Report of the Industrial School for Colored Girls*. Peake's Turnout, VA, 1923.

———. *The Twelfth Annual Report of the Industrial School for Colored Girls*. Peake's Turnout, VA, 1927.

———. *The Fourteenth Annual Report of the Industrial School for Colored Girls*. Peake's Turnout, VA, 1929.

———. *The Twentieth Annual Report of the Industrial School for Colored Girls*. Peake's Turnout, VA, 1935.

———. *The Twenty-First Annual Report of the Industrial School for Colored Girls*. Peake's Turnout, VA, 1936.

———. *The Twenty-Third Annual Report of the Industrial School for Colored Girls*. Peake's Turnout, VA, 1938.

———. *Pictorial Record of the Virginia Industrial School*. Richmond, VA: Division of Purchase and Printing, 1922.

Bashford, Alison. *Imperial Hygiene: A Critical History of Colonialism, Nationalism, and Public Health*. London: Palgrave Macmillan, 2004.

Bauerkemper, Joseph. "Narrating Nationhood: Indian Time and Ideologies of Progress." *Studies in American Indian Literatures* 19, no. 4 (2007): 27–53.

Bellingham, Bruce. "Institution and Family: An Alternative View of Nineteenth-Century Child Saving." *Social Problems* 33, no. 6 (October–December 1986): S33–57.

Berlant, Lauren. *Cruel Optimism*. Durham, NC: Duke University Press, 2011.

———. "The Pedagogies of 'Pedagogy of Buddhism.'" *Supervalent Thought*, March 18, 2010. www.supervalentthought.com.

———. *The Queen of America Goes to Washington City: Essays on Sex and Citizenship*. Durham, NC: Duke University Press, 1997.

Berlant, Lauren, and Michael Warner. "Sex in Public." *Critical Inquiry* 24, no. 2 (1998): 547–66.

Bernstein, Robin. *Racial Innocence: Performing American Childhood from Slavery to Civil Rights*. New York: New York University Press, 2011.

Berthold, Dana. "Tidy Whiteness: A Genealogy of Race, Purity, and Hygiene." *Ethics and the Environment* 15, no. 1 (Spring 2010): 1–26.

"The Bookshelf." *Christian Science Monitor*, February 17, 1945, 12.

The Booster 32, no. 2 (May 1948).

Brackeen v. Haaland. SCOTUSblog, November 9, 2022. https://www.scotusblog.com/case-files/cases/brackeen-v-haaland/.

Bradway, Tyler, and Elizabeth Freeman. "Introduction: Kincoherence/Kin-aesthetics/Kinematics." In *Queer Kinship: Race, Sex, Belonging, Form*, edited by Bradway and Freeman, 1–22. Durham, NC: Duke University Press, 2022.

Brenzel, Barbara. *Daughters of the State: A Social Portrait of the First Reform School for Girls in North America, 1856–1905*. Cambridge, MA: MIT Press, 1983.

Breslow, Jacob. *Ambivalent Childhoods: Speculative Futures and the Psychic Life of the Child*. Minneapolis: University of Minnesota Press, 2021.

Briggs, Laura. *Somebody's Children: The Politics of Transracial and Transnational Adoption*. Durham, NC: Duke University Press, 2012.

———. *Taking Children: A History of American Terror*. Oakland: University of California Press, 2020.

Brim, Matt. *Poor Queer Studies: Confronting Elitism in the University*. Durham, NC: Duke University Press, 2020.

Bristow, Nancy. *Making Men Moral: Social Engineering during the Great War*. New York: New York University Press, 1966.

Broadwaycom. "Tarell Alvin McCraney & Jeremy Pope on Bringing CHOIR BOY to Broadway." YouTube, January 30, 2019. https://youtu.be/ZQZOOLQTkY4.

Brown, Claude. "Harlem, My Harlem." *Dissent*, Summer 1961, 378–82.

———. *Manchild in the Promised Land*. 1965. New York: Simon & Schuster, 2012.

Bruhm, Steven, and Natasha Hurley, eds. *Curiouser: On the Queerness of Children*. Minnesota: University of Minnesota Press, 2004.

Burch, Susan. *Committed: Remembering Native Kinship in and beyond Institutions*. Chapel Hill: University of North Carolina Press, 2021.

Burch, Susan, and Lindsey Patterson. "Not Just Any Body: Disability, Gender, and History." *Journal of Women's History* 25, no. 4 (Winter 2013): 122–37.

Bush, Erin. "'Attracted by the Khaki': War Camps and Wayward Girls in Virginia, 1918–1920." *Current Research in Digital History* 1 (2018). https://doi.org/10.31835/crdh.2018.07.

Butler, Judith. "Critically Queer." *GLQ: A Journal of Lesbian and Gay Studies* 1 (1993): 17–32.

Byrd, Jodi A. "Loving Unbecoming." In *Critically Sovereign: Indigenous Gender, Sexuality, and Feminist Studies*, edited by Joanne Barker, 207–28. Durham, NC: Duke University Press, 2017.

Carson, Warren. "Albert Murray: Literary Reconstruction of the Vernacular Community." *African American Review* 50, no. 4 (Winter 2017): 890–98.

Carter, Julian. *The Heart of Whiteness: Normal Sexuality and Race in America, 1880–1940*. Durham, NC: Duke University Press, 2007.

Castronovo, Russ. *Necro Citizenship: Death, Eroticism, and the Public Sphere in the Nineteenth Century United States*. Durham, NC: Duke University Press, 2001.

Chamberlain, Chelsea. "Challenging Custodialism: Families and Eugenic Institutionalization at the Pennsylvania Training School for Feeble-Minded Children at Elwyn." *Journal of Social History* 55, no. 2 (2021): 484–509.

Chambers-Letson, Joshua, Tavia Nyong'o, and Ann Pellegrini. "Foreword: Before and After." In *Cruising Utopia*, 10th anniv. ed., by José Esteban Muñoz, ix–xvi. New York: New York University Press, 2019.

Chinn, Sarah. "Gender, Sex, and Disability from Helen Keller to Tiny Tim." *Radical History Review* 94 (Winter 2006): 240–48.

———. "'I Was a Lesbian Child': Queer Thoughts about Childhood Studies." In *The Children's Table: Childhood Studies and the Humanities*, edited by Anna Mae Duane, 149–66. Athens: University of Georgia Press, 2013.

Chinn, Sarah, and Anna Mae Duane, eds. "Child." Special issue of *WSQ: Women's Studies Quarterly* 43, nos. 1–2 (2015).

"Claude Brown 1937–2002." *Journal of Blacks in Higher Education* 35 (Spring 2002): 105.

Cobb, Michael. "Childlike: Queer Theory and Its Children." *Criticism* 47, no. 1 (2005): 119–30.

Collins, Patricia Hill. *Black Feminist Thought: Knowledge, Consciousness, and the Politics of Empowerment*. New York: Routledge, 2000.

———. "The Meaning of Motherhood in Black Culture and Black Mother-Daughter Relationships." *SAGE* 4, no. 2 (Fall 1987): 3–10.

Cooper, Tova. *The Autobiography of Citizenship: Assimilation and Resistance in U.S. Education*. New Brunswick, NJ: Rutgers University Press, 2015.

Crenshaw, Kimberlé Williams, Priscilla Ocen, and Jyoti Nanda. "Black Girls Matter: Pushed Out, Overpoliced, and Underprotected." New York: Center for Intersectionality and Social Policy Studies, 2015.

Cvetkovich, Ann. *Archive of Feelings: Trauma, Sexuality, and Lesbian Public Cultures*. Durham, NC: Duke University Press, 2003.

———. *Depression: A Public Feeling*. Durham, NC: Duke University Press, 2012.

Daley, Maxine. "The Cardozo Project." *Negro American Literature Forum* 1, no. 2 (Winter 1967): 17.

Davis, J. E. "A Virginia Asset." *Southern Workman* 49, no. 8 (August 1920): 357–64.

Dawson, Melanie. "The Miniaturizing of Girlhood: Nineteenth-Century Playtime and Gendered Theories of Development." In *The American Child: A Cultural Studies Reader*, edited by Caroline Levander and Carol Singley, 63–84. New Brunswick, NJ: Rutgers University Press, 2003.

DeGout, Yasmin. "Masculinity and (Im)maturity: 'The Man Child' and Other Stories in James Baldwin's Gender Studies Enterprise." In *Re-viewing James Baldwin: Things Not Seen*, edited by D. Quentin Miller and David Adams Leeming, 128–53. Philadelphia: Temple University Press, 2002.

DeJong, David. *If You Knew the Conditions: A Chronicle of the Indian Medical Service and American Indian Health Care, 1908–1955*. Lanham, MD: Lexington Books, 2008.

———. "'Unless They Are Kept Alive': Federal Indian Schools and Student Health, 1878–1918." *American Indian Quarterly* 31, no. 2 (2007): 256–82.

Deloria, Vine. *God Is Red*. Wheat Ridge, CO: Fulcrum, 1994.

D'Emilio, John. "Capitalism and Gay Identity." In *Families in the US: Kinship and Domestic Politics*, edited by Karen V. Hansen and Anita Ilta Garey, 131–41. Philadelphia: Temple University Press, 1983.

———. *In a New Century: Essays on Queer History, Politics, and Community Life*. Madison: University of Wisconsin Press, 2014.

"Dialogue in Washington." *Architectural Forum*, October 1966, 38–42.

Dinshaw, Carolyn. *How Soon Is Now? Medieval Texts, Amateur Readers, and the Queerness of Time*. Durham, NC: Duke University Press, 2012.

Douglas, Mary. *Purity and Danger: An Analysis of Concepts of Pollution and Taboo*. 1966. New York: Routledge Classics, 2002.

Doyle, Dennis. *Psychiatry and Racial Liberalism in Harlem, 1936–1968*. Rochester, NY: University of Rochester Press, 2016.

Driskill, Qwo-Li. "Stolen from Our Bodies: First Nation Two Spirits/Queers and the Journey to a Sovereign Erotic." *Studies in American Indian Literatures* 16, no. 2 (2004): 50–64.

Duane, Anna Mae. "Introduction." In *The Children's Table: Childhood Studies and the Humanities*, edited by Anna Mae Duane, 1–14. Athens: University of Georgia Press, 2013.

Du Bois, W. E. B. *Morals and Manners among Negro Americans*. 1904. Lanham, MD: Lexington Books, 2010.

Eaton, Kristi. "Can an All-Black Boarding School Bring an Education Revolution?" *Ozy*, January 15, 2021. www.ozy.com.

Edelman, Lee. *No Future: Queer Theory and the Death Drive*. Durham, NC: Duke University Press, 2004.

Edwards, George C. "The Private School in American Life." *Education Review* 23 (March 1902): 264–80.

Elman, Julie Passanante. *Chronic Youth: Disability, Sexuality, and U.S. Media Cultures of Rehabilitation*. New York: New York University Press, 2016.

Eng, David. *The Feeling of Kinship: Queer Liberalism and the Racialization of Intimacy*. Durham, NC: Duke University Press, 2010.

Fass, Paula S. "Foreword." In *Children and Youth During the Gilded Age and Progressive Era*, edited by James Marten, vii–ix. New York: New York University Press, 2014.

Fawaz, Ramzi. "Stripped to the Bone: Sequencing Queerness in the Comic Strip Work of Joe Brainard and David Wojnarowicz." *ASAP/Journal* 2, no. 2 (May 2018): 335–67.

Ferguson, Roderick. *Aberrations in Black: Toward a Queer of Color Critique*. Minneapolis: University of Minnesota Press, 2003.

———. "Of Our Normative Strivings: African American Studies and the Histories of Sexuality." *Social Text* 23, nos. 3–4 (2005): 85–100.

Fielder, Brigitte. *Relative Races: Genealogies of Interracial Kinship in Nineteenth-Century America*. Durham, NC: Duke University Press, 2020.

"file, v." *OED Online*, June 2022.

"The Final Four: African American Boarding Schools on the Verge of Extinction." *HBCUMoney*, September 22, 2014. https://hbcumoney.com.

Finley, Chris. "Decolonizing the Queer Native Body (and Recovering the Native Bull-Dyke): Bringing 'Sexy Back' and Out of Native Studies' Closet." In *Queer Indigenous Studies: Critical Interventions in Theory, Politics, and Literature*, edited by Qwo-Li Driskill, Chris Finley, Brian Joseph Gilley, and Scott Lauria Morgensen, 31–42. Tucson: University of Arizona Press, 2011.

Fischel, Joseph. *Sex and Harm in the Age of Consent*. Minneapolis: University of Minnesota Press, 2017.

Fleetwood, Nicole. *Marking Time: Art in the Age of Mass Incarceration*. Cambridge, Mass.: Harvard University Press, 2020.

Folks, Homer. *The Care of Destitute, Neglected, and Delinquent Children*. New York: Macmillan, 1902.

Foucault, Michel. *Discipline and Punish: The Birth of the Prison*. 1977. Translated by Alan Sheridan. New York: Vintage, 1995.

———. *The History of Sexuality, Volume 1: An Introduction*. 1976. Translated by Robert Hurley. New York: Vintage, 1990.

———. "Of Other Spaces: Utopias and Heterotopias." *Architecture/Mouvement/Continuite*, October 1984, 1–9.

———. *"Society Must Be Defended": Lectures at the College de France, 1975–1976*. Translated by David Macey. New York: Picador, 2003.

Franke, Katherine. *Wedlocked: The Perils of Marriage Equality*. New York: New York University Press, 2017.

Freedman, Estelle. *Their Sisters' Keepers: Women's Prison Reform in America, 1830–1930*. Ann Arbor: University of Michigan Press, 1984.

Freeman, Damon. "Reconsidering Kenneth B. Clark and the Idea of Black Psychological Damage, 1931–1945." *Du Bois Review* 8, no. 1 (2011): 271–83.

Freeman, Elizabeth. "Introduction." *GLQ: A Journal of Lesbian and Gay Studies* 13, nos. 2–3 (2007): 159–76.

———, ed. "Queer Temporalities." Special issue of *GLQ: A Journal of Lesbian and Gay Studies* 13, no. 2 (2007).

———. *Time Binds: Queer Temporalities, Queer Histories*. Durham, NC: Duke University Press, 2011.

Gilbert, Jen. *Sexuality in School: The Limits of Education*. Minneapolis: University of Minnesota Press, 2014.

Gill-Peterson, Jules. *Histories of the Transgender Child*. Minneapolis: University of Minneapolis Press, 2018.

Gill-Peterson, Jules, Rebekah Sheldon, and Kathryn Bond Stockton, eds. "The Child Now." Special issue of *GLQ: A Journal of Lesbian and Gay Studies* 22, no. 4 (2016).

———. "What Is the Now, Even of Then?" *GLQ: A Journal of Lesbian and Gay Studies* 22, no. 4 (2016): 495–503.

Giroux, Henry. "From *Manchild* to *Baby Boy*: Race and the Politics of Self-Help." *JAC: A Journal of Composition Theory* 22, no. 3 (Summer 2002): 527–60.

Glazer, Nona, and Carol Creedon. *Children and Poverty: Some Sociological and Psychological Perspectives*. Chicago: Rand McNally, 1968.

Goeman, Mishuana. "Ongoing Storms and Struggles." In *Critically Sovereign: Indigenous Gender, Sexuality, and Feminist Studies*, edited by Joanne Barker, 99–126. Durham, NC: Duke University Press, 2017.

Goffman, Erving. *Asylums: Essays on the Social Situation of Mental Patients and Other Inmates*. New York: Anchor, 1961.

Goldman, Robert, and William Crano. "Black Boy and Manchild in the Promised Land: Content Analysis in the Study of Value Change over Time." *Journal of Black Studies* 7, no. 2 (December 1976): 169–80.

Gould, Stephen Jay. "Carrie Buck's Daughter." *Constitutional Commentary* 2, no. 331 (1985): 331–39.

Gregory, Chase. "Critics on Critics." *GLQ: A Journal of Lesbian and Gay Studies* 25, no. 1 (2019): 101–6.

Gross, Kali, and Cheryl Hicks. "Introduction—Gendering the Carceral State: African American Women, History, and the Criminal Justice System." *Journal of African American History* 100, no. 3 (2015): 357–65.

Hagedorn, Herman, ed. *The Works of Theodore Roosevelt: Presidential Addresses and State Papers (Part 5)*. New York: P. F. Collier, 1926.

Halberstam, J. Jack. *In a Queer Time and Place*. New York: New York University Press, 2005.

———. *The Queer Art of Failure*. Durham, NC: Duke University Press, 2011.

Haley, Sarah. "'Like I Was a Man': Chain Gangs, Gender, and the Domestic Carceral Sphere in Jim Crow Georgia." *Signs* 39, no. 1 (Autumn 2013): 53–77.

Harkins, Gillian. *Virtual Pedophilia: Sex Offender Profiling and U.S. Security Culture*. Durham, NC: Duke University Press, 2020.

Hartman, Saidiya. *Scenes of Subjection*. Oxford: Oxford University Press, 1997.

———. "Venus in Two Acts." *Small Axe* 12, no. 2 (2008): 1–14.

———. *Wayward Lives, Beautiful Experiments: Intimate Histories of Social Upheaval*. New York: Norton, 2020.

Hayden, Ruth R. *The Braille Code: A Guide to Grade Three*. Lexington, KY: American Printing House for the Blind, 1958.

———. *Erma at Perkins*. Boston: Chapman & Grimes, 1944.

———. "What to Do for the Mentally Retarded Pupil." *Teachers Forum for Instructors of Blind Children* 13 (May 1941): 82–90.

Hayes, Jarrod. "The Marxist Bedroom: Sex and Class Struggle." *Minnesota Review* 48–49 (Spring–Fall 1997): 207–16.

Herron, Antwan. "Baldwin Documentary 'I Am Not Your Negro' Is Mostly for White People." *Wear Your Voice*, February 21, 2017. http://wearyourvoicemag.com.

Hicks, Cheryl. "'Bright and Good-Looking Colored Girl': Black Women's Sexuality and 'Harmful Intimacy' in Early-Twentieth-Century New York." *Journal of the History of Sexuality* 18, no. 3 (2009): 418–56.

Highway, Tomson. *Kiss of the Fur Queen*. Norman: University of Oklahoma Press, 1998.

Hogan, John C., and Mortimer D. Schwartz. "In Loco Parentis in the United States 1765–1985." *Journal of Legal History* 8, no. 3 (1987): 260–74.

Holmes, Rufus. "Don't Knock Homosexuals." *Jet Magazine* 41, no. 5 (October 28, 1971): 4.

hooks, bell. *Ain't I a Woman: Black Women and Feminism*. 1981. New York: Routledge, 2015.

———. *Black Looks: Race and Representation*. Boston: South End, 1992.

Howe, Samuel Gridley. *Sixteenth Annual Report of the Trustees of the Perkins Institution and Massachusetts Asylum for the Blind*. Cambridge: Metcalf and Company, 1848.

———. *Seventeenth Annual Report of the Trustees of the Perkins Institution and Massachusetts Asylum for the Blind*. Cambridge: Metcalf and Company, 1849.

———. *Thirty-Fifth Annual Report of the Trustees of the Perkins Institution and the Massachusetts School for the Blind*. Boston: Wright & Potter, 1867.

———. *Forty-Second Annual Report of the Trustees of the Perkins Institution and the Massachusetts School for the Blind*. Boston: Wright & Potter, 1873.

———. *Forty-Third Annual Report of the Trustees of the Perkins Institution and the Massachusetts School for the Blind*. Boston: Wright & Potter, 1874.

———. *Eighty-First Annual Report of the Trustees of the Perkins Institution and the Massachusetts School for the Blind*. Boston: Wright & Potter, 1912.

———. *Eighty-Second Annual Report of the Trustees of the Perkins Institution and the Massachusetts School for the Blind*. Boston: Wright & Potter, 1913.

Hurley, Nat. "Childhood and Its Discontents: An Introduction." *ESC: English Studies in Canada* 38, nos. 3–4 (2012): 1–24.

Jacobs, Margaret. *White Mother to a Dark Race: Settler Colonialism, Maternalism, and the Removal of Indigenous Children in the American West and Australia, 1880–1940*. Lincoln: University of Nebraska Press, 2009.

James, Robin. *Resilience and Melancholy: Pop Music, Feminism, and Neoliberalism*. Winchester, UK: Zero Books, 2015.

Jarrett, Hobart. "Review: To Live Is to Experience." *Phylon* 27, no. 2 (1966): 205–7.

Jerng, Mark. *Claiming Others: Transracial Adoption and National Belonging*. Minneapolis: University of Minnesota Press, 2010.

Johnson, E. Patrick. "Introduction." In *No Tea, No Shade: New Writings in Black Queer Studies*, edited by E. Patrick Johnson, 1–27. Durham, NC: Duke University Press, 2016.

Justice, Daniel Heath. "Fear of a Changeling Moon: A Rather Queer Tale from a Cherokee Hillbilly." In *Me Sexy: An Exploration of Native Sex and Sexuality*, edited by Drew Hayden Taylor, 87–108. Vancouver: Douglas & McIntyre, 2008.

Kafer, Alison. *Feminist, Queer, Crip*. Bloomington: Indiana University Press, 2013.

Kahan, Benjamin. *Celibacies: American Modernism and Sexual Life*. Durham, NC: Duke University Press, 2013.

Kazanjian, David. *The Colonizing Trick: National Culture and Imperial Citizenship in Early America*. Minneapolis: University of Minnesota Press, 2003.

Keeling, Kara. *Queer Times, Black Futures*. New York: New York University Press, 2020.

Kent, Kathryn. *Making Girls into Women: American Women's Writing and the Rise of Lesbian Identity*. Durham, NC: Duke University Press, 2003.

Khan, Aisha. "Dark Arts and Diaspora." *Diaspora: A Journal of Transnational Studies* 17, no. 1 (2008): 40–63.

Kim, Eunjung. "Asexuality in Disability Narratives." *Sexualities* 14, no. 4 (2011): 479–93.

Kincaid, James R. *Erotic Innocence: The Culture of Child Molesting*. Durham, NC: Duke University Press, 1998.

Kleege, Georgina. *Blind Rage: Letters to Helen Keller*. Washington, DC: Gallaudet University Press, 2006.

Kline, Wendy. *Building a Better Race: Gender, Sexuality, and Eugenics from the Turn of the Century to the Baby Boom*. Oakland: University of California Press, 2001.

Koestler, Frances A. *The Unseen Minority: A Social History of Blindness in the United States*. Arlington, VA: American Foundation for the Blind, 2004.

Korn, Richard. *Juvenile Delinquency*. New York: Crowell, 1968.

Kunzel, Regina. *Criminal Intimacy: Prison and the Uneven History of Modern American Sexuality*. Chicago: University of Chicago Press, 2008.

———. *Fallen Women, Problem Girls: Unmarried Mothers and the Professionalization of Social Work, 1890–1945*. New Haven, CT: Yale University Press, 1993.

———. "Situating Sex: Prison Sexual Culture in the Mid-Twentieth-Century United States." *GLQ: A Journal of Lesbian and Gay Studies* 8, no. 3 (2002): 253–70.

Kyungwon Hong, Grace, and Roderick Ferguson, eds. *Strange Affinities: The Gender and Sexual Politics of Comparative Racialization*. Durham, NC: Duke University Press, 2011.

The Lantern 13, no. 4 (June 15, 1944).

Lehrer, Riva. "Golem Girl Gets Lucky." In *Sex and Disability*, edited by Robert McRuer and Anna Mollow, 231–55. Durham, NC: Duke University Press, 2012.

Lewis, Stephen Johnson. *Undaunted Faith: The Story of Jennie Dean*. 1941. Manassas, VA: Manassas Museum, 1994.

Lira, Natalie. *Laboratory of Deficiency: Sterilization and Confinement in California, 1900–1950s*. Oakland: University of California Press, 2022.

Lomotey, Kofi, ed. *Encyclopedia of African American Education*. Vol. 1. Thousand Oaks, CA: SAGE, 2009.

Lord, Alexandra. "Models of Masculinity: Sex Education, the United States Public Health Service, and the YMCA, 1919–1924." *Journal of the History of Medicine and Allied Sciences* 58, no. 2 (2003): 123–52.

Lorde, Audre. *Sister Outsider: Essays and Speeches*. 1984. New York: Random House, 2007.

————. "Uses of the Erotic: The Erotic as Power." 1984. In *Sister Outsider: Essays and Speeches by Audre Lorde*, 53–59. New York: Random House, 2007.

Lott, Eric. *Love and Theft: Blackface Minstrelsy and the American Working Class*. 1993. Oxford: Oxford University Press, 2013.

Love, Heather. "Close but Not Deep: Literary Ethics and the Descriptive Turn." *New Literary History* 41, no. 2 (2010): 371–91.

————. *Feeling Backward: Loss and the Politics of Queer History*. Cambridge, MA: Harvard University Press, 2009.

————. "Feminist Criticism and Queer Theory." In *A History of Feminist Literary Criticism*, edited by Gill Plain and Susan Seller, 301–21. Cambridge: Cambridge University Press, 2007.

————. "Truth and Consequences: On Paranoid Reading and Reparative Reading." *Criticism* 52, no. 2 (2010): 235–41.

Lowe, Lisa. *The Intimacies of Four Continents*. Durham, NC: Duke University Press, 2015.

Lubin, Joan. "Haircut Theory: Living with Judith Butler's Gender Trouble." *Post45*, May 19, 2020. www.post45.org.

Lundquist, Harry. *Education: Readings in the Processes of Cultural Transmission*. Boston: Houghton Mifflin, 1970.

"Manassas Industrial School." *Crisis* 2, no. 4 (August 1911): 277.

Manassas Industrial School. *1915–1916 Annual Report*. 1916.

————. *1907 Financial Report, Donors' List and Statement of Current Needs*. 1907.

————. *1908 Financial Report, Donors' List and Statement of Current Needs*. 1908.

————. *1910 Financial Report, Donors' List and Statement of Current Needs*. 1910.

————. *Manassas Bulletin* 7, no. 4 (February 1912).

————. *Manassas School Journal* 1, no. 3 (January 1905).

"man-child, n." *OED Online*, June 2022.

Manion, Jen. "Gendered Ideologies of Violence, Authority, and Racial Difference in New York State Penitentiaries, 1796–1844." *Radical History Review*, no. 126 (2016): 11–29.

Markotić, Nicole, and Robert McRuer. "Leading with Your Head: On the Borders of Disability, Sexuality, and the Nation." In *Sex and Disability*, edited by Robert McRuer and Anna Mollow, 165–82. Durham, NC: Duke University Press, 2012.

Mathes, William. "A Negro Pepys." *Antioch Review* 25, no. 3 (Autumn 1965): 456–62.

McBride, Dwight. "Straight Black Studies: On African American Studies, James Baldwin, and Black Queer Studies." In *Black Queer Studies: A Critical Anthology*, edited by E. Patrick Johnson and Mae G. Henderson, 68–89. Durham, NC: Duke University Press, 2005.

McClintock, Anne. *Imperial Leather: Race, Gender, and Sexuality in the Colonial Conquest*. New York: Routledge, 1995.

McCraney, Tarell Alvin. *Choir Boy*. New York: Theater Communications Group, 2015.

McKegney, Sam. "From Trickster Discourses to Transgressive Politics." *Studies in American Indian Literature* 17 (Winter 2005): 79–113.

McLachlan, James. *American Boarding Schools: A Historical Study*. New York: Charles Scribner's Sons, 1970.

Menon, Madhavi. *Indifference to Difference: On Queer Universalism*. Minneapolis: University of Minnesota Press, 2015.

Meyers, Sidney, director. *The Quiet One*. Film Documents Inc., 1948. https://archive.org.

Michaels, Walter Benn. *Our America: Nativism, Modernism, and Pluralism*. Durham, NC: Duke University Press, 1995.

Million, Dian. "Felt Theory: An Indigenous Feminist Approach to Affect and History." *Wicazo Sa Review* 24, no. 2 (Fall 2009): 53–76.

———. *Therapeutic Nations: Healing in an Age of Indigenous Human Rights*. Tucson: University of Arizona Press, 2013.

Milloy, John Sheridan. *A National Crime: The Canadian Government and the Residential School System, 1879 to 1986*. Winnipeg: University of Manitoba Press, 1999.

Miranda, Deborah A. "Dildos, Hummingbirds, and Driving Her Crazy: Searching for American Indian Women's Love Poetry and Erotics." *Frontiers* 23, no. 2 (2002): 135–49.

Mollow, Anna. "Is Sex Disability?" In *Sex and Disability*, edited by Robert McRuer and Anna Mollow, 285–312. Durham, NC: Duke University Press, 2012.

Moraga, Cherríe. *Loving in the War Years: lo que nunca pasó por sus labios*. Boston: South End Press, 1983.

Morgensen, Scott Lauria. "Settler Homonationalism: Theorizing Settler Colonialism within Queer Modernities." *GLQ: A Journal of Lesbian and Gay Studies* 16, nos. 1–2 (2010): 105–31.

Morris, Monique. *Pushout: The Criminalization of Black Girls in Schools*. New York: New Press, 2009.

Moynihan, Daniel Patrick. *The Negro Family: The Case for National Action*. Washington, DC: Department of Labor, Office of Policy Planning and Research, 1965.

Muñoz, José Esteban. *Cruising Utopia: The Then and There of Queer Futurity*. New York: New York University Press, 2009.

Murray, Albert. *The Omni-Americans: Some Alternatives to the Folklore of White Supremacy*. 1970. Boston: Da Capo Press, 2020.

Nealon, Christopher. *Foundlings: Lesbian and Gay Historical Emotion before Stonewall*. Durham, NC: Duke University Press, 2001.

Nelson, Emmanuel. *African American Autobiographers: A Sourcebook*. Westport, CT: Greenwood, 2002.

Nolte-Odhiambo, Carmen. "'I Be Home': Childhood Belonging and Un/becoming in Hawaiʻi." *Children's Literature Association Quarterly* 43, no. 4 (Winter 2018): 377–94.

"Notable Books of 1965." *ALA Bulletin* 60, no. 3 (March 1966): 284–85.

Nyongʼo, Tavia. "Punkʼd Theory." *Social Text* 23, nos. 3–4 (2005): 19–34.

Opager Baughn, Jennifer. "A Modern School Plant: Consolidated Schools in Mississippi, 1910–1955." *Buildings & Landscapes* 19, no. 1 (Spring 2012): 43–72.

Ordover, Nancy. *American Eugenics: Race, Queer Anatomy, and the Science of Nationalism*. Minneapolis: University of Minnesota Press, 2003.

Ovington, Mary White. *Portraits in Color*. New York: Viking, 1927.

Owen, Gabrielle. *A Queer History of Adolescence: Developmental Pasts, Relational Futures*. Athens: University of Georgia Press, 2020.

"Peabody Bimonthly Booknotes." *Peabody Journal of Education* 22, no. 3 (1944): 184–90.

Peck, Raoul, director. *I Am Not Your Negro*. Magnolia Pictures and Amazon Studios, 2016.

Penrose, Lionel. "Mental Disease and Crime: Outline of a Comparative Study of European Statistics." *British Journal of Medical Psychology* 18 (1939): 1–15.

Perkins Institution. *Perkins Institution Scrapbook of Clippings*. January 1943–December 1946. https://archive.org.

Platt, Anthony. *The Child Savers: The Invention of Delinquency*. 1970. New Brunswick, NJ: Rutgers University Press, 2009.

Poupart, Lisa M. "The Familiar Face of Genocide: Internalized Oppression among American Indians." *Hypatia* 18, no. 2 (2003): 86–100.

Povinelli, Elizabeth A. *The Empire of Love: Toward a Theory of Intimacy, Genealogy, and Carnality*. Durham, NC: Duke University Press, 2006.

Pratt, Richard H., and Robert M. Utley. *The Indian Industrial School, Carlisle, Pennsylvania: Its Origins, Purposes, Progress, and the Difficulties Surmounted*. 1908. Carlisle, PA: Cumberland County Historical Society, 1979.

Probyn, Elspeth. "Suspending Beginnings: Of Childhood and Nostalgia." *GLQ: A Journal of Lesbian and Gay Studies* 2, no. 4 (1995): 439–65.

"promised land, n." *OED Online*, June 2022.

Przybylo, Ela. *Asexual Erotics: Intimate Readings of Compulsory Sexuality*. Columbus: Ohio State University Press, 2019.

Puar, Jasbir. "The Cost of Getting Better: Suicide, Sensation, Switchpoints." *GLQ: A Journal of Lesbian and Gay Studies* 18, no. 1 (2011): 149–58.

———. *Terrorist Assemblages: Homonationalism in Queer Times*. Durham, NC: Duke University Press, 2017.

Rampersad, Arnold. "Afterword." In *Rite of Passage*, by Richard Wright, 117–44. New York: HarperTeen, 1994.

Raney, David. "Encroaching Dark: Germs and Race in Twentieth-Century American Literature and Culture." *Interdisciplinary Literary Studies* 6, no. 2 (2005): 1–23.

Rayback, Joseph. *A History of American Labor*. New York: Free Press, 1966.

Reddy, Chandan. *Freedom with Violence: Race, Sexuality, and the US State*. Durham, NC: Duke University Press, 2011.

Reuschling, Wyndy Corbin. "'Trust and Obey': The Danger of Obedience as Duty in Evangelical Ethics." *Journal of the Society of Christian Ethics* 25, no. 2 (Fall/Winter 2005): 59–77.

Rhoades, Everett. *Report on Indian Health, Task Force Six: Final Report to the American Indian Policy Review Commission*. Washington, DC: Government Printing Office, 1976.

Rifkin, Mark. *Erotics of Sovereignty*. Minneapolis: University of Minnesota Press, 2012.

———. "Queering Indigenous Pasts, or Temporalities of Tradition and Settlement." In *The Oxford Handbook of Indigenous American Literature*, edited by James H. Cox and Daniel Heath Justice, 137–51. Oxford: Oxford University Press, 2014.

———. *When Did Indians Become Straight? Kinship, the History of Sexuality, and Native Sovereignty*. Oxford: Oxford University Press, 2011.

Ritchie, John, and Joseph Caldwell. *Primer of Hygiene*. 1910. Toronto: W. J. Gage, 1927.

Roberts, Dorothy. "The Paradox of Silence and Display: Sexual Violation of Enslaved Women and Contemporary Contradictions in Black Female Sexuality." In *Beyond Slavery: Overcoming Its Religious and Sexual Legacies*, edited by Bernadette Brooten, 41–60. London: Palgrave Macmillan, 2010.

Rogin, Michael. *Fathers and Children: Andrew Jackson and the Subjugation of the American Indian*. 1975. Piscataway, NJ: Transaction, 2008.

Rohy, Valerie. *Anachronism and Its Others: Sexuality, Race, Temporality*. Albany: State University of New York Press, 2010.

Ross, Marlon. "Some Glances at the Black Fag: Race, Same-Sex Desire, and Cultural Belonging." *Canadian Review of Comparative Literature* 21, nos. 1–2 (March–June 1994): 193–219.

Rotella, Carlo. *October Cities: The Redevelopment of Urban Literature*. Oakland: University of California Press, 1998.

Rowell, Charles. "An Interview with Henry Louis Gates, Jr." *Callaloo* 14, no. 2 (Spring 1991): 444–63.

"rub, v." *OED Online*, June 2022.

Rubin, Gayle. "Thinking Sex." In *Pleasure and Danger: Exploring Female Sexuality*, edited by Carole S. Vance, 267–319. Boston: Routledge and Kegan Paul, 1984.

Sánchez, Marta. *"Shakin' Up" Race and Gender: Intercultural Connections in Puerto Rican, African American, and Chicano Narratives and Culture (1965–1995)*. Austin: University of Texas Press, 2006.

Schneider, Bethany. "Introduction: Bethany's Take." *GLQ: A Journal of Lesbian and Gay Studies* 16, nos. 1–2 (2010): 13–22.

———. "A Modest Proposal: Laura Ingalls Wilder Ate Zitkala-Ša." *GLQ: A Journal of Lesbian and Gay Studies* 21, no. 1 (2015): 65–93.

———. "Pleasures and Frictions from the Queer Middles." Paper presented at the American Studies Association annual meeting, Los Angeles, November 2014.

Schoen, Johanna. *Choice and Coercion: Birth Control, Sterilization, and Abortion in Public Health and Welfare*. Chapel Hill: University of North Carolina Press, 2007.

Schuller, Kyla. *The Biopolitics of Feeling: Race, Sex, and Science in the Nineteenth Century*. Durham, NC: Duke University Press, 2018.

Sedgwick, Eve Kosofsky. *Epistemology of the Closet*. Berkeley: University of California Press. 1990.

———. *Tendencies*. Durham, NC: Duke University Press, 1993.

———. *Touching Feeling*. Durham, NC: Duke University Press, 2003.

Shaw, Stephanie. "Black Club Women and the Creation of the National Association of Colored Women." *Journal of Women's History* 3, no. 2 (1991): 11–25.

Sheldon, Rebekah. *The Child to Come: Life after the Human Catastrophe*. Minneapolis: University of Minnesota Press, 2016.

Smith, Andrea. "Queer Theory and Native Studies: The Heteronormativity of Settler Colonialism." *GLQ: A Journal of Lesbian and Gay Studies* 16, nos. 1–2 (2010): 41–68.

Smith, Mark. *Mastered by the Clock: Time, Slavery, and Freedom in the American South.* Chapel Hill: University of North Carolina Press, 1997.

Soderberg, Laura. *Vicious Infants: Dangerous Childhoods in Antebellum U.S. Literature.* Amherst: University of Massachusetts Press, 2021.

Somerville, Siobhan B. *Queering the Color Line: Race and the Invention of Homosexuality in American Culture*. Durham, NC: Duke University Press, 2000.

"The Status of African Americans at the Nation's Most Prestigious Boarding Schools." *Journal of Blacks in Higher Education* 14 (Winter 1996–97): 26–28.

St. Félix, Doreen. "The Troubled Teens of Netflix's *Girls Incarcerated*." *New Yorker*, April 30, 2018. www.newyorker.com.

Stockton, Kathryn Bond. *Beautiful Bottom, Beautiful Shame: Where "Black" Meets "Queer."* Durham, NC: Duke University Press, 2006.

———. *The Queer Child, or Growing Sideways in the Twentieth Century*. Durham, NC: Duke University Press, 2009.

Stoler, Ann Laura. *Race and the Education of Desire: Foucault's* History of Sexuality *and the Colonial Order of Things*. Durham, NC: Duke University Press, 1995.

Story, Kaila Adia. "On the Cusp of Deviance: Respectability Politics and the Cultural Marketplace of Sameness." In *No Tea, No Shade: New Writings in Black Queer Studies*, edited by E. Patrick Johnson, 362–79. Durham, NC: Duke University Press, 2016.

Stowe, Harriet Beecher. *Uncle Tom's Cabin*. 1852. Mineola, NY: Dover, 2005.

Stubblefield, Anna. "'Beyond the Pale': Tainted Whiteness, Cognitive Disability, and Eugenic Sterilization." *Hypatia* 22, no. 2 (2007): 162–81.

Sykes, Gresham, and Thomas Drabek. *Law and the Lawless: A Reader in Criminology.* New York: Random House, 1969.

Taylor, Diana. *The Archive and the Repertoire*. Durham, NC: Duke University Press, 2003.

Terkel, Studs, and Claude Brown. "Claude Brown Talks with Studs Terkel." *Studs Terkel Radio Archive*, September 13, 1965. https://studsterkel.wfmt.com.

Thompson, E. P. "Time, Work-Discipline, and Industrial Capitalism." *Past and Present* 38 (December 1967): 56–97.

Thompson, Jane. "Letter to William Loeb." December 13, 1908. Manassas Industrial School Collection, Manassas Museum, Manassas, VA.

Tilley, Heather. "Portraying Blindness: Nineteenth-Century Images of Tactile Reading." *Disability Studies Quarterly* 38, no. 3 (2018).

Trodson, Lars. "The 'Quiet' Man: Eliot Man Recalls a 'Masterpiece' Film." *Seacoastonline*, August 3, 2008. www.seacoastonline.com.

Trustees. *Annual Report of the Trustees of the New-England Institution for the Education of the Blind*. Boston: J.T. Buckingham, 1835.

———. *Fifth Annual Report of the Trustees of the New-England Institution for the Education of the Blind*. Boston: Press of the Boston Courier, 1837.

Trustees of Dartmouth College v. Woodward. February 2, 1819. www.law.cornell.edu.

Tucker, Holly. *Blood Work: A Tale of Medicine and Murder in the Scientific Revolution*. New York: Norton, 2012.

Viego, Antonio. *Dead Subjects: Toward a Politics of Loss in Latino Studies*. Durham, NC: Duke University Press, 2007.

"Virginia Industrial School for Colored Girls." In *Juvenile Institutions*. Richmond, VA: Children's Bureau of the State Department of Public Welfare, 1941.

Wallace, Michele. "Race, Gender, and Psychoanalysis in Forties Film: *Lost Boundaries, Home of the Brave* and *The Quiet One*." In *Black American Cinema*, edited by Manthia Diawara, 257–71. New York: Routledge, 1993.

Ward, Geoff. *The Black Child-Savers: Racial Democracy and Juvenile Justice*. Chicago: University of Chicago Press, 2012.

Washington, Booker T. *Up from Slavery*. 1902. Oxford: Oxford University Press, 1995.

———. *Working with Your Hands*. New York: Doubleday & Page, 1904.

Webster, Crystal Lynn. *Beyond the Boundaries of Childhood: African American Children in the Antebellum North*. Chapel Hill: University of North Carolina Press, 2021.

Weinstein, Deborah. *The Pathological Family: Postwar America and the Rise of Family Therapy*. Ithaca, NY: Cornell University Press, 2003.

Wexler, Laura. *Tender Violence: Domestic Visions in an Age of U.S. Imperialism*. Chapel Hill: University of North Carolina Press, 2000.

Whaley, Elizabeth Gates. "What Happens When You Put the Manchild in the Promised Land? An Experience with Censorship." *English Journal* 63, no. 5 (May 1974): 61–65.

Wiegman, Robyn. "Eve's Triangles, or Queer Studies Beside Itself." *differences: A Journal of Feminist Culture* 26, no. 1 (2015): 48–73.

Wiegman, Robyn, and Elizabeth A. Wilson. "Introduction: Antinormativity's Queer Conventions." *differences: A Journal of Feminist Culture* 26, no. 1 (2015): 1–25.

Willis, Paul. *Learning to Labor: How Working Class Kids Get Working Class Jobs*. New York: Columbia University Press, 1977.

Willrich, Michael. "The Two Percent Solution: Eugenic Jurisprudence and the Socialization of American Law, 1900–1930." *Law and History Review* 16, no. 1 (Spring 1998): 63–111.

Wolcott, David. "Juvenile Justice before Juvenile Court: Cops, Courts, and Kids in Turn-of-the-Century Detroit." *Social Science History* 27, no. 1 (Spring 2003): 109–36.

Wolfe, Patrick. "Settler Colonialism and the Elimination of the Native." *Journal of Genocide Research* 8, no. 4 (2006): 387–409.

Worth, Robert. "Claude Brown, Manchild of the Promised Land, Dies at 64." *New York Times*, February 6, 2002.

Woubshet, Dagmawi. *The Calendar of Loss: Race, Sexuality, and Mourning in the Early Era of AIDS*. Baltimore: Johns Hopkins University Press, 2015.

———. "The Imperfect Power of *I Am Not Your Negro*." *Atlantic*, February 8, 2017. www.theatlantic.com.

Wright, Nazera Sadiq. *Black Girlhood in the Nineteenth Century*. Urbana: University of Illinois Press, 2017.

Wright, Richard. *Rite of Passage*. New York: HarperTeen, 1994.

Yagoda, Ben. *Memoir: A History*. New York: Riverhead Books, 2009.

Young, Vernetta, and Rebecca Reviere. "Black Club Women and the Establishment of Juvenile Justice Institutions for Colored Children: A Black Feminist Approach." *Western Journal of Black Studies* 39, no. 2 (2015): 102–13.

Yousman, Bill. "Blackophilia and Blackophobia: White Youth, the Consumption of Rap Music, and White Supremacy." *Communication Theory* 13, no. 4 (November 2003): 366–91.

Zipf, Karen. *Bad Girls at Samarcand: Sexuality and Sterilization in a Southern Juvenile Reformatory*. Baton Rouge: Louisiana State University Press, 2016.

Zitkala-Ša (Gertrude Simmons Bonnin). *American Indian Stories, Legends, and Other Writings*. 1921. New York: Penguin, 1992.

INDEX

Abate, Michelle Ann, 241n7
ability. *See* disability
abuse, 17, 25, 28, 30, 43, 47, 55, 72, 91, 105,
    188–91, 194, 207–9, 212, 276n101
Adoptive Couple v. Baby Girl, 217
adulthood, 12, 14, 48, 76, 82–83, 161–62,
    200, 257n75
African American boys. *See* child(ren):
    Black
African American girls. *See* child(ren):
    Black
Agyepong, Tera, 49, 248n7, 248n20,
    248n26, 249n29
Ahmed, Sara, 27, 84–85, 245n91,
    256nn52–55, 256nn59–60
AIDS, 215, 228, 277n136
Alexander, M. Jacqui, 38, 188, 208,
    247nn140–41
Alexie, Sherman, 42, 191, 218
Allen, Edward, 121
Althusser, Louis, 36, 105, 247nn133–34,
    247n136, 259n144
Amar, Paul, 3, 241n13
Amin, Kadji, 15–16, 18, 27, 234, 243n44,
    243n47, 244nn55–56, 245n90, 278n18
Andrews, William, 269n50
Antin, Mary, 255n47
antinormativity, 13
Anzaldúa, Gloria, 1, 241n4
apprentices/apprenticeship, 32, 40, 47
archives, 6, 8, 11–13, 15, 19–20, 167, 191, 202,
    243n38
Aries, Philippé, 33–34, 246n121
Armstrong, General Samuel Chapman, 30

asexual/ity, 33, 88, 116, 149
assimilation, 7, 9–10, 15, 18, 31, 43, 45, 48,
    56, 70, 75, 115, 118, 168, 185, 187, 193–94,
    197, 223
Atlanta Compromise, 152, 267n20

Bailey, Hannah, 253n90
Baker, Houston, 79, 254n15, 254n23, 254n25
Baldwin, James, 79, 147–50, 181–82, 255n47,
    266n1, 267n8, 272n129
Barker, Joanne, 186, 272n6
Barrett, Janie Porter, 47, 49–51, 53–64,
    67–70, 110, 248n11, 249n31, 249nn35–37,
    249n39, 249n41, 250nn45–56,
    251nn57–60, 251nn62–64, 252n69,
    252nn71–78, 253nn91–96, 253n98–99
Bashford, Alison, 268n40
Bauerkemper, Joseph, 201, 275n72
Belafonte, Harry, 147
Bellingham, Bruce, 38, 246nn104–5,
    246n109, 247n142, 247n146\
Berlant, Lauren, 156–57, 230–32, 241n7,
    242n30, 247n3, 269nn41–42, 273n37,
    278n7
Bernstein, Robin, 244n70
Berthold, Dana, 268n40
Bethune, Mary McLeod, 110, 251n61
"biophilanthropy," 24, 196
biopolitics, 9, 11, 21–22, 24, 26, 38, 191, 193,
    214
Black studies, 17, 27, 182–83, 225
boarding schools. *See* schools
"body praxis," 38
Brackeen v. Haaland, 218, 277n141

ABOUT THE AUTHOR

MARY ZABORSKIS is Assistant Professor of American Studies and Gender Studies in the Program in American Studies at the Pennsylvania State University, Harrisburg. Her work has appeared in *GLQ: A Journal of Lesbian and Gay Studies*, *Signs: Journal of Women in Culture and Society*, *WSQ*, *Jump Cut*, and *Feminist Formations*.